The Essent

CW00546637

UNDERWATER GUIDE
to
NORTH WALES

Volume One

Barmouth to South Stack

Chris Holden

CALGO PUBLICATIONS
(2003)

www.calgopublications.co.uk

Photography Credits

Paul Kay - 1, 13, 16, 18, 20, 23, 28, 32, 33, 35, 37, 39, 41, 46, 54, 72, 73, 77, 85, 89, 95, 103, 111, 102, 116, 121, 123, 125, 127, 130, 140, 143, 148, 151, 158, 159, 164, 167, 173, 177, 182, 186, 187, 200, 221, 228, 230

Chris Holden - 1, 15, 17, 20, 30, 36, 38, 39, 41, 44, 45, 46, 47, 48, 49, 50, 51, 52, 53, 56, 58, 59, 60, 61, 62, 63, 64, 65, 66, 69, 71, 72, 74, 75, 76, 77, 78, 84, 86, 88, 90, 93, 94, 95, 96, 97, 98, 99, 100, 102, 107, 108, 109, 113, 115, 117, 118, 122, 128, 129, 131, 133, 134, 135, 136, 137, 138, 139, 140, 141, 142, 143, 144, 145, 146, 148, 149, 154,155, 157, 158, 160, 161, 162, 163, 164, 165, 166, 168, 169, 171, 172, 176, 177,178, 179, 180, 181, 184, 185, 186, 191, 193, 196, 197, 198, 200, 201, 202, 204,205, 206, 207, 208, 209, 210, 211, 212, 213, 214, 215, 216, 217, 218, 219, 220, 221, 228, 229, 235

Richard Bufton - 21 Mandy McMath - 7, 50 Simon Fielding - 25, 203, 204

Neil O'May - 207 Roslyn Cossons - 21 Derek Haslam - 81 Martin Turtle - 34, 40

Gwynedd Archives - 97, 183 John Clarkson - 112, 147, 195

Echo-sounder traces by Chris Holden and Richard Bufton

Charts & maps by Pinpoint Creative

Published by Calgo Publications 33, Meadowcroft, Higher Kinnerton, Chester. CH4 9AY
Tel: 01244 660579 web: www.calgopublications.co.uk e-mail: info@calgopublications.co.uk

Graphic Design by Pinpoint Creative
Haven Buidings, Chester Road West, Queensferry, Flintshire, North Wales. CH5 3UD
Tel: 01244 834877 Fax: 01244 831606 e-mail: info@pinpointcreative.co.uk

Printed and bound in the United Kingdom by Amadeus Press Ltd.

This book has been produced with financial support from the Countryside Council for Wales

All charts in this book have been reproduced from Admiralty charts, numbers 1971, 1970, 1464, and 1413. By permission of the controller of Her Majesty's Stationery Office and the Uk Hydrographic Office (www.ukho.gov.uk)

Llywodraeth Cynulliad Cymru
Welsh Assembly Government
CORFF NODDEDIG | SPONSORED BODY

Cyngor Cefn Gwlad Cymru
Countryside Council for Wales

Pinpoint
Creative

Contents

Section 1 - Dive Sites

Charts are based on the appropriate Admiralty Chart for that area and are reproduced with the permission of the Controller of Her Majesty's Stationery Office.

Acknowledgments

This series of books could not have been made possible without the assistance of many others, both divers and non-divers, who have given help or advice in one form or another.

In particular, I would like to thank (in alphabetical order) - Roger Amsden; Rod Aspinall; Mike Bowyer; John Boylett; Mike Breathen; Richard Bufton; Jeremy Carroll; Pete Drury; Graham Farley; John Farley; Richard Frost; Al Gray; Dave Hanson; Jon Holden; Bill Huyton; Ian James; Dr. Cecil Jones; Paul and Lucy Kay; Frank Little; Doug McElvogue; Brendan Maguire; Graham McLeod; Neil O'May; Martin & Caroline Sampson; Peter Stone; John Stubbs; Stewart & Joyce Tattersall; John Taylor; Wally Waldron; John Walsh and Dave Warner.

My thanks must also go to all past and present members of Chester Sub-Aqua Club for their patience and help, as well as for the many wonderful days that I have spent diving with them.

In addition, I would like to thank all the local library and archives staff who have provided valuable assistance with the historical research for this book.

The support and guidance provided by the Countryside Council for Wales is gratefully acknowledged.

Without the perseverance, expert knowledge and dedication shown by Mike Sedgwick of Pinpoint Creative, this book would not have been made possible.

Lastly, to my wife Lesley and son Andrew, who have spent countless hours on windswept beaches, been repeatedly drenched in dive-boats by rain and spray, and have even been persuaded to join me underwater. Thank You.

Why?

North Wales has a great variety of excellent dive sites, which under the right conditions can be dived for twelve months of the year. Many local divers have accumulated a great deal of information regarding tides, currents, weather, wrecks, and reefs but little accurate information is readily available to visiting divers.

I first enquired about purchasing a diving guide for North Wales in 1983. At that time, a book was being prepared by Alan Watkinson, a former National Diving Officer of the British Sub-Aqua Club, so I volunteered to collect and pass on any relevant information to Alan. Unfortunately, Alan was unable to complete the book, so I simply continued to accumulate as much information as possible. At this time, my 'word-processor' was a £1,000,000 mainframe computer that I had access to in my work as a computer engineer. After another false start in 1991 and having read many more books on the maritime history of North Wales, I decided to produce this guide myself. Fortunately, computer technology has progressed dramatically since beginning this venture, but from start to finish, this book has taken 20 years to put into print.

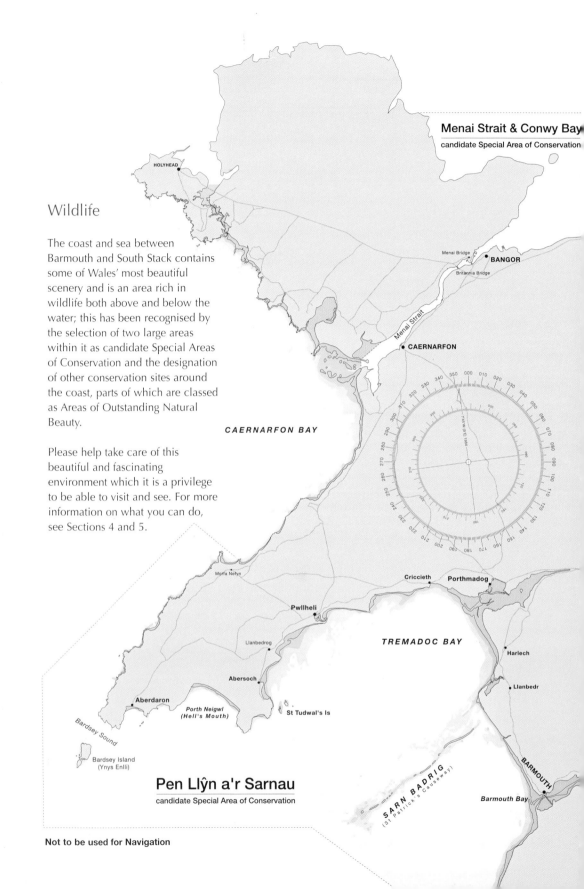

Wildlife

The coast and sea between
Barmouth and South Stack contains
some of Wales' most beautiful
scenery and is an area rich in
wildlife both above and below the
water; this has been recognised by
the selection of two large areas
within it as candidate Special Areas
of Conservation and the designation
of other conservation sites around
the coast, parts of which are classed
as Areas of Outstanding Natural
Beauty.

Please help take care of this
beautiful and fascinating
environment which it is a privilege
to be able to visit and see. For more
information on what you can do,
see Sections 4 and 5.

Menai Strait & Conwy Bay
candidate Special Area of Conservation

HOLYHEAD

Menai Bridge
BANGOR
Britannia Bridge

Menai Strait

CAERNARFON

CAERNARFON BAY

Criccieth Porthmadog

Morfa Nefyn

Pwllheli

Llanbedrog

TREMADOC BAY

Harlech

Abersoch

Llanbedr

Aberdaron

*Porth Neigwl
(Hell's Mouth)*

St Tudwal's Is

Bardsey Sound

Bardsey Island
(Ynys Enlli)

Pen Llŷn a'r Sarnau
candidate Special Area of Conservation

*SARN BADRIG
(St Patrick's Causeway)*

BARMOUTH

Barmouth Bay

Not to be used for Navigation

Dyma'r cyntaf o gyfres o arweinlyfrau sy'n bwriadu rhoi gwybodaeth am yr amgylchedd tanddwr o gwmpas arfordir Cymru o'r Bermo hyd at aber Afon Dyfrdwy. Er ei fod wedi'i anelu'n bennaf at deifwyr-sgwba, mae gwybodaeth ynddo a fydd yn ddefnyddiol i snorcelwyr, pysgotwyr môr, caiacwyr môr ac unrhyw un arall â diddordeb yn ein hamgylchedd morol neu hanes morwrol Gogledd Cymru.

Mae amrywiaeth eang o safleoedd wedi'u cynnwys yn yr arweinlyfr hwn. Safleoedd da, safleoedd go lew, safleoedd gwael, a'r rheiny na fyddaf i fyth yn ymweld â nhw eto. Gobeithiaf y bydd hwn yn rhoi gwybodaeth i'r darllenydd ynghylch ble i ddeifio, ond lawn cyn bwysiced, ble a phryd i beidio â deifio. Nid oes unrhyw ddiben ailadrodd y camgymeriadau lu rwyf i ac eraill eisoes wedi'u gwneud. Yn y llyfr hwn, rwyf wedi cynnwys cynifer o'r llongau drylliedig oddi ar y glannau ag sy'n bosibl, ond rwyf wedi cyfyngu'r niferoedd i gynnwys dim ond y rheiny sy'n gorwedd mewn 30 metr o ddyfnder neu lai. Bydd safleoedd deifio dŵr croyw yn cael eu cynnwys yng nghyfrolau'r dyfodol, ond nid yw hyn yn golygu bod gennych hawl mynediad i'r afonydd, y llynnoedd neu'r chwareli tanddwr hyn, felly rhaid cael caniatâd ymlaen llaw cyn croesi tir preifat.

Byddai'n amhosibl ysgrifennu arweinlyfr hollol gyflawn i'r amgylchedd tanddwr o gwmpas Gogledd Cymru ac nid yw'r llyfr hwn yn honni ei fod yn un. Ni allaf hawlio fy mod wedi cynnwys pob un safle plymio, rîff, llong ddrylliedig, llyn, chwarel, a phwll yng Ngogledd Cymru, ond un o bleserau deifio yw bod cymaint i'w archwilio, gan fynd ar ôl yr anhysbys neu'r hyn sydd heb ei ddarganfod drwy'r amser ac weithiau'n cael hyd i'r annisgwyl. Nid oes bwriad chwaith iddo fod yn llyfr am fioleg tanddwr, gan fod llawer o lyfrau eraill gryn dipyn yn fwy awdurdodol ar y pwnc. Gweler y llyfryddiaeth am ragor o fanylion. Fodd bynnag, rwy'n gobeithio y bydd fy sylwadau i lluniau gwych Paul Kay yn darparu gwybodaeth ddefnyddiol ar gyfer deifwyr, selogion bywyd y môr, pysgotwyr, ac unrhyw un arall sy'n mwynhau arfordir Gogledd Cymru.

Deifiwr efo pysgodyn darn arian   Diver with a 'John Dory'

Preface - The Book

This is the first of a series of guides which aim to pass on information about the underwater environment around the Welsh coastline from Barmouth to the Dee Estuary. Although primarily aimed at scuba-divers, there is information of use to snorkellers, sea anglers, sea kayakers, and anyone interested in our marine environment or the maritime history of North Wales.

A wide variety of sites have been covered in this guide. Good sites, mediocre sites, bad sites, and those that I won't ever visit again. Hopefully, this will inform the reader as to where to dive, but just as importantly where and when not to dive. There is simply no point in repeating the many mistakes that have already been made by myself and others. In this book, I have included as many of the offshore wrecks as possible, but have restricted the numbers to include only those resting in depths of 30 metres or less. Freshwater dive-sites will be included in future volumes, but this does not imply the right of access to these rivers, lakes, or flooded quarries, so prior permission must be obtained before crossing private land.

It would be impossible to write a totally complete guide to the underwater environment around North Wales and this book makes no pretence to be one. I cannot claim to have included every single dive-site, reef, wreck, lake, quarry, pond and puddle within North Wales, but one of the great joys of diving is that there is so much to explore, always chasing the unknown or undiscovered and occasionally finding the unexpected. Nor is it meant to be a book on underwater biology, as there are many other books that are far more authoritative on the subject. See the bibliography for further details. However, I do hope that my own observations and Paul Kay's superb photographs will provide useful information for divers, marine-life enthusiasts, anglers, and anyone else who simply enjoys the North Wales coast.

Safety

Diving is by nature an adventurous sport and should only be undertaken after completing the appropriate training and by using equipment suitable for the depth and type of dive being undertaken. In particular, the flooded quarries of North Wales have claimed far too many lives and should be treated with the greatest respect. These freshwater dive-sites will be described in further volumes of this diving guide. These quarries are deep, cold and dangerous, so don't become yet another diving statistic. Dive within your own and your buddy's capability and ensure that your equipment is up to the task. Diving equipment must be designed to operate in cold water and, where appropriate, divers must have back-up equipment such as octopus regulators, pony-cylinders or twin cylinders and regulators.

The seas around North Wales have their own hazards, especially in the narrow channels of Bardsey Sound and the Menai Strait. These geographical features funnel the tidal flow through a narrow gap to produce extremely strong currents. I have been in a boat that was travelling forwards on the plane, but was actually being taken backwards by the force of the tide. Other natural features such as the exposed headlands at Pen-y-Cil, Bardsey Island, Braich-y-Pwll, the Fangs and South Stack create whirlpools, tide-rips and overfalls big enough to swamp even a rigid-hull inflatable, so avoid these dangerous areas whenever possible. Outboard motors will always fail at the most inopportune moment; so think in advance what will happen when an engine does fail. Fit twin engines or an additional 'pony' engine, and remember that two boats are always safer than just one.

Why not register your boat with the Coastguard before you dive this area? Use the Safety Identity Scheme (CG66) using form MSF6000, copies of which are available on the web or from Coastguard Stations.

Vast amounts of unexploded munitions have been dumped in the Irish Sea, as well as the lakes, quarries and rivers of North Wales. These bombs, bullets and shells have mostly originated from ammunition dumps, shipwrecks and military exercises, or are from Second World War bombing-ranges. Others explosives have been illegally dumped or have resulted from an accident. Flares and other pyrotechnics, some containing phosphorous, may be seen underwater or washed up on the shoreline. Leave any suspicious objects well alone. Phosphorous is especially dangerous if it is allowed to dry out.

Further safety advice is available regarding boats, engines, munitions and diving. Check the web, or read the many excellent leaflets produced by the Maritime & Coastguard Agency (MCA) and the Royal National Lifeboat Institution (RNLI). In short, think carefully before you go out for a dive, check the weather forecast, check the tides, and check your equipment. Read the warnings given in this book. Above all else, set out for an enjoyable day's diving, rather than aiming for a specific dive-site or depth and be prepared to alter your plans if the conditions are worse than expected. Remember, this is meant to be a leisure-sport, not an endurance test.

Tides & Tide Tables

- Tide times are based on Laver's Liverpool tide-tables, as these booklets are more readily available than Holyhead or Pwllheli tide tables.

- Slack-water times and the direction of tidal streams, unless otherwise stated, are based on personal observations, but they may be inaccurate on the day due to prevailing weather conditions and tidal height.

- Local high-water and low-water times given can only be approximate as they will vary according to the time of day, the tide height and prevailing weather conditions. Check www.easytide.com or www.bbc.co.uk/weather/marine/tides beforehand.

- Note that the tidal-range at Liverpool is always greater than at any of the dive-sites mentioned in this book. For a more accurate calculation of the water-depth at the dive-site, again use www.easytide.com for the nearest harbour.

Standards Used in this Book

- Depths and measurements are given in metres.

- Short distances are given in metres. Longer distances in nautical miles.

- One nautical mile = 1.1516 Statue Miles = 1,853 metres

- Dive-site positions are given in degrees, minutes, and decimal parts of a minute. (To three decimal places). They are NOT given as degrees, minutes and seconds.

- Land-based positions such as slipways, shore-dives, quarries, dive-shops and air-stations are given as degrees, minutes, and decimal parts of a minute, followed by the six-figure Ordnance Survey position.

- If you are unsure as to how to work out the Ordnance Survey system, a worked example is usually given on the inside cover of any Ordnance Survey map.

Charts and Maps

Charts and diagrams shown in this book are meant for schematic purposes only and should not be used for navigation. The chart extracts must only be used in conjunction with the appropriate Admiralty Chart for that area and are subject to Crown Copyright.

Bad Weather and Underwater Visibility

Past and present weather conditions have a tremendous effect on diving conditions around North Wales. Southwesterly winds can prevent a boat from being launched at several slipways. Strong northwesterly winds and spring-tides can wipe-out many of our dive-sites due to poor underwater visibility, but there is always an alternative dive-site in North Wales, if only a flooded slate-quarry.

The quality and enjoyment of most of these locations will depend on the present and previous tide and weather conditions, so always check the weather forecast beforehand, especially the wind direction and strength.

Corrections and Updates

All GPS positions have been checked, double-checked and triple-checked but gremlins have been known to play on my computer keyboard. (Other people call them mistypes, mess-ups or other unprintable names)

As time moves on, things do change, especially transits. Drawings for the reef off Pen-y-Chain headland at Pwllheli had to be totally redrawn when the chair lift and terminal building were demolished. For the last 20 years, I have used a chimney on the cliff-top at Aberdaron to re-locate the wreck of the 'Glenocum' and have issued these transits to other divers with good results. Unfortunately, in the summer of 2002, this chimney and the adjacent cottage were demolished and rebuilt, making my original transits no longer valid.

Great care has been taken to ensure that the facts given in this guide are up to date and correct, but I would welcome any additional information, updates or corrections. Please let me know of any useful information so that we can save others time and money, or perhaps even a totally wasted day. There is nothing more frustrating than spending a day searching for a wreck or reef, only to find that your original data is wrong.

The author can be contacted via e-mail at info@calgopublications.co.uk or by searching the web under 'Calgo Publications North Wales Diving'. All corrections & updates will be published on the web-site, www.calgopublications.co.uk

Spellings

With only a few exceptions, the spelling of place-names has been taken from the current Ordnance Survey maps, with others being obtained from Hydrographic Office charts, the Internet, and local guidebooks. In many instances, there are several variations in the spelling, so please accept my apologies for any inaccuracies. If possible, I have tried to use both the Welsh and English spellings, and where historic information has been included, the spelling in use at that time has been used. Hence the town of Caernarfon may have one of the following spellings:- 'Caernarfon', 'Caernarvon' or 'Carnarvon'.

Decca Positions, GPS Positions and Datums

Wreck locations have always been a jealously guarded secret, but in the past, even when a wreck has been located and the position is known, returning to the exact spot has always proved difficult. My early attempts at finding the charted wrecks in Liverpool bay were total failures. This was before the days of the satellite-based Global Position System (GPS), so we were using the ground-based Decca Navigator system. At that time, we did not realise that charted positions were different to Decca positions, causing us to make several dives 'in the vicinity of the wreck', but not on the actual wreck itself. Only later, by applying corrections to the charted positions, we actually started to dive on shipwrecks.

The Decca Navigator transmitters closed down in the late 1990's, so Decca receivers are no longer useable and any position previously taken by this system can only be an approximation.

The introduction of the Global Position System (GPS) in the early 1990's greatly improved the accuracy of our position fix, but it was still impossible to obtain a totally accurate reading due to the imposition of 'Selective Availability'. This degradation in position accuracy was deliberately imposed by the United States Military, giving a position that could be over a hundred metres away from the true location. Re-locating small wrecks such as the submarine 'Resurgam' off Rhyl was still very hit-and-miss. Differential GPS (DGPS) became available at extra cost, based locally on a transmitter at Point Lynas, Anglesey. This aerial broadcasts a signal telling our own GPS receiver how much degradation or error in position accuracy is being applied, therefore allowing our own GPS to correct the offset. At last, we had an accurate, but more expensive way of accurately locate and relocate the offshore wrecks.

One of the last decrees of the Bill Clinton presidential term of office was to abolish 'Selective Availability', thus giving us a cheap, consistent and accurate means of locating shipwrecks. Now, thanks to Bill, we have a GPS system that enables us to return to almost exactly the same position time and time again. Perhaps the former President should be better remembered for this reason rather than for his other, better-publicised, exploits.

So what does this mean and how does it affect us if we are given a GPS position? Is it a Decca position or a GPS position? Was the positions taken while 'Selective Availability' was still being applied? None of these will not be totally accurate and should be treated with caution. Only those positions taken by a Differential-GPS or one that was taken after 'Selective Availability' was abolished (i.e. after May 2000) should be treated as truly accurate and then only if the same datum is being used. All GPS positions given in this book are from personal observations and are believed to be accurate. Check our website for updates or corrections.

Snorkelling

Snorkelling in Wales? You must be joking! We tend to associate the sport of snorkelling with warmer climates and clearer water, but under the right conditions, there are some very interesting snorkelling sites in North Wales. This was actually my own introduction to the underwater world, having purchased a cheap mask and snorkel combination from a newsagent in Abersoch. Peering under the surface in around a metre of water off Porth Ceiriad beach, I was totally amazed at just how much marine-life there is around our coast. This led me to further snorkelling off Anglesey and eventually into diving.

Several of the dive-sites described in this book are some distance from the nearest road and with full diving-gear, they are only accessible from a boat. However, these sites are much easier to reach on foot when carrying only a wetsuit, a mask, a snorkel and a pair of fins. Wait for a calm summer's day and try it. You may be surprised!

How to use this book

- Section One of this book is organised into 13 chapters, running geographically clockwise around the North Wales coast from Barmouth to South Stack Lighthouse.

- Each chapter starts with a (hopefully) relevant quotation from the past, followed by what I consider to be a list of essential information for that area. Read and understand this first.

- Each chapter then continues with a list of shore dives for that area, followed by boat dives. Again, all dives are listed geographically clockwise.

- Each dive has a group of icons to indicate the type of diving that will be encountered. eg. Deep-water ⊕ marine-life 🐟 See the inside front cover for a full list.

- Section Two covers 'Launch-sites' throughout the area. Read and understand the notes beforehand. It is a long way to travel, only to find out you can't launch because you don't have your insurance certificate available, the tide is out, or that you really do need a four-wheel drive vehicle.

- Section Three covers the local diving services available to divers, such as Dive Shops, Air Supplies and Charter-boat operators.

- Section Four covers 'Diving with a Purpose' in North Wales (Marine Biology and Nautical Archaeology).

- Section Five covers the role of the Countryside Council for Wales, Legislation applicable to the area and Codes of Conduct

- Section Six – Bibliography & Index

Archaeology

The remains of various ships have been recorded at a number of dive sites referred to in this book – further details are provided for the individual sites. Remember that all wreckage that is salvaged should be reported to the Receiver of Wreck.

Diver & compass jellyfish

Yes, I love it.
The sea is everything.
It covers seven-tenths of the terrestrial globe.
Its breath is pure and healthy.
It is an immense desert where man is never alone,
for he feels life, quivering around him on every side.
There is supreme tranquillity.

The sea does not belong to despots.
On its surface iniquitous rights can still be exercised,
men can fight there, devour each other there,
and transport all terrestrial horrors there.
But at thirty feet below its level, their power ceases,
their influence dies out, their might disappears.
Ah, Sir, live in the bosom of the waters!
There alone is independence.
There I recognise no masters!
There I am free.

Jules Verne - 20,000 Leagues Under the Sea

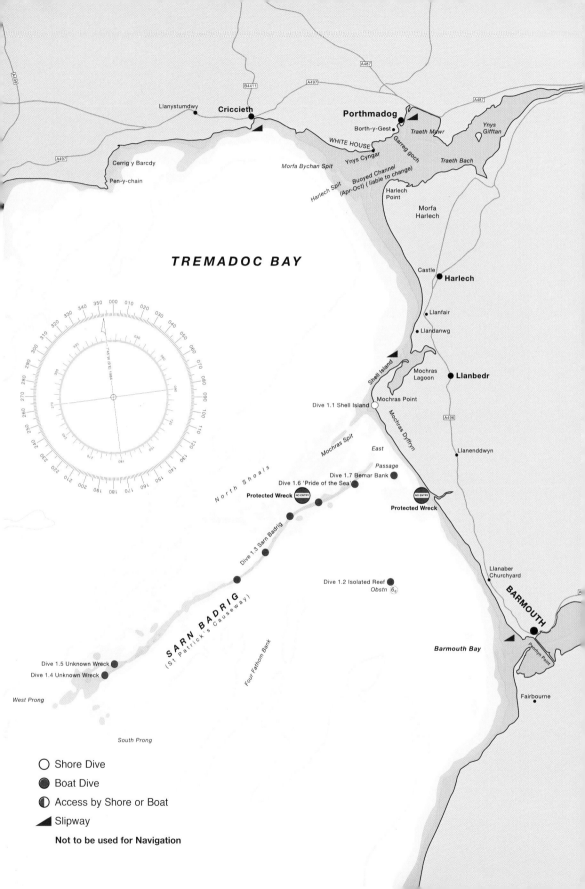

TREMADOC BAY

Llanystumdwy
Criccieth
Llansystumdwy
B4411
A497
A487
A497
Cerrig y Barcdy
Pen-y-chain

Porthmadog
Borth-y-Gest
Traeth Mawr
Ynys Gifftan
WHITE HOUSE
Ynys Cyngar
Garreg goch
Morfa Bychan Spit
Traeth Bach
Harlech Spit
Buoyed Channel
(Apr-Oct) (liable to change)
Harlech Point
Morfa Harlech

Castle
Harlech
Llanfair
Llandanwg

Shell Island
Mochras Point
Dive 1.1 Shell Island
Mochras Lagoon
Llanbedr
A496

N=4.5° W (B'E) 1984

Mochras Spit
Mochras Dyffryn
East
Passage
Dive 1.7 Bemar Bank
Llanenddwyn
North Shoals
Dive 1.6 'Pride of the Sea'
Protected Wreck NO ENTRY
NO ENTRY
Protected Wreck

Dive 1.3 Sarn Badrig
Dive 1.2 Isolated Reef
Obstn 6₆
Llanaber Churchyard

SARN BADRIG
(St Patrick's Causeway)
BARMOUTH

Four Fathom Bank
Barmouth Bay
Fegynyn Point
Dive 1.5 Unknown Wreck
Dive 1.4 Unknown Wreck

West Prong
Fairbourne

South Prong

○ Shore Dive
● Boat Dive
◑ Access by Shore or Boat
◣ Slipway

Not to be used for Navigation

CHAPTER ONE

Barmouth to Porthmadog

'Abundance of vessels have been lost in this bay, owing in a great measure to Captain Collin's charts, which make ten and seventeen fathom water in the very middle of this foul ground, which comes dry last quarter ebb. In which he is followed by all our mercenary chart contrivers, none of whom ever saw the places they pretend to describe. This is a crime equal to making false lights to mislead vessels for the sake of wreck, and like parricide among the ancient Romans, there is no law against it'.

Lewis Morris, 1748

General Description

The low-lying coastal area between Barmouth and Porthmadog consists of sandy beaches backed by extensive sand-dunes. The north-eastern skyline is dominated by the mountains of Snowdonia, while the peaks of Rhinog Fawr, Rhinog Fach, Y Llethr, and Diffws show on the

eastern horizon. Rivers flow into the sea at Barmouth, Mochras (Shell Island), and Porthmadog, with each of their estuaries having extensive, drying sandbanks. At the time of writing, this is a main training area for the Royal Air Force, so look out for the low-flying aircraft which are often seen chasing radio-controlled, pilot-less target aircraft.

RAF pilot-less aircraft

There are few places to dive from the shore, so most diving is done from RIBs or from the commercial dive-boats that operate out of Pwllheli.

The main underwater feature of the area is Sarn Badrig (St. Patrick's Causeway), a 10-mile long, narrow reef that partially dries out at low-water on spring-tides. Various myths abound about the original formation of this reef, including the legend that it was part of the dykes which surrounded the long-lost land of Cantre'r Gwaelod. A more likely explanation is that the reef is simply the remains of glacial deposits, left behind after the Ice Age. Away from the causeway, the seabed is mostly flat, but there are several small yet interesting reefs which are all alive with fish and crustaceans. Marine-life enthusiasts should check these reefs carefully, as there is much to see in Cardigan Bay, with rare but confirmed sightings of seahorses and leatherback turtles.

Essential Information:-

- Barmouth, Shell Island and Porthmadog slipways are only viable for around 2 and a half to 3 hours either side of high-water, restricting boating time to a maximum of 5 or 6 hours unless you 'lock out' for the low-tide period. Alternative sites at Black Rock Sands and Criccieth are available at all tidal states.

- The underwater visibility rapidly diminishes during westerly winds.

- Parts of Sarn Badrig dry out at low-water, even up to ten miles offshore. The surface disturbance caused by the reef can be seen from a boat in calm conditions, but not in rough weather. Take care when navigating near the reef and keep a close watch on the echo sounder.

- Although tidal streams in this area are generally weak, strong currents may be found at the entrances to the major rivers and in the East Channel between Sarn Badrig and Shell Island. There is fast-flowing water over the top of Sarn Badrig reef.

- Marine speed limits apply off most of the popular beaches, so read the appropriate notices and maintain a low speed inshore of the yellow buoys.

- Lobster fishing is a well established local industry, so beware of the pot-buoys. Note that the bag limit for unregistered fishermen (including divers) is two lobsters per person per day throughout North Wales

- There is a closed-season for taking scallops. (July 1st until December 31st.)

- There are two Protected Wrecks in this area, the Bronze Bell wreck and a wreck on Sarn Badrig, possibly the 'Diamond'.

- This is the northern part of Cardigan Bay, one of our most important areas for dolphins and porpoise. These are often seen while out in a boat, so please report any sightings to the Seawatch Foundation on 01865 717276
  or check their website on www.seawatchfoundation.org.uk

- Charts required – 'Cardigan Bay North' (Number 1971) and 'Plans on the Llŷn Peninsula' (Number 1512)

- Maps – Ordnance Survey Outdoor Leisure Map number OL18

Harlech Beach

Shore Dives or Snorkelling Sites

1.1 - Shell Island (Mochras)

Latitude	52° 48.750'N	Longitude	004° 09.080'W
O.S. Reference	SH	550E	261N

Many years ago, Shell Island was cut off from the mainland but now remains an island in name only. The Earl of Winchelsey cut a new river channel in 1819 to allow vessels to sail up to Pensarn Wharf to load slate and stone. This diversion of the Artro river channel converted the area into a peninsula which is now reached by a Tarmac road across a sandy estuary. At high-water on spring-tides, the road becomes submerged, so check the tidal information on notice boards alongside the road, or check out the Shell Island web site on www.shellisland.co.uk.

The island comprises 300 acres of camping sites, large areas of sand dunes, a long sandy beach, and a sheltered but tidal estuary. The campsite has a holiday centre with tavern, snack bar, licensed restaurant, and a games room. Although it caters for tents and motor-homes, caravans are not allowed on the island.

Mochras Point

Mochras Point at Shell Island provides a shallow, easy shore dive in good weather, but a south-westerly to north-westerly wind soon creates surf to give poor visibility for some distance offshore. In calm weather, there is good snorkelling in the shallow water around the rocks at low-tide, with entry to the water being easiest from the sandy beach close to these rocks. Scuba-diving from the shore entails a long swim to reach a depth of more than 5 metres. On a really low tide, Mochras Spit shows only 1.3 metres of water in a position more than a mile offshore from Mochras Point. Having shallow water means that your air will last for a long time, especially on a sunny day, when shallow water and a sandy seabed combine to produce pleasantly warm water. A boat is useful for diving here, but the slipway at Shell Island can only be used for just over 2 hours either side of high-water. This means you either have to operate within a 4-hour window, or remain at sea until the tide again reaches the slipway on the next flood-tide. Surface marker-buoys should always be used as a warning sign for any traffic heading to or from the river mouth at Shell Island.

Away from the rocks, the flat, sandy seabed has a sprinkling of large boulders, but you may also come across large areas of ephemeral (here to-day, gone tomorrow) mussel-beds, along with their attendant, hungry starfish. Large shoals of small fish such as sand-eels are common, with the odd lobster lurking among the boulders. In midsummer, monkfish and sea-bream visit the area, with seals and dolphins farther offshore. Shoals of mullet sweep in and out of the estuary, while divers have even seen stingrays here.

Directions: Shell Island is situated off the A496, about 7 miles north of Barmouth and 3 miles south of Harlech. Turn westwards at Llanbedr for Mochras / Shell Island. Follow the road over the railway and past the airfield onto the roadway that runs across the estuary to Shell Island. Note that the island may be cut off from the mainland at high-water on spring-tides. After paying the entry fee (£5.00 in 2002), bear left up the hill and follow the road running parallel to the sea. Park on the cliff-top as close as possible to where the rocky beach changes to flat sand. Vehicles are not allowed onto the beach, so there is a short scramble down the cliff to the sea.

So why do I like Shell Island?

My first ever dive was in 15 metres of water, from a boat moored near the Skerries, 6 miles off Holyhead. No shot-line to hang onto, insufficient weight, a leaky twin-hose regulator, and a cold, homemade wetsuit all combined to make the experience somewhat un-nerving. My second and third dives were in the River Dee in 1 metre visibility, with not a lot to see. I was ill for a week afterwards and began to wonder what this 'fun' sport was all about.

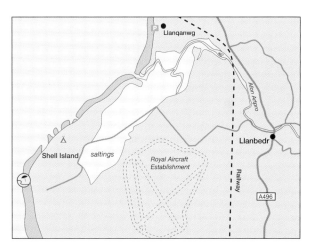

My fourth dive was from the beach at Shell Island on a fine, sunny day, following a long spell of calm weather. Once underwater, I could see for miles! Breathing was much easier from my new-fangled, single-hose Snark-2 regulator. This was a whole new world full of crabs, lobsters, plaice, wrasse, and sand-eels. I was hooked!

Edible crab hiding amongst mussels

Boat Dives - Where to Dive

1.2 - Isolated reef, charted as Obstn 6.6

Latitude	52° 44.355'N	Longitude	004° 08.180'W
Position Fix	Differential-GPS	Datum	WGS84

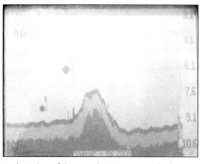

Isolated reef (metres) Note expanded trace

This is an isolated reef located about 3.5 miles west-north-west of Barmouth, where it is charted as an obstruction with a minimum depth of 6.6 metres. In calm weather, underwater visibility can be excellent, and the shallow depth means you can fully explore this reef in a single dive.

The surrounding seabed is mainly flat sand at a depth of about 10 metres, with the top of the reef at about 8 metres. The circular reef is around 50 metres in diameter and consists of millions of worn and broken pieces of tufa. These are all strangely shaped, some looking like a tangled mass of reindeer antlers, while others resemble hull-plates from a shipwreck. As a result, there are many crevices to provide shelter for the abundant marine-life. At least one large conger-eel inhabits the reef, along with many goldsinnys, tompot blennies, pout, sea-bream, and even large plaice. Scores of dogfish lie around the outer fringes of the reef and huge ballan wrasse hide under the flat sheets of rock. There are many lobster-pots scattered around the area which are connected together by underwater ropes, so care must be taken not to swim under any of the submerged lines with a surface marker-buoy. Several old lobster-pots and their connecting ropes will be found on the seabed, having lost their own lobster-pot buoy.

WRECKING - During Thursday and Friday the l4th and l5th, a large quantity of the contents of the Caroline, was washed ashore from Harlech to Mochras: consisting of staves & co., tobacco leaf, puncheons of rum, Hollands etc. As much as could be secured from the hands of the wreckers was taken possession of by Mr. E. S. Jones, Collector of the Customs, of Barmouth, and placed in safe custody. We regret to state that the inhuman and illegal practice of 'wrecking' was carried on to a most unlimited extent by the country people many of whom were in good circumstances, and the work was carried on in a barefaced and unblushing manner. The pockets of the three bodies, which had undoubtedly died since coming on shore, were ransacked. The number of people congregated on the shore was incredible, and we have heard it said, that it would have required a regiment of soldiers to prevent them thieving. It is also said, that watches are in abundance all about the country. When will this most disreputable and dishonest practice cease to disgrace this country?

Carnarvon & Denbigh Herald, March 23, 1844.

1.3 - Sarn Badrig (St. Patrick's Causeway)

Latitude (1)	52° 46.840'N	Longitude (1)	004° 09.680'W
Latitude (2)	52° 46.790'N	Longitude (2)	004° 09.760'W
Latitude (3)	52° 46.675'N	Longitude (3)	004° 09.970'W
Latitude (4)	52° 46.640'N	Longitude (4)	004° 10.045'W
Position Fix	Differential-GPS	Datum	WGS84

Sarn Badrig at low-water on a spring tide

Sarn Badrig is a shallow, ribbon-shaped reef which runs for about 10 miles out to sea, south-west from Mochras Point (Shell Island) near Harlech. A west cardinal buoy marks the south-western tip, and much of the reef dries out at low-water on spring-tides, even at a point 10 miles from the nearest dry land. Hydrographic charts for the area suggest a maximum tidal stream of only 1.5 knots, but faster currents flow across the top of the reef and in the East Passage channel off Shell Island, where the reef comes close to the shore. Fast drift-dives are possible in the area, either parallel to the reef or directly across it, depending on the tidal flow.

This dangerous reef was incorrectly charted for many years. As a result, many vessels were stranded and wrecked. As recently as August 1998, a large part of an old wooden rudder was found on the shore at Barmouth. Now displayed at Barmouth Maritime Museum, it still has the rudder-pintles attached and is believed to date from the early 1800s. A more recent item, found on the nearby beach during 1993, is a paravane, which was formerly used for mine-clearance work and is now on display at Maes Artro Museum, Llanbedr. In 1748, the hydrographer Lewis Morris published a set of charts on which he made the comments at the beginning of this chapter. In other words, the charts before 1748 showed deep water in an area where there was actually a reef which dried out at low-water. No wonder dozens of vessels have been wrecked here.

Old wooden rudder at Barmouth Maritime Museum

Sarn Badrig and two other smaller reefs in Cardigan Bay, form a reef structure that is unique to UK waters. The causeway provides a home to a wide and plentiful variety of marine-life including seals, dolphins, bass, pollack, sea-bream, dogfish, pipefish, whelks and cuttlefish. The seabed along the causeway consists of coarse gravel, small rocks and boulders. Bootlace and pod weed grows along the shallowest part of the reef, forming a dense, swaying jungle in only a few metres of water, but in deeper water, the amount of weed rapidly diminishes to almost nil. Note that many different species of weed are found here, to form a seaweed meadow, instead of the usual impenetrable tangle of kelp.

The following sites (1.4, 1.5 and 1.6) are specific locations along the reef where ships have been lost, but for anyone fascinated by our marine-life, almost anywhere near the reef will prove to be of interest. Sample GPS positions for Sarn Badrig are given opposite.

1.4 - Unknown Wreck

Name	Boiler wreck	Type	Steamer
Date Lost	Unknown	Location	Sarn Badrig
Cause	Unknown	How Lost	Ran aground
Hull	Wood	Weight	Unknown
Cargo	Unknown	Access	Boat only
Latitude	52° 42.295′N	Longitude	004° 19.655′W
Position Fix	Differential-GPS	Datum	WGS84
Seabed	3 metres (low neaps)	Wreck Height	2.5 metres
Charted as	Drying wreck		
Slipway (1)	Barmouth	Distance	10 miles
Slipway (2)	Black Rock Sands	Distance	13.5 miles
Slipway (3)	Abersoch	Distance	9 miles
Tidal Data	Slack 2 hours before low-water at Liverpool		

There is a drying wreck shown on the chart near the west end of the causeway, about 10 miles due west of Barmouth and 9 miles south-east of Abersoch. Note that the true location is further west than that shown on the chart. These are the remains of a steam-driven vessel, believed to have run aground in the 1890's. At low-water on a spring-tide, the single boiler dries out and can be seen from some distance. At low-water on neap-tides, it cannot be seen since it lies about half a metre under the surface, so take care when navigating in this area.

Low water (neap-tide)

Low water (spring-tide)

"Let another's shipwreck be your seamark".

17th century saying.

As low-water approaches, several seals are often seen waiting for the tide to drop sufficiently for them to rest on the boiler. Underwater, there is only a small amount of wreckage, lying immediately west of the boiler. Apart from the engine, there is no nearby sign of the hull or other fittings, although other wreckage has been reported away to the east-north-east. The wreck has been salvaged over the years. The condenser, steam-valves and engine bearing-caps were removed many years ago, but several of the brass boiler-tubes remain in place.

As with most of the Sarn Badrig reef, the surrounding seabed is covered with bootlace weed. During the summer months, a tangled spaghetti of more than 50 dogfish may be seen on the seabed close to the boiler, as well as wrasse, pout, goldsinnys, blennies, crabs, and lobster. Unless a drift-dive is envisaged, the best time to dive is at low-water slack, about 2 hours before low tide at Liverpool.

1.5 - Unknown Wreck

Name	Unknown	Type	Unknown
Date Lost	Unknown	Location	Sarn Badrig
Cause	Unknown	How Lost	Ran aground
Hull	Iron	Weight	Unknown
Cargo	Unknown	Access	Boat only
Latitude	52° 42.715'N	Longitude	004° 18.655'W
Position Fix	Differential-GPS	Datum	WGS84
Seabed	9 metres (low neaps)	Wreck Height	0.5 metres max
Charted as	Uncharted		
Slipway (1)	Barmouth	Distance	10 miles
Slipway (2)	Black Rock Sands	Distance	13 miles
Slipway (3)	Abersoch	Distance	9 miles
Tidal Data	Slack 2 hours before low-water at Liverpool		

This wreck is well scattered and mostly buried under the shingle, with only the edges of several iron plates projecting just above the sea-bed. It lies about 30 to 50 metres north of the drying part of the causeway and just clear of the bootlace weed which grows on the shallower part of the reef. The main part of the vessel may be totally buried, and was only located with a magnetometer, as nothing significant shows on the echo-sounder. It is very easy to swim around this site without seeing a single sign of a shipwreck. As yet, no artefacts have been recovered to identify the vessel. Any new information will be posted on our web-site.

Large cuttlefish have been seen here, expertly camouflaged among the weed and wreckage, as they rapidly change colour to blend in with the background. Should you be fortunate to locate one on a sunny day, watch it closely as a cloud passes over and blocks out the sun, making the cuttlefish instantly darken its colour. If there are no clouds, simply use your hand at a distance to block out the sun's rays, then move your hand away again. It's quite an amazing sight as the cuttlefish immediately changes its disguise! As with all dives along the reef, packs of dogfish are always present, but do look upwards as well as downwards as, on one dive, a shoal of about a dozen bass was seen cruising overhead. At a different dive-site, bass have attacked a diver's exhaust-bubbles, presumably mistaking the small silver spheres for food. I bet that gave them buoyancy problems, as well as wind!

In September 1988, a large turtle was found dead on the beach beneath Harlech castle. It was reported to the Nature Conservancy Council for Wales and taken to the National Museum of Wales, where it proved to be the largest and heaviest turtle ever recorded. It measured 113.5 inches (291 centimeters) in total length and 108 inches (277 centimeters) from flipper tip to flipper tip, and weighed 2,106 pounds (916 kilograms). Now on display in Cardiff, this

specimen is currently recognized as the world's largest and heaviest turtle by the Guinness Book of Records. The turtle seen above was washed ashore at Rhosneigr, Anglesey.

1.6 - Wreck (possibly the 'Pride of the Sea')

Name	Pride of the Sea	Type	Sailing vessel
Date Lost	8/12/1854	Location	Sarn Badrig
Cause	Ran aground in fog	How Lost	Caught fire
Hull	Wood	Weight	1,660 tons (net)
Cargo	Cotton	Access	Boat only
Latitude	52° 46.685'N	Longitude	004° 09.955'W
Position Fix	With SA	Datum	WGS84
Seabed	4 metres (low neaps)	Wreck Height	0.25 metres
Charted as	Uncharted		
Slipway (1)	Barmouth	Distance	6 miles
Slipway (2)	Black Rock Sands	Distance	8 miles
Slipway (3)	Abersoch	Distance	12 miles
Tidal Data	Slack 2 hours before low-water at Liverpool		

On the 8th of December, 1854, the Baltimore clipper 'Pride of the Sea' hit the causeway about 3 miles offshore and later caught fire. It had successfully crossed the Atlantic from New Orleans, with a cargo of cotton, only to be totally destroyed so close to its destination of Liverpool.

Wreckage, presumed to be the remains of the 'Pride of the Sea', still lies in only a few metres of water, just off the eastern side of the causeway where it may even dry out at low-water on spring-tides. The vessel was constructed of wood and since it caught fire, very little now remains of the hull, masts or fittings. Numerous metal bars lie scattered on a coarse, sandy seabed, but these are difficult to identify, being mostly covered in sea-weed. Divers have excavated the wreck in recent years, with several synthetic ropes still being attached to items of wreckage.

The GPS position given above, was taken several years ago when Selective Availability (SA) was still in force and therefore could be over 100 metres away from the true position. (See pages 10-11) Extensive searches in 2003 failed to relocate the wreck, so it is possible that the vessel has sunk into the seabed. Further information, when available, will be placed on our web site. Even without any wreckage there is much marine-life here, with pipefish, whelks, dragonets and dogfish in abundance. One huge monkfish was observed during our search for the wreck.

Pwllheli - At daybreak on Saturday morning the 9th instant, two large ships were observed from a place near this town to have stranded during the storm and thick weather on the previous night, on the Eastern part of St Patrick's Causeway not far asunder. The ship nearest to Barmouth is reported to be cotton laden from New Orleans. The other ship, timber laden from St John's, New Brunswick. Early on Monday morning the former ship was observed to be on fire and continued so for at least 24 hours. Not a vestige of her can now be seen. The latter ship is still on the causeway with no hopes of getting her off until next spring tides, should the weather prove moderate.

Carnarvon and Denbigh Herald, 16th December, 1854

1.7 - Bemar Bank

Latitude (1)	52° 46.770'N	Longitude (1)	004° 08.240'W	
Latitude (2)	52° 46.870'N	Longitude (2)	004° 08.320'W	
Position Fix	Differential-GPS	Datum	WGS84	

This small reef, about 100 to 150 metres in diameter, lies in the East Passage between the coastline and Sarn Badrig. Charted with a minimum depth of 0.7 metres with 6 metres close by, it lies outside the exclusion zone for the 'Bronze Bell' protected wreck-site. The two positions given above are for different parts of the reef. Being so shallow, it could easily catch any vessel attempting to pass inshore of Sarn Badrig, but extensive searches have failed to reveal any other wrecks close by. A dive at high-water on a neap-tide varied from 8.1 metres off the reef, to 5.2 metres on the shallowest part.

The reef is composed of small boulders covered in weed and has a wide variety of marine-life including tub gurnard, goldsinnys, dogfish, pollack, wrasse and squat lobsters. Diving on a neap-tide does not cause any problems, but the current on spring-tides can be quite strong as the reef lies in the restricted channel of the East Passage between Sarn Badrig and Mochras Point. The best time to dive is around 2 to 3 hours before low-water at Liverpool, but there is a shorter period of slack around 4 hours before high-water at Liverpool.

The Hydrographic Department lists the wreck of a schooner called the N.D. at 52° 47.400'N 004° 09.660'W. This position lies between Mochras Point (Shell Island) and the north-eastern part of Sarn Badrig, in at least 6 metres of water. A report dated 14th December, 1926, says the wreck had been dispersed and a marker-buoy withdrawn. This suggests that the wreck originally posed a danger to navigation and was deliberately destroyed at this position rather than being refloated. The report almost certainly refers to the 'Notre Dame de Boulogne', a French ketch lost in this area on the 14th of September, 1924.

Barmouth lifeboat in a gale.

Rescue of French sailors - After nine hours struggle with sea, the Barmouth lifeboat returned on Sunday night, having rescued four French sailors of the ketch 'Notre Dame de Boulogne', which had stranded on St Patrick's Causeway, eight miles from Barmouth. The vessel left Porthmadog on Sunday morning with 70 tons of slates. Two hours later, the vessel was seen signalling in distress on the treacherous causeway. Mountainous waves were washing over the vessel, which was in a perilous position. After four hours fight against the gale, the lifeboat got alongside the vessel, taking the captain and three members of the crew, including a boy of 16, on board. The vessel by that time was in a sinking condition. They were landed at Barmouth quay, which was crowded with visitors and residents. A collection was taken on behalf of the shipwrecked crew, who were taken under the care of the Shipwrecked Mariners Society. Subsequently the vessel drifted off the causeway and on Monday, only the mast was visible, the ketch being about a mile from shore.

Carnarvon and Denbigh Herald, 19th September, 1924.

The author, butty time. Cardigan Bay

Why don't I trust electronics and engines?

On a trip out to Sarn Badrig, the weather was rough but 10 miles from home my main engine was even rougher. When the outboard finally died, no amount of tinkering would get it to start. (Faulty optical sensor in the ignition circuit) Never mind, run home on the auxiliary engine. After 5 miles, that also failed. (Timing-advance rod broken) Fortunately we had two boats, so our boat was towed home. Back at the beach, one of our vehicles wouldn't start. (Salt water on the ignition-key immobilised the immobiliser)

Moral – salt water, electronics, and engines don't mix too well.

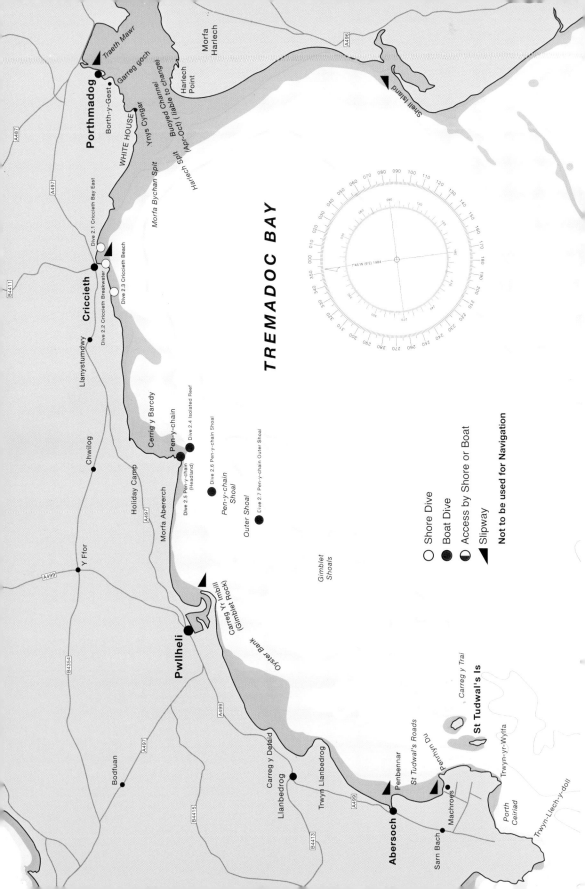

CHAPTER TWO

Porthmadog to Llanbedrog

'After another mile's ride, reach Pwllheli, the best town in this country and the magazine of goods which supplies all this tract. It lies close on the shore and has a tolerable harbour for vessels of about sixty tons. The entrance is by a high rock called The Gimlet, a mile from land to which it is joined by a range of sand-hills'.

Thomas Pennant, 1781

General Description

This is also a low-lying coastline, with sandy beaches backed by dunes and low lying drifts, while the northern skyline is dominated by the hills of the Llŷn Peninsula. Rivers flow into the sea at Porthmadog, Llanystumdwy and Pwllheli. Apart from Criccieth, there are few places to dive from the shore, so most diving is done either from RIBs and inflatables or from commercial dive boats, operating out of Pwllheli. The seabed consists mainly of flat sand or a mixture of pebbles and boulders, with little bedrock showing.

Essential Information:-

- Launch sites are available at Porthmadog, Black Rock Sands, Criccieth, Pwllheli and Abersoch.

- This south-facing coastline can provide excellent, shallow, shore-diving as long as there is settled weather or the wind direction is from the north. There are several offshore reefs, but maximum depths are all less than 15 metres.

- Tidal streams in the area are generally weak, so they do not cause major problems.

- South-westerly winds stir up the seabed to give poor underwater visibility.

- The area is popular with jet-skis and other power-craft, but don't assume that they know the significance of the Divers 'A' flag!

- Marine speed limits apply off most beaches. Read the appropriate notices and maintain a low speed inshore of the yellow buoys.

- Lobster fishing is a well-established local industry, so beware of the pot-buoys. Note that the bag limit for unregistered fishermen (including divers) is two lobsters per person per day throughout North Wales

- There is a close season for taking scallops. (July 1st until December 31st.)

- Charts required – 'Cardigan Bay North' (Number 1971) and 'Plans on the Llŷn Peninsula' (Number 1512)

- Maps – Ordnance Survey Explorer Maps numbers 12 (Lleyn Peninsula West) & 13 (Lleyn Peninsula East).

Shore Dives or Snorkelling Sites

2.1 - Criccieth Bay East

Latitude	52° 55.180'N	Longitude	004° 13.430'W
O.S. Reference	SH	505E	382N

At high-water and in calm weather, it is possible to snorkel amongst the rocks and boulders by the Moranedd Café at the east end of Criccieth. Many of the boulders are awash at high-water, but dry-out completely as the tide falls.

Directions: Take the A497 from Porthmadog, heading west towards Criccieth. As you enter Criccieth, turn left opposite the Texaco garage and cross the railway line. Park along the seafront and walk eastwards past the Moranedd Café.

Criccieth Bay (Snorkelling site in foreground, opposite the Moranedd Café).

2.2 - Criccieth Breakwater

Latitude	52° 55.040'N	Longitude	004° 13.825'W
O.S. Reference	SH	502E	379N

Although not a particularly inspiring site, the seaward side of Criccieth Breakwater offers a useful dive-site between the breakwater and the castle. At high-water and in calm conditions, it is ideal for a first sea-dive or as a training dive where there will be a maximum depth of only 4 or 5 metres. High-water at Criccieth occurs about 3 hours before high-water at Liverpool. Avoid low-water as, even after swimming 50 metres off-shore, there will be only 2 or 3 metres of water. Surface marker-buoys should be used to warn off the boat traffic coming in and out of Criccieth Harbour, while divers should keep towards the castle to avoid the anglers who fish from the breakwater. The seabed is a mixture of sand and shingle, with many large boulders covered in small mussels and bladder-wrack weed. Masked crabs lie buried in the sand, with flatfish such as plaice, solonettes, and thornback rays often seen while diving here.

Avoid diving here in southerly or south-westerly winds, as the underwater visibility is soon reduced to nil. There is room to unload near the breakwater, but do not block the access as the slipway is used by the RNLI.

Directions: Take the A497 from Porthmadog, heading west. As you enter the 40 mph speed limit in Criccieth, turn left opposite the Texaco garage. Cross the railway line and bear to the right, along the seafront. The breakwater is opposite the lifeboat station, so unload the diving gear and park back along the promenade.

2.3 - Criccieth Beach

Latitude	52° 54.930'N	Longitude	004° 14.390'W
O.S. Reference	SH	494E	378N

The beach to the west of Criccieth Castle provides an easy shore dive, suitable for novices or for a shallow night-dive. It is also suitable for snorkelling, being shallow with lots of life. Best dived at local high-water (3 hours before Liverpool) during calm weather or if the wind is from a northerly direction, this sand and shingle beach has rocks at low-water and wooden groynes running seawards. Southerly winds soon reduce the visibility to nil. Marine-life is surprisingly plentiful, with many dogfish, pollack, pipefish, tompot blennies, crabs, prawns and lobsters in depths of up to about 8 metres of water. Between 75 and 100 metres directly out from the entry point, there are several large rocks, jealously guarded by numerous shannies. These small fish are easily distinguished from most other blennies by the lack of tufts on their heads. During the summer months, rhizostomidae (barrel) jellyfish will be seen slowly drifting with the tide, looking just like huge blobs of wobbly jelly.

Cars can be parked by the beach shelter at the west end of the promenade and diving gear carried down the steps onto the flat concrete strip. More steps lead onto a gravel beach broken up by wooden groynes. The only difficult part of this site is the steep climb back up 40 steps to the car park.

A line of yellow buoys off the beach marks the marine 4 mph speed-limit area. The bay is a popular site for jet-skis, so surface marker-buoys should be used - but note that on occasions, the jet-skis have treated them as a slalom course. Lobster-pot markers will also be seen off the beach.

As mentioned, this makes an easy night-dive. On a calm night, the tide line can be seen sparkling from the blue-light given off by the bioluminescent creatures in the water. This is a perfectly natural occurrence, so don't report it to the authorities as radioactive pollution. Others have done so! A report headed 'Glowing Sea Starts a Scare' in the Daily Post of 24th September 1984 says that Police, the Fire Service, Coastguards and the Water Authorities were all called out to investigate this natural phenomenon.

Directions: From Porthmadog, take the A497 into Criccieth, passing the main shopping area, the garage on the left and Plas Newydd. Turn left (signposted 'Traeth/Beach' & 'Castle'), cross over the railway and the car park is on the right, immediately after the sharp left-hand bend by the Abereistedd Hotel. From Pwllheli, take the A497 for Criccieth and Porthmadog. Immediately after entering the 30 mph speed limit at Criccieth, turn right - signposted 'Traeth/Beach', 'Castle' and 'Lon Fel'. Cross the railway and the car park is on the right, immediately after the sharp left-hand bend.

2.4 - Isolated Reef, close to Pen-y-Chain Headland

Latitude	52° 53.490'N	Longitude	004° 19.440'W
Position Fix	Differential - GPS	Datum	WGS84

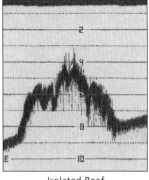

Isolated Reef
off Pen-y-Chain (metres)

Pen-y-Chain Headland is situated about half-way between Criccieth and Pwllheli and is easily identified by the chalets of the former 'Butlins Star-Coast World' holiday camp, now known as 'The Haven' or 'Hafan-y-Mor'.

The low, rocky headland drops onto a shallow, sandy seabed, but slightly to the east, there is a kelp-covered reef that provides an interesting dive suitable for novices or for a second dive. The reef is about 5 metres high in only 9 to 10 metres of water. It is almost awash at chart datum, so care is needed to avoid propeller damage at low-water on spring-tides. Chart 1512 shows the reef as having 3 separate peaks, marked as 0.6 metres, 1.4 metres, and 1.6 metres. In good conditions, kelp growing on the rock may be seen through the water, or a disturbance on the surface of the sea may indicate the location of the site. Otherwise, locate the reef by the transit or the GPS in conjunction with an echo-sounder.

It is possible to explore the whole circumference of the reef in about 30 minutes simply by keeping to the boundary between the rock and the surrounding sand. Marine-life is quite prolific with pipefish, two-spotted blennies, huge rhizostomidae (barrel) jellyfish (in summer), and a few crustaceans. Tidal streams in the area are generally fairly weak, but at full flow there can be strong currents across the top of the reef. At this time, shelter can usually be found around the base of the reef.

Visibility is usually quite good, especially when the wind is from the north-west or the north-east. The area does not suffer greatly from plankton blooms, as found in parts of Anglesey or Liverpool Bay. Hence, it is a useful dive-site for May or June when these other areas may be impossible to dive due to poor visibility, but this area should be avoided in south-westerly winds.

Location: Head towards Pen-y-Chain headland, keeping the small building partially obscured. The reef gives a good indication on the echo-sounder.

Transit for Isolated Reef, close to Pen-y-Chain Headland. Small building (inset) is partly obscured

2.5 - Pen-y-Chain Headland

Latitude (West)	52° 53.495'N	Longitude (W)	004° 19.860'W
Latitude (East)	52° 53.490'N	Longitude (E)	004° 19.665'W
Position Fix	Differential-GPS	Datum	WGS84

Pen-y-Chain headland consists of two rocky outcrops which provide shallow dives with a maximum depth of only about 5 metres against the cliffs. The headland is a popular site for anglers, so keep watch for their lines and hooks. Despite the lack of deep water, there is still a good variety of marine-life. Pipefish are common, along with small lobsters and the occasional salmon. The site is sheltered from the north, but is very exposed to south and south west.

When investigating this site, I once found several large roofing-slates jammed together amongst the rocks, suggesting that a vessel may have been wrecked here - probably when outbound from Porthmadog. Unfortunately, I was unable to find any further evidence of a wreck, such as timbers or an anchor.

2.6 - Pen-y-Chain Shoal

Latitude	52° 52.955'N	Longitude	004° 20.660'W
Position Fix	Differential-GPS	Datum	WGS84

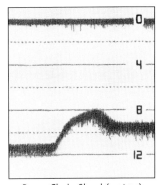

Pen-y-Chain Shoal (metres)

This shallow shoal lies less than a mile south-west of Pen-y-Chain headland. Although not a brilliant dive-site, it provides an interesting site for anyone wishing to observe a wide variety of small marine creatures. Many small boulders provide shelter for squat lobster, edible-crabs, hermit-crabs, and the occasional juvenile lobster. At high-water, the shallowest part of the reef is only about 8 metres deep, dropping off to around 12 metres. A tidal diamond for this location is shown on chart 1971 and gives the maximum current on a spring-tide of only 0.5 knots, so the reef can be dived at almost any time. Note that the tidal data given on chart 1971 is with reference to high-water at Milford Haven and not Liverpool or Holyhead. High-water at Milford is around 5 hours earlier than Liverpool.

2.7 - Pen-y-Chain Outer Shoal

Latitude	52° 52.145'N	Longitude	004° 21.440'W
Position Fix	Differential-GPS	Datum	WGS84

Pen-y-Chain Outer Shoal lies about 1.75 miles south-west of Pen-y-Chain Headland. Despite being so far offshore, the shallowest part is charted at a minimum depth of only 3.6 metres. The top of the reef is covered in large stones and green weed, but these fade away to coarse gravel as the depth gradually increases to around 10 metres. The site is over-run with dogfish, while several tub-gurnard have been observed here, noticeable by their beautiful blue fins. Look carefully for the small spider-crabs, with their camouflage coating of weed. Again, tidal streams are weak, allowing the reef to be dived at any time.

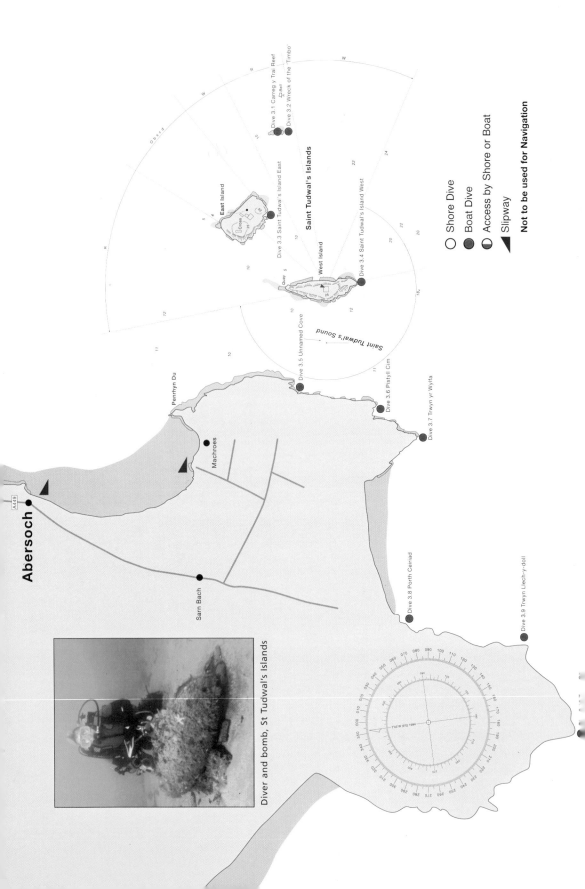

Abersoch

A499

Penrhyn Du

Machroes

Sarn Bach

Diver and bomb, St Tudwal's Islands

East Island

Cross

West Island

Quay

Saint Tudwal's Islands

Dive 3.1 Carreg y Trai Reef
Dive 3.2 Wreck of the 'Timbo'

Dive 3.3 Saint Tudwal's Island East

Dive 3.4 Saint Tudwal's Island West

Dive 3.5 Unnamed Cove

Saint Tudwal's Sound

Dive 3.6 Pistyll Cim

Dive 3.7 Trwyn yr Wylfa

Dive 3.8 Porth Ceiriad

Dive 3.9 Trwyn Llech-y-doll

○ Shore Dive

● Boat Dive

◑ Access by Shore or Boat

▲ Slipway

Not to be used for Navigation

CHAPTER THREE

Abersoch, Porth Ceiriad and the Saint Tudwal's Islands

'This is reckoned to be one of the best roads in Great Britain, it being a good outlet and so extensive that it would contain the whole Royal Navy of England'

Lewis Morris, 1748.

General Description

Moving westwards from Abersoch, the coastline changes to rocky cliffs with offshore islands at St. Tudwal's Island East and St Tudwal's Island West. Long, sandy beaches are found at the popular tourist venue of Abersoch and also at Porth Ceiriad.

Abersoch Bay faces towards the east and, in combination with the islands, gives almost total shelter from south-westerly winds. The area has provided a sheltered anchorage for hundreds of years, but is now used mainly for leisure craft rather than the working vessels of old. During the summer months, many cruising yachts and powerboats lie afloat to the east of the islands, while dinghy racing takes place around the islands and anchorage. Dive-boat coxswains need to be aware of other water-users, keeping clear of them or warning them off as necessary. Make sure the 'A' flag is flown whenever divers are in the water.

Lobster at Carreg-y-Trai reef

Essential Information:-

- There are two slipways at Abersoch, but larger RIBS should use Pwllheli for launching.

- Apart from the Tudwal Islands, there is very little shelter from southerly or easterly winds.

- There were several Second World War bombing ranges here. Leave any munitions well alone, as the contents can become unstable if allowed to dry out.

- Beware of the drying reef at Carreg-y-Trai (St. Tudwal's Islands).

- Marine speed limits apply off most beaches. Read the appropriate notices and maintain a low speed inshore of the yellow buoys.

- The area is popular with jet-skis and power-boats, but don't assume they know the significance of the diver's 'A' flag!

- Lobster fishing is a well established local industry, so beware of the pot-buoys. Note that the bag limit for unregistered fishermen (including divers) is two lobsters per person per day throughout North Wales

- There is a close season for taking scallops (July 1st until December 31st).

- The gate to the main slipway in Abersoch is locked at 8pm.

- Dinghy racing is popular off Abersoch, so keep well clear during contests. Race-time in midsummer can be chaotic.

- Dolphins and porpoise are frequently encounted here. Please follow the Seawatch Foundation code of conduct to avoid disturbing them.

- Charts required – 'Cardigan Bay North' (Number 1971) and 'Plans on the Llŷn Peninsula' (Number 1512).

- Maps – Ordnance Survey Explorer Map number 12 (Lleyn Peninsula West).

Shore Dives or Snorkelling Sites

There are no really interesting shore-dives in this area, as the only easy shore-access is on to a series of sandy beaches.

The St Tudwal's Islands & Abersoch Bay

Boat Dives - Where to Dive

3.1 - Carreg-y-Trai reef, St. Tudwal's Islands

Latitude (North)	52° 48.200'N	Longitude	004° 27.020'W
Latitude (Middle)	52° 48.150'N	Longitude	004° 26.985'W
Latitude (South)	52° 48.130'N	Longitude	004° 27.020'W
Position Fix	Differential-GPS	Datum	WGS84

This reef lies about 400 metres south-east of St. Tudwal's Island East. It provides an excellent dive-site, with a mix of wreckage, rocks and varied marine-life. Located about two miles from Abersoch slipway, it is charted as a rock that dries by 3.3 metres in about 15 metres at low-water. At low-tide, two separate rocks will be seen above the surface, but the underwater reef continues for some distance to the north. Three GPS positions are given above. One is for the north peak, one for the shallow channel between the peaks, and one for the very top of the southern-most peak of the reef. These are all completely covered at high-water, but there is a red, can-shaped 'Bell-buoy' moored about 400 metres to the east, to give some warning of the danger. At low-water, two or three dozen seals can be seen on the rocks, but they leave their resting place to feed as the tide rises. Divers then often see them underwater, and some of the juvenile seals have been known to tug on a diver's fins. If you suffer from sea-sickness, stay upwind of the reef at low-water to avoid the stench of decaying fish given off by the seals as they laze upon the rocks. They may look cute, but they do have bad breath and body odour!

During the 1970's, a small boat overturned between the reef and St. Tudwal's Island East, throwing a quantity of diving equipment into the water. Occasionally, remnants of old diving equipment are found and recovered, but please leave the live aerial torpedo and other unexploded munitions well alone! See photo page 32.

Two or more vessels lie wrecked on or around the reef, details of these wrecks and the tides being given within the following dive-site.

3.2 - Wreck of the British Steamer 'Timbo'

Name	Timbo	Type	Steamer
Date Lost	15/11/1922	Location	Carreg-y-Trai
Cause	Bad Weather	How Lost	Hit rock
Hull	Iron	Weight	295 tons (gross)
Cargo	In ballast	Access	Boat only
Latitude	52° 48.110'N	Longitude	004° 27.000'W
Position Fix	Differential-GPS	Datum	WGS84
Seabed	14 metres (low neaps)	Wreck Height	2 metres
Charted as	Uncharted		
Slipway (1)	Abersoch	Distance	2 miles
Slipway (2)	Pwllheli	Distance	6 miles
Tidal Data	Slack 3 to 3.5 hours before low-water at Liverpool		

The 'Timbo'. High and dry at Dinas Dinlle

The 'Timbo' memorial in Rhoscolyn.

The British screw-steamer 'Timbo' was first involved in a major disaster in December, 1920, when it was stranded high and dry on Dinas Dinlle beach near Caernarfon. During a rescue attempt by the Rhoscolyn Lifeboat, five members of the lifeboat crew tragically lost their lives, along with four crew-members from the 'Timbo'.

A memorial to the sacrifice made by the lifeboat crew can be seen in Rhoscolyn Churchyard, near Holyhead. The ship remained stranded high and dry until a wooden launching ramp could be constructed and, with the aid of tugs, the 'Timbo' was eventually refloated. It continued to trade around the Welsh and Lancashire coasts, but did not survive long and was finally wrecked on Carreg-y-Trai reef.

Bound for London, the 'Timbo' had just left Pwllheli when she ran on to Carreg-y-Trai reef during darkness on the evening of 15th November, 1922. The crew quickly abandoned ship and everyone reached the shore in safety. Lloyd's Agents initially reported that the ship could be refloated if powerful pumps could quickly be sent to the scene, but by 21st November, the situation had deteriorated and the ship was described as being underwater at half-tide.

Built at Newcastle during 1883, the 'Timbo' had its boiler and engine mounted amidships to power a single propeller. The vessel also carried a spare, 2-metre diameter iron propeller, which can still be found immediately south of the reef in around 14 metres of water. The 3-metre wide boiler, two large winches, a length of propeller shaft and a tangled mass of ribs, hull-plates and girders all lie close by. The valuable condenser has already been recovered, while other heavy items such as the crankshaft have been moved and put to further use as mooring weights in Abersoch Bay. Surprisingly, a small, unmarked bell was recovered from the site as recently as May 2002, and may be from the 'Timbo'.

Even without the lure of a shipwreck, this is an excellent dive-site with a variety of sponges, fan worms and other marine-life as well as many pollack, goldsinny wrasse, cuckoo wrasse and tompot blennies. In addition to the fish life, it's almost inevitable that one or more of the local seals will investigate you, checking up on the wide-eyed, bubble-blowing, clumsy visitor to their hunting grounds.

The remains of a wooden vessel and its cargo of roofing slates lie scattered among the wreckage of the 'Timbo'. This was probably the 'Omnibus', which was reportedly wrecked on Half-Tide Rocks (Carreg-y-Trai) on October 2nd, 1869, when all the crew were fortunately saved. A quantity of musket-balls or grapeshot has also been recovered from among the kelp at this site, but it would seem unlikely that these have come from either a steamship or a wooden coaster with a cargo of roofing slates. More modern .22 and .303-calibre bullets also litter the area.

Timing: On spring-tides, strong currents will be found around Carreg-y-Trai, so unless you fancy a long drift-dive, stick to neap-tides and keep close to the rocks, or dive at low-water slack, around 3 to 3.5 hours before low water at Liverpool.

Location: The easiest way to locate the wreck is to visit the site at low-water when the reef will be clearly visible, with the 'Timbo' lying only a crab's scuttle to the south-east of the reef. The thick kelp seen on the reef at low-water will have cleared by the time you have dropped down the near-vertical cliffs to reach the wreck. See photo overleaf.

At high-water, use the GPS and echo-sounder to locate the south edge of Carreg-y-Trai, with the wreck lying at the GPS position given opposite, on the flat seabed immediately to the south of the reef.

Diving on the 'Timbo'

The St. Tudwal's Islands – General Information

For the marine-life enthusiast, either of the St. Tudwal's islands provides ample opportunities for observing and photographing the local wildlife. Seals have become used to the presence of divers and are regularly seen underwater, suddenly appearing out of the gloom to liven up the dive. A local diver, peering into a small cave to inspect a lobster, was totally surprised when he was barged out of the way by a seal that wanted to know what all the fuss was about.

On a calm, summer's evening, both islands can provide a very pleasant night-dive, but you will need to recover your boat at the Machroes slipway as the main slipway in Abersoch is locked at 8pm.

Long drift-dives can be enjoyed around the islands or through the channel between St. Tudwal's Island East and St. Tudwal's Island West. The minimum depth in this channel is only around 6 metres, slowly dropping away to more than 20 metres as you drift southwards. The channel between the islands and the coast, Tudwal's Sound, has a minimum charted depth of around 12 metres, where long drift-dives are also possible.

Divers have found several unexploded bombs or shells in this area, so leave any unidentified lumps of metal well alone. The visiting diver who took one live, explosive-shell ashore did not realise that the contents become unstable as they dry out. Fortunately, it was noticed in the back of his car and reported to the correct authorities for safe disposal.

Several large anchors lie out on the sand, either lost from vessels taking refuge here, or from the many shipwrecks that have occurred locally.

3.3 - St. Tudwal's Island East

Latitude (North)	52° 48.470'N	Longitude (N)	004° 27.780'W
Latitude (South)	52° 48.230'N	Longitude (S)	004° 27.515'W
Position Fix	Differential-GPS	Datum	WGS84

St Tudwal's Island - East. Carreg-y-Trai reef and Timbo wreck in foreground

St. Tudwal's Island East is a small diamond-shaped island, only 1.5 miles from Abersoch slipway. It is the site of an old priory, but landing is not permitted as the island is privately owned. 'Chapel Bay', on the east of the island, is often used as a sheltered anchorage during the summer months. The whole east side of the island is rather shallow, with a flat seabed where a variety of creatures live in the sand. The west and south parts of the island offer better diving, where there is more rock and marine-life. Isolated lumps of concreted wreckage will be found in a small bay on the north-west side of the island.

There is a small underwater cave near the southern tip of the island (at 52° 48.200' N 004° 27.600'W) where the rocks drop away steeply to around 14 metres, but take care if diving here when a sea-swell is running. Beware of the shallow reef and drying rock located close to the cave. The cave is an excellent but shallow dive site, as there are often several seals to be seen underwater. The sea bed in the gully leading to the cave is full of rounded boulders which have 'shot-blasted' the

bedrock smooth. Dahlia and Jewel anemones cling to the bedrock, while in the nesting season you will find guillimot and seagull eggs which have fallen fron the precarious nest on the cliffs above. The local starfish appear to have quite an appetite for these eggs.

3.4 - St. Tudwal's Island West

Latitude (North)	52° 48.165'N	Longitude (N)	004° 28.280'W
Latitude (South)	52° 47.750'N	Longitude (S)	004° 28.190'W
Position Fix	Differential-GPS	Datum	WGS84

St Tudwal's Island - West

St. Tudwal's Island West is a small teardrop-shaped island, about 2 miles from Abersoch slipway. It has a prominent lighthouse instead of a chapel and is again privately owned, so landing is not permitted here either.

The east side of the island is shallow, allowing long dive-times for the marine-life enthusiast or underwater photographer. A shallow, kelp-covered reef runs out from the north tip of the island, where strong currents can be found. This makes a good starting point for a long drift-dive along the east or west coasts of the island. If you fancy such a dive, there will be a strong southwards-running current between 1 and 3 hours before high-water at Liverpool. As you are carried along, you will see many dead-men's fingers, sponges, wrasse, pollack, dogfish and spiny spider-crabs, as well as a few lobsters and crabs. Farther away from the island and in about 15 metres of water, the seabed changes to coarse gravel with less conspicuous marine-life, except where there are clusters of large boulders.

As with St. Tudwal's Island East, the western side of the island offers better diving than the east, with several small underwater caves.

3.5 - Un-named cove

Latitude	52° 48.065'N	Longitude	004° 29.045'W
Position Fix	Differential - GPS	Datum	WGS84

Sheltered from the west, this is a shallow bay with a sandy seabed and little current. Landing is not possible due to the rocky cliffs, where there is a small cave, but this is a useful site for snorkelling or for a training dive in only a few metres of water. Keep within the bay to avoid passing boat traffic.

3.6 - Pistyll Cim

Latitude	52° 47.640'N	Longitude	004° 29.270'W
Position Fix	Differential - GPS	Datum	WGS84

Another sheltered and shallow bay suitable for novice training, Pistyll Cim is again accessible only by boat. Maximum depths are only 9 or 10 metres and this bay has a small waterfall if you fancy an after-dive shower! Keep close inshore to avoid the boat traffic.

Although the water is shallow, there is ample marine-life, with even the occasional conger eel. If you enjoy seafood, take a fishing rod for the shoals of mackerel that run through Tudwal's Sound during the summer months.

3.7 - Trwyn yr Wylfa

Latitude	52° 47.455'N	Longitude	004° 29.535'W
Position Fix	Differential - GPS	Datum	WGS84

Porth Ceiriad, Trwyn yr Wylfa and the St Tudwal's Islands

The cliff-face to the north-west of Trwyn yr Wylfa provides an excellent dive-site, which drops off rapidly to a sandy seabed at about 10 metres. This cliff faces south-west and should be avoided if the wind is from that direction. Large underwater boulders form small caves, gullies, overhangs and tunnels, all sandblasted smooth by strong currents and surges. Strong currents will be found, especially off the point, where an underwater reef continues southwards. Sponges, sea-squirts and other marine animals attach themselves to the reef. Shoals of large pollack are usually seen, along with large ballan wrasse, spiny spider-crabs and large dahlia anemones.

3.8 - Porth Ceiriad

Latitude	52° 47.500'N	Longitude	004° 31.000'W
Position Fix	Differential - GPS	Datum	WGS84

Porth Ceiriad is a wide, south-facing, sandy bay that drops off to a depth of only around 10 metres. On warm summer days, it can be extremely popular with jet-skis, power-boats and yachts. Porth Ceiriad is useful for shallow training-dives where there is plenty of marine-life against the rocks, but the large sandy areas are less interesting.

3.9 - Trwyn Llech-y-doll

Latitude	52° 46.895'N	Longitude	004° 31.100'W
Position Fix	Differential - GPS	Datum	WGS84

Trwyn Llech-y-Doll

The western point of Porth Ceiriad is known as Trwyn Llech-y-Doll, where - despite the impressive, grey, coastal cliffs - the seabed slowly drops off to a depth of only about 15 metres. Close inshore, there are kelp-covered rocks which give way to a seabed of coarse, undulating sand. Look out for fan worms, wrasse, dogfish and 2-spotted gobies.

Strong currents will be found here, so use the area for a fast drift-dive, although some slack will be found around 3 hours before low-water at Liverpool.

3.10 - Trwyn Cilan

Latitude	52° 46.645'N	Longitude	004° 31.840'W
Position Fix	Differential - GPS	Datum	WGS84

Trwyn Cilan

The southernmost headland along this stretch of coast, Trwyn Cilan has impressive cliffs above the water and a pleasant, rocky terrain for divers. There are several small underwater reefs and a stony, shale seabed farther offshore. Look out for the large bull-huss usually found here.

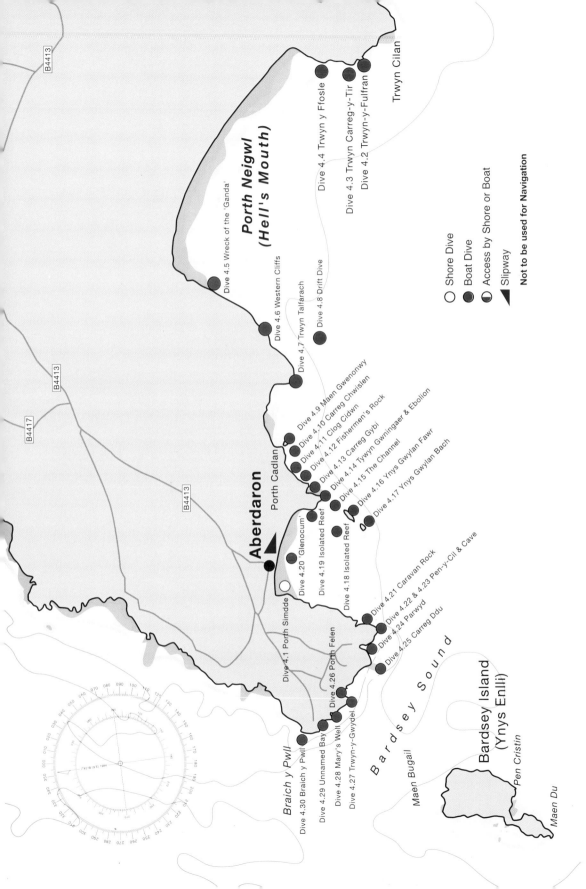

Porth Neigwl
(Hell's Mouth)

Dive 4.5 Wreck of the 'Ganda'
Dive 4.6 Western Cliffs
Dive 4.7 Trwyn Talfarach
Dive 4.8 Drift Dive

Dive 4.4 Trwyn y Ffosle
Dive 4.3 Trwyn Carreg-y-Tir
Dive 4.2 Trwyn-y-Fulfran

Trwyn Cilan

Dive 4.9 Maen Gwenonwy
Dive 4.10 Carreg Chwislen
Dive 4.11 Clog Cidwn
Dive 4.12 Fishermen's Rock
Dive 4.13 Carreg Gybi
Dive 4.14 Tywyn Gwningaer & Ebolion
Dive 4.15 The Channel
Dive 4.16 Ynys Gwylan Fawr
Dive 4.17 Ynys Gwylan Bach

Aberdaron
Porth Cadlan

Dive 4.20 'Glenocum'
Dive 4.19 Isolated Reef
Dive 4.18 Isolated Reef

Dive 4.21 Caravan Rock
Dive 4.22 & 4.23 Pen-y-Cil & Cave
Dive 4.24 Parwyd
Dive 4.25 Carreg Ddu

Dive 4.1 Porth Simdde
Dive 4.26 Porth Felen
Dive 4.30 Braich y Pwll
Dive 4.29 Unnamed Bay
Dive 4.28 Mary's Well
Dive 4.27 Trwyn-y-Gwydel

Braich y Pwll

Bardsey Sound

Bardsey Island
(Ynys Enlli)

Maen Bugail
Pen Cristin
Maen Du

○ Shore Dive
● Boat Dive
◑ Access by Shore or Boat
▲ Slipway

Not to be used for Navigation

B4413
B4413
B4417
B4413

CHAPTER FOUR

Hell's Mouth to Braich-y-Pwll

'In the promontory, Penrhyn Du, on the points of this bay, have been considerable adventures for lead ore and of late years, attempts to drain the mines by means of a fire-engine: but the expenses proved superior to the gains. A little beyond this is another bay, called Hell's Mouth, dreaded by mariners, being the Scylla to the Charybdis of Sarn Badrig whose extremity lies nearly opposite'.

Thomas Pennant, 1781

General Description

Long, south-westerly facing, sandy beaches are found at Hell's Mouth (Porth Neigwl) and Aberdaron, where there are steep cliffs of soft clay. Between these sandy beaches, there are many impressive headlands, coves and high cliffs featuring notable volcanic-rock formations. The offshore islands of Ynys Gwylan Fawr, Ynys Gwylan Bach (The Seagull Islands) and Bardsey Island (Ynys Enlli) are also composed of volcanic rock.

There is spectacular wildlife to be seen both above and below the surface. Look out for seals, dolphins, porpoise, puffins, razorbills, guillemots, choughs and buzzards.

Thomas Pennant, in his 'A Tour in Wales', published in 1781, compares the dual dangers of Hell's Mouth and Sarn Badrig to those of Scylla and Charybdis in Homer's Tales, where the mariner avoids one but is trapped by the other. Chapter One discussed the wrecks on Sarn Badrig, but many other vessels came to grief in Hell's Mouth. Unfortunately for divers, most were wrecked on the sandy beach and subsequently salvaged.

Although this is not the easiest of diving areas, there are many superb dives to be enjoyed.

Essential Information:-

- There are no easy shore dives along this coastline, so all diving is done from RIBs or inflatables launched at Abersoch or Aberdaron. If you don't have a boat, contact any of the hard-boats operating out of Pwllheli or ring 'Waterline', who can provide a RIB and coxswain. See Section 3 for details.

- There were several Second World War bombing ranges here. Leave any munitions well alone.

- There are very strong currents and heavy overfalls in Bardsey Sound. Avoid the exposed sites on spring-tides.

- Fog banks may suddenly appear in Bardsey Sound, reducing surface visibility to as little as 50 metres.

- There is very little shelter from southerly or south-westerly winds.

- Beware of drying rocks at Carreg Chwislen (Porth Cadlan), Ebolion and Mary's Well.

- There is a close season for taking scallops (July 1st until December 31st.).

- Lobster fishing is a well-established local industry, so watch out for pot-buoys.

- Launching can be very difficult in Aberdaron, where the car park usually closes at 7pm (read the notes in Section 2 carefully before attempting to launch here).

- If you launch at Abersoch, remember that the gate to the main slipway is locked at 8pm.

- Charts required – 'Cardigan Bay North' (Number 1971).

- Maps – Ordnance Survey Explorer Map number 12 (Lleyn Peninsula West).

Shore Dives or Snorkelling Sites

4.1 - Porth Simdde (Western corner of Aberdaron Bay)

Latitude	52° 48.160'N	Longitude	004° 43.160'W	
O.S. Reference	SH	167E	263N	

At low-water and in calm weather, the cliffs at the west end of Aberdaron Bay provide easy snorkelling in an area well away from the main boat traffic heading for Aberdaron slipway. It would be a long way to carry diving gear. The site is sheltered from the north and west by the high cliffs, but is exposed to the south and south-west.

The stumps of the supporting legs of an old wooden pier appear on the beach at low-water, and there are many boulders within easy distance of the shoreline. The water is shallow for some distance offshore, allowing snorkellers to see sand-eels, wrasse, pollack and crabs.

Directions: Park in Aberdaron and walk westwards (to the right) along the beach to the cliffs at the far end. Note that at high-water, there is no access along the beach. At other times, you will have to paddle across a stream.

Porth Simdde (foreground)
& the Seagull Islands
Note - 2 rows of 'Stumps' on the beach

Boat Dives - Where to Dive

Hell's Mouth (General description)

Hell's Mouth

Hell's Mouth (Porth Neigwl) comprises a three and a half mile wide south-west facing sandy bay, with rocky cliffs to the east and west. It was appropriately named, and feared by generations of seamen. Any sailing ship unfortunate enough to be swept into the bay during a south-westerly gale would have had great difficulty in escaping, and would be faced with the choice of running into the cliffs or on to the beach. Most ships opted for the latter, with the 1850s Ordnance Survey map clearly stating 'Transit wrecked in 1839'. Other vessels known to have been beached are the 'Arfestone' (1840), the 'Aggravator' (1898), the 'Twelve Apostles' (also 1898), the 'Margaret & Elizabeth' (1912) and the 'Trader' (1917). Most of these would have been pounded to pieces on the beach and scavenged for scrap, but some items - such as the boiler from the 'Aggravator' - can still be seen at the high-water mark.

Although there are some areas of small rocks scattered along the beach, these are very limited in extent and are home only to the odd shoal of sand-eels. Realistically, the only useful dive-sites are off the cliffs to the east or west of the bay, along with a few isolated reefs further out to sea.

Dive-sites on the eastern side of Hell's Mouth (All boat dives)

This area can be reached only by boat. The nearest slipways are Abersoch and Aberdaron. The east side of Hell's Mouth bay has impressive cliffs, with abandoned mines on the hillside above and mysterious, rocky caves at sea level. The blue-grey patches on the cliff face are manganese ore, which was mined in this area in the early 1900s and exported by sea.

4.2 - Trwyn-y-Fulfran

Latitude	52° 47.045'N	Longitude	004° 32.500'W
Position Fix	Differential - GPS	Datum	WGS84

Trwyn-y-Fulfran has steep, rocky cliffs above water and a succession of underwater gullies and ridges lying close inshore, where some shelter can be found from the currents that sweep the east side of Hell's Mouth. Note that the tidal flow away from the cliffs can be quite fierce, even though the surface conditions appear quite calm. Against the cliffs, this area gives a pleasant, easy dive for newcomers to our sport. Depths vary from around 5 to 15 metres.

4.3 - Trwyn Carreg-y-Tir

Latitude	52° 47.180'N	Longitude	004° 32.595'W
Position Fix	Differential - GPS	Datum	WGS84

Hells Mouth - eastern cliffs

The seabed at Trwyn Carreg-y-Tir

Trwyn Carreg-y-Tir has two small islets close to the cliffs at the eastern side of Hell's Mouth. This is an excellent diving area in 15 to 20 metres of water, where you have the choice of keeping close inshore and out of the current, or undertaking a long drift-dive along the outer edge of the islets.

Close inshore, there are many large boulders and rocky ridges, mostly about 2 or 3 metres high, which can give some shelter from the current. The gully between the islets and the cliffs is particularly interesting. As you rummage under the rocks, don't miss the seals that occasionally swoop past the dry-suit clad intruder to their territory. Just what is the diving signal for 'There's a seal performing an underwater ballet-dance right behind you'? Look out for wrasse, dogfish, pollack, spiny spider-crabs, starfish and the occasional sunfish.

Strong currents are encountered off the islets, providing an exhilarating drift over a varied seabed. But don't stray too far offshore, as there are extensive areas of flat sand further out. Off the islets, where the currents are strongest, the rocks have been worn smooth and are covered with dead-men's fingers. Following the edge of the rocks takes you to a maximum depth of around 20 metres.

4.4 - Trwyn y Ffosle

Latitude	52° 47.615'N	Longitude	004° 32.560'W
Position Fix	Differential - GPS	Datum	WGS84

Still on the east side of Hell's Mouth, and heading northwards towards the sandy beach, the seabed off Trwyn y Ffosle is a mass of large boulders covered in dense kelp. Don't dive here if there is any swell running, as you will perform an underwater waltz, constantly crashing into the boulders. I still have the bruises!

Hell's Mouth beach

The shallow and sandy expanse of Hell's Mouth beach is more than 3 miles wide, with scattered pieces of shipwreck lying on the sand around the high-water line. Extensive magnetometer searches from a boat have revealed only several old targets from the bombing range that was established here during the Second World War.

4.5 - Wreck of an old steamer at the western end of Hell's Mouth

Name	Ganda	Type	Steamer
Date Lost	5/8/1904	Location	Hell's Mouth (West)
Cause	Broke from moorings	How Lost	Blown ashore
Hull	Iron	Weight	474 tons (gross)
Cargo	Manganese ore	Access	Boat only
Latitude	52° 48.915'N	Longitude	004° 37.055'W
Position Fix	Differential-GPS	Datum	WGS84
Seabed	4 to 6 metres	Wreck Height	2 metres (boiler)
Charted as	Uncharted		
Slipway (1)	Abersoch	Distance	8 miles
Slipway (2)	Aberdaron	Distance	4 miles
Tidal Data	Little current		

During the late 1800s and early 1900s, manganese ore was mined at the western side of Hell's Mouth on the hillside above the village of Rhiw. The cover photograph of 'The Manganese Mines of Gwynedd' (see bibliography) shows vessels loading this ore at Rhiw Pier. The mineral was transported by an aerial runway and loaded on to ships at a wooden pier north-east of the rocky outcrop of Graig Ddu. Obsolete mining equipment, including a boiler, still lies scattered along the hillside. A few wooden piles from the pier can still be seen at low-water. At least one vessel got into difficulty while loading in such an exposed location, and now lies wrecked among the kelp only 50 metres or so from the low-water mark. Some divers have difficulty believing that an iron steamship can be found this close inshore, while others have failed to find the wreck because they are unwilling to delve among the thick kelp. The vessel is probably the S.S. 'Ganda', a Belgian-registered vessel of 474 tons which was wrecked here on 5th August, 1904, while loading manganese ore.

The 'Ganda' broke from her mooring during the night, tangled the mooring-rope around her propeller and drifted ashore. On the following day, the rope was cleared and she steamed away, heading for a safe anchorage at the St. Tudwal's Islands. Unfortunately, she was found to be leaking badly and so returned to the pier where she grounded on a stony seabed, split her hull and filled with seawater.

The wreck can usually be seen when snorkelling, since the least depth of water over the single boiler is only 3 metres. The outer casing of the boiler is slowly falling apart to reveal the inner boiler-tubes. Through the summer months, a thick layer of kelp grows around the wreck, partially or fully hiding any sign of a ship. The hull and fittings have been salvaged over the years, so most of the non-ferrous metal, including the condenser, has already been removed. The riveted steel hull is almost totally flattened or covered in boulders, but it is possible to swim into the forward hold where samples of manganese ore are still found. Despite the hundreds of boulders that have piled up around the bow section, the forward hold remains relatively clear. There is a 2-metre drop into this hold, where you can swim through gaps in the vertical hull-plates and explore under the horizontal decking.

The main identifiable part of the wreck is the 4-metre wide boiler that has partly split open, to reveal the internal tubing. There is no apparent sign of the engine. Unless it lies hidden under the kelp, this valuable piece of machinery was probably salvaged in 1904.

'Bitts'

Heading roughly north from the boiler, the propeller-shaft leads past a pair of bitts to the stern-post, thrust bearing, rudder and a single, 4-bladed, iron propeller. These lie at an angle of about 45 degrees to provide a dark hiding place for a shoal of pout. Make sure you take a torch to shine into this man-made underwater cave. The 'Ganda' was only 52 metres long and, as the prop-shaft is about 16 metres long, the engine and boiler must have been mounted amidships.

To get the most out of this dive-site, you really need to delve among the kelp to see the wreck and the huge spur-dogs which shelter here. Expect to see wrasse, pollack and spiny spider-crabs.

The underwater visibility can be extremely good in settled weather, but south-westerly winds produce a heavy swell and poor visibility. Currents are very weak, so the site can be dived at any tidal state. There are numerous lobster-pots in the area, many of which have long, floating lines attached, and a seemingly magnetic attraction to a boat's propeller.

Location: At the western side of Hell's Mouth, head north-east along the rocky shore, looking for the pronounced rocky knoll of Graig Ddu. Slightly further to the north you will see a distinct, sandy-coloured patch immediately above the high-water mark. If you look carefully, you can see a line of wooden posts hammered into the shingle beach. Head towards these posts using transit A and anchor about 50 metres offshore. In good surface visibility, use transit B to line-up the small hump on the cliff top, with the right hand shoulder of the far mountain.

The wreck does not show up on the echo-sounder as it is very close to the shore and totally overgrown with kelp.

The Ganda transits

Transit A

Transit B

4.6 - Western cliffs of Hell's Mouth

Latitude (North)	52° 48.030'N	Longitude (N)	004° 38.450'W	
to	52° 47.900'N	to	004° 38.910W	
Position Fix	Differential-GPS	Datum	WGS84	

The western edge of Hell's Mouth has a steep hillside with low, rocky cliffs at the water's edge, and provides a pleasant site for a drift-dive as the tidal stream runs parallel to the shore. The south west end of the cliffs is known as Trwyn Talfarach. The seabed in shallow water consists of dense kelp, attached to a collection of large boulders that have tumbled from the hillside above. These boulders get progressively smaller as the depth increases, finally levelling out on to a flat gravel and sand seabed at about 18 to 20 metres. Further out, the seabed is mainly gravel and small boulders, but in places the whole area is carpeted with a mass of feather stars, all with their arms extended upwards to feed in the current.

Marine-life is plentiful, with an abundant supply of snakelocks anemones, ross coral, gurnards, pipefish, gobies, goldsinnys, top-knots and spider-crabs, as well as what is probably the biggest population of sea-urchins along this coast. In July and August, dozens of sea-hares will be seen here.

A period of slack water will be found from around 4 to 4 and a half hours after high-water at Liverpool, but why not utilise the current for a long, enjoyable drift-dive?

4.7 - Trwyn Talfarach - West Point

Latitude	52° 47.960'N	Longitude	004° 39.025'W	
Position Fix	Differential - GPS	Datum	WGS84	

Trwyn Talfarach

When there is a strong westerly current along Trwyn Talfarach headland, this area provides a convenient, sheltered dive-site, just north-west of the point. Beware of the anglers who cast out from the rocks. Large, kelp-covered boulders lie close inshore, down to a depth of about 10 metres, with many crevices and overhangs among the kelp. The seabed then changes to a mixture of coarse gravel and rock, with several isolated boulders at a depth of about 15 metres. There are usually many lobster-pots in the area. Sightings are often made of large sea-urchins, dogfish, conger eels, top-knots, goldsinnys, ballan wrasse and cuckoo wrasse. Further out to sea there are many dead-men's fingers, indicating strong currents, but the more obvious marine-life decreases as the seabed drops away to a depth of around 30 metres.

The current runs in a westerly direction for a longer period than it does to the east, so use the site for a long drift-dive, or dive at slack-water, around 4 hours after high-water at Liverpool.

4.8 - Drift-dives off Trwyn Talfarach, Hell's Mouth

Latitude	52° 47.730'N	Longitude	004° 38.750'W
Position Fix	Differential - GPS	Datum	WGS84

Excellent drift-dives are possible in Hell's Mouth, about half a mile south of Trwyn Talfarach at a depth of around 20 metres. The GPS position given is a typical example of a starting point for a drift-dive, but anywhere in the vicinity will give a similar dive. The seabed varies considerably, with large areas covered in brittle stars, other areas covered in feather stars, and some areas with no starfish of any kind. Sea urchins and spider-crabs are common, though edible-crabs and lobsters are rarely seen. Dogfish are plentiful, while john dories, octopus and thornback rays have occasionally been encountered. Large colonies of ross coral will be seen, some almost as large as a football. These are very brittle, so take care not to damage them. During calm periods in mid-summer, the water clarity tends to be quite good. Visibility of 15 metres or more makes it feel just like swimming in a fish tank

A 'John Dory'

Basically, you simply dive here at any time and 'go with the flow' in whatever direction the current decides to take you, covering anything up to a mile underwater. Obviously, surface marker-buoys and reliable boats are essential.

4.9 - Maen Gwenonwy

Latitude	52° 48.020'N	Longitude	004° 40.150'W
Position Fix	Differential - GPS	Datum	WGS84

Carreg Chwislen ●

The Seagull Islands   Ebolion   Maen Gwenonwy

Maen Gwenonwy is a huge, square-cut and dark-coloured rock that can be easily distinguished from more than a mile away. Connected to the mainland by a short causeway, it becomes an island only at high-water on a spring-tide.

The dive-site lies immediately to the south of Maen Gwenonwy, where close inshore there is shelter from northerly and westerly winds, with little current. There are many boulders between 1 and 3 metres high, all hidden in a dense kelp forest inhabited by a variety of marine-life including scores of sea-hares. More than a dozen have been counted on a single rock. The site is strewn with lobster-pots, so there are generally few large crustaceans to be seen, but large ballan wrasse will always appear out of nowhere to follow a diver round the site.

Further offshore, strong currents will be found for long drift-dives, but the seabed is mostly flat sand and gravel, with occaional large boulders.

4.10 - Carreg Chwislen

Latitude	52° 47.965'N	Longitude	004° 40.360'W
Position Fix	Differential - GPS	Datum	WGS84

Situated slightly south-west of Maen Gwenonwy, the small reef known as Carreg Chwislen can be seen at low-water, becoming hidden as the tide rises to create a danger to navigation. It provides an interesting dive-site which can be circumnavigated during a single dive in a maximum depth of around 12 to 14 metres. There is a sheltered area to the west of the rock where there are many large boulders with deep clefts underneath. These boulders are often covered in small starfish. Among the rocks, the seabed provides shelter for many wrasse and dogfish, while a shoal of large pollack cruises over the kelp. Thornback rays have occasionally been noticed out on the flat sand.

Long drift-dives on a sandy seabed can be undertaken south of Carreg Chwislen in depths of only 12 to 15 metres. Large colonies of ross coral will be encountered, in an area where the current tends to run towards the west for a far longer period than it does to the east.

4.11 - Clog Cidwm (Wolf Rock)

Latitude	52° 47.970'N	Longitude	004° 40.710'W
Position Fix	Differential - GPS	Datum	WGS84

This small reef does not appear on the Admiralty chart but is marked on the large-scale Ordnance Survey map. The reef runs southwards from the cliff base and partially dries as the tide falls, causing potential danger to any boats passing this close to the shore. The site is sheltered from northerly and westerly winds, but is very exposed to the south. There is little current close to the reef, but strong currents will be found immediately to the south. At high-tide, there is only about 5 metres of water over the reef with the surrounding seabed at only 10 to 12 metres. At this depth, ross coral, common-dogfish and bull-huss are regularly seen, while the reef itself has many large boulders that provide shelter for small lobsters and crabs.

4.12 - Fishermen's Rock

Latitude	52° 47.770'N	Longitude	004° 40.970'W
Position Fix	Differential - GPS	Datum	WGS84

Between Clog Cidwm (Wolf Rock) and the eastern entrance to Aberdaron Bay, there is a narrow footpath leading down the hillside to a small promontory. This site is very popular with anglers and is therefore often off-limits to divers. Over the years, these anglers have lost many fishing weights, enabling me to collect more than thirty on my first dive here. The rocky shore quickly drops off to a depth of about 12 metres, being initially covered in kelp but with broken rock, sand and gravel further out. Mackerel and pollack can be seen swimming just off the rocks - hence the popularity with anglers - but look closely at the seabed for the telltale black dorsal fins of the poisonous weever-fish.

4.13 - Carreg Gybi

Latitude	52° 47.670'N	Longitude	004° 41.200'W
Position Fix	Differential - GPS	Datum	WGS84

Carreg Gybi is a large rock that forms a small island just off the high cliffs. This is an interesting site for observing marine-life, where the rocks drop off rapidly to 12 to 15 metres on to flat, coarse sand with a scattering of large boulders. Other rocks form small islands, with several reefs being seen only as the tide falls. Beware of motoring inshore of these islands because some of the rocks are shallow enough to damage a propeller even at high-water.

Anchor in the bay just south of Carreg Gybi, where there will be about 8 metres of water, and shelter from the current. Exploring around the rocks will reveal many small caves formed by the tumble of boulders, while cracks and crevices in the bare rock are full of squat-lobsters, prawns, small edible-crabs and undersized lobsters. Dead-men's fingers will be found out in the current flow, but away from the rocks there is flat sand and relatively little marine-life.

4.14 - Trwyn Gwningaer & Ebolion

Latitude	52° 47.565'N	Longitude	004° 41.280'W
Position Fix	Differential - GPS	Datum	WGS84

Ebolion at low-water

Trwyn Gwningaer is a rocky headland on the northern edge of the eastern channel into Aberdaron Bay. Strong currents run through the channel, but there is some shelter in the bay immediately west of the headland. Don't take a boat too close to the cliffs as there is an outer rock (Ebolion), lying just under the surface as the tide falls.

Enjoy a fast drift-dive round the headland, but beware of the pot-buoys in the channel as they will entangle a diver's SMB, and are difficult to see from a boat.

4.15 - Channel between Ynys Gwylan Fawr and Ebolion

Latitude	52° 47.435'N	Longitude	004° 41.400'W
Position Fix	Differential - GPS	Datum	WGS84

The channel between the Llŷn Peninsula and Ynys Gwylan Fawr is about 600 metres wide, consisting mainly of a flat sandy seabed and a scattering of boulders. It is best used for a fast drift-dive on a westerly moving current as the seabed is deeper to the east of the channel than to the west. Depths range from 24 metres in the east, rising to 10 metres in the channel and then slightly deeper to around 12 to 14 metres in Aberdaron Bay. As always around here, watch out for semi-submerged lobster-pot buoys.

Several bombs have been found by divers drifting in the channel, but these were used only for practice and hopefully do not contain explosive material. However, take care if you do find one.

Ynys Gwylan Fawr and Ynys Gwylan Bach (The Seagull Islands)

These two rocky islands provide pleasant, scenic diving only about a mile south-east of Aberdaron slipway. From a distance, Ynys Gwylan Fawr (the larger, more easterly of the two) resembles a battleship, being long, narrow and with a central peak. Only the guns, aerials and flags are missing. Probably because of this resemblance to a ship, the islands were used for target practice during the Second World War. Bombs, bullets and detonators are regularly found in the vicinity.

Ynys Gwylan Fawr   'Seagull Islands'   Ynys Gwylan Bach

The area is much more tranquil these days, so the islands are home to a wide variety of seabirds. The brightly-coloured puffins really are entertaining, as they bob about on the waves, dive out of sight or stagger off as they attempt to become airborne. The islands are an important nesting site, so do not go ashore here. A small group of seals will be encountered sheltering in a gully on the south side of the smaller island, while further offshore a school of dolphins occasionally rides the bow-wave of a passing boat. Check the Seawatch Foundation website for their code of conduct.

In decent weather, there is always somewhere to dive here, despite the strong currents and back-eddies. Shelter from these currents can usually be found close to the islands, while long drift-dives can be enjoyed parallel to the islands or out across the bay. Slack-water is about the same time as high-water at Liverpool and does not coincide with high-water at Aberdaron. The currents tend to run towards the west for a greater period than they do to the east, probably the result of a back-eddy during the ebb-tide.

4.16 - Ynys Gwylan Fawr

Latitude	52° 47.335'N	Longitude	004° 41.520'W
Position Fix	Differential - GPS	Datum	WGS84

'Puffin Island' would probably be a better name for Ynys Gwylan Fawr because hundreds of these entertaining little birds breed here. They are often seen flying back to their nests with beaks crammed full of sand-eels. Razorbills, guillemots, cormorants and gulls also nest here. In the late 1980s, a pair of white rabbits was frequently seen on the island, presumably domestic ones which had been set free. No one would believe the story until they actually saw one, but the rabbits did survive this Robinson Crusoe existence for several years.

Lying roughly parallel to the coast, the north side of the island gives shelter from southerly winds, but the diving is not as good as on the south side. There is loose rock in the shallower water which then changes to sand and gravel at around 10 metres. Swimming quite a way north from the island, you will move into the area swept by the fast channel through Gwylan Sound. There is less obvious marine-life here. Off this north side of the island, one diver has reported a large anchor that sits almost upright on the seabed and is large enough to swim under. Spent cartridge cases have been found here, so presumably the islands were strafed as well as bombed during the last war.

On the southern side of the island, the thick kelp close inshore thins out at a depth of about 8 metres. Moving deeper, the currents increase and the seabed becomes covered in dead-men's fingers, urchins, spider-crabs, squat lobsters, feather-stars and brittle-stars. Pollack and dogfish

Spiny Spider crab

are always present, and well-camouflaged angler-fish are sometimes seen on the seabed off the island. A rarely-seen sunfish has been spotted here, lazily drifting just under the surface with only the dorsal fin showing above water. Further out, there are beds of large mussels with their accompanying predatory pack of starfish.

Halfway down the south side of the island, a small cave is worth a quick look. Although in shallow water against the cliffs, it provides a home for several large wrasse. Nearby, another large anchor has been reported, this one lying close inshore and well hidden among the kelp.

There is a narrow channel between Ynys Gwylan Fawr and Ynys Gwylan Bach. It is only about 8 metres deep at low-water but gives a hair-raising drift-dive at full current. Start your drift on the southern side of Ynys Gwylan Fawr on a westward current. You will fly over the rocks and gullies at a considerable rate, before zooming through the channel and out towards the middle of Aberdaron Bay. It is quite amazing how large boulders suddenly emerge out of the gloom and directly in your path, but the current takes you over or around the obstruction without harm. Always use surface marker-buoys, but watch out for lobster-pot buoys in the channel.

4.17 - Ynys Gwylan Bach

Latitude	52° 47.050'N	Longitude	004° 41.915'W
Position Fix	Differential - GPS	Datum	WGS84

There is a small inlet on the south side of Ynys Gwylan Bach, which provides shelter from the current for a small group of seals. Just off the inlet, the seabed consists of gullies and rocks before it flattens out at a depth of about 15 metres.

The north-west side and the south-west point of the island do give some shelter from the westerly current. Large boulders and dense kelp are found in the shallows. At about 8 metres, this changes to cobble-sized rocks which are clear of kelp and finally to clean sand at about 13 metres. It is well worth spending a few minutes investigating the mass of life under the cobbles, where you will see many thousands of miniature squat-lobsters, brittle-stars, green-crabs, edible-crabs and spider-crabs. These all run for cover when they sense the presence of an invader to their territory. Corkwing wrasse cruise around this area and will fearlessly approach a diver. They have even been known to bite a diver's glove, dart away and then dash in for another nibble.

The rusty remains of several Second World War bombs can be found scattered around the seabed at 52° 47.050'N 004° 41.915'W. At least one looks remarkably intact, so leave it well alone. Although it is assumed that they are not armed, this is uncertain because some of the metallic objects found here appear to be the remains of detonators.

Fast drift-dives may be undertaken from the south-west tip of Ynys Gwylan Bach, heading west towards Bardsey Sound on a mussel-covered reef that is an underwater extension of the two islands. The reef near the smaller island is about 5 metres high and consists of boulders and bare rock. As you drift westward and away from the island, the seabed becomes almost totally covered in dead-men's fingers at a depth of around 18 to 20 metres. You will see even more bombs in this area, as the seabed gradually drops away to a depth of more than 30 metres.

4.18 - Isolated reef in Aberdaron Bay

Latitude	52° 47.565'N	Longitude	004° 41.840'W
Position Fix	Differential - GPS	Datum	WGS84

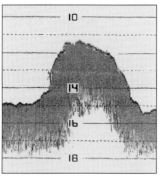

'Isolated Reef' in Aberdaron bay.
Note - expanded scale

There are several small, isolated reefs in the middle of Aberdaron Bay. This one lies to the north of Ynys Gwylan Fawr and rises from a flat seabed at 15 metres to a rocky, kelp-covered peak at a depth of about 11 metres. The reef shows well on the echo-sounder and is often marked by one or more lobster-pots. Pollack, wrasse, dogfish, spiny spider-crabs and pipefish are usually seen, but away from the reef there is less life on a flat seabed which has only a scattering of weed-covered boulders.

4.19 - Isolated Reef and unidentified wreck

Latitude	52° 47.700'N	Longitude	004° 41.725'W
Position Fix	Differential - GPS	Datum	WGS84

ABERDARON BAY (EAST)   EBOLION

Isolated reef

'Isolated Reef - shoreline view'. Reef is about 200 metres offshore of the white marks

There is an uncharted reef at the eastern entrance to Aberdaron Bay which rises from flat sand at a depth of about 8 metres to only 2 metres at low-water on a spring-tide. At this time, in calm conditions, the dark patch indicating the kelp-covered rock can be seen from the boat or, when there is a strong current running, a ripple on the surface may be noticed.

Strong currents may be found on top of the rock, but there will be some shelter around the sides. A period of slack water will be found at about 3 to 3.5 hours after high-water at Liverpool.

The reef has many gullies and crevices, but in the shallows you will need to delve among the thick kelp. Some of the gullies have been worn smooth where the underwater surge has rolled a boulder round and round to shot-blast the bedrock, but most of the gullies have sharp and jagged edges. These shelter a variety of small marine-life such as prawns and squat-lobsters, but one area provides a home for a fully visible, 2-metre long conger eel which lies sideways in a rocky crevice. Pipefish, wrasse and pollack will be seen, while large bull-huss doze on the flat sand around the reef.

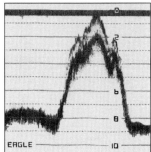

EAGLE   10

'Isolated Reef' - East (metres)

At some time in history, the master of a small sailing vessel must have had the shock of his life when he ran on to the reef. This ship's cargo of roofing slates lies scattered around the rock, with the greatest concentration to the south. Most of the slates are broken, but several complete ones have been recovered, each measuring either 20, 22 or 24 inches long, and all about 8 inches wide. The slate is purple, so with further research it should be possible to identify which quarry the slates came from and perhaps even the identity of the vessel. Small pieces of ship's timber with brass screws have been found close to this reef, along with a substantial piece of metal. This was thought on first inspection to be a cannon, but proved otherwise and is now not believed to be associated with the wreck. Although there appears to be nothing major left of the ship itself, part of a copper-sheathed wooden keel was washed up on the nearby beach in July, 2002.

Location: The reef lies about 200 metres directly off the white marks on the cliff-face. See Photo

4.20 - Wreck in Aberdaron Bay, believed to be the 'Glenocum'

Name	Glenocum	Type	Steamer
Date Lost	23/5/1883	Location	Aberdaron Bay
Cause	Hit rock	How Lost	Beached
Hull	Iron	Weight	344 tons (gross)
Cargo	Iron bars	Access	Boat
Latitude	52° 48.025'N	Longitude	004° 42.550'W
Position Fix	Differential-GPS	Datum	WGS84
Seabed	8 metres	Wreck Height	4 metres
Charted as	+ PA		
Slipway (1)	Aberdaron	Distance	0.2 miles
Slipway (2)	Abersoch	Distance	11 miles
Tidal Data	Little current		

Aberdaron - A steamer sunk. About 6 o'clock last Wednesday morning, the steamer 'Glen Okum' of London, bound from Newport to Liverpool with railway bars, went ashore at Porth Cadlan. She sank soon afterwards. She was 200 tons register and belongs to London. The crew managed to save some of the effects.

Carnarvon and Denbigh Herald, 2nd June 1883

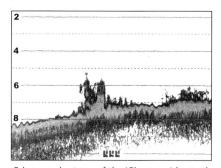

Echo-sounder trace of the 'Glenocum' (metres)

Usually referred to as 'The Wreck in the Bay', I believe that this is the remains of the 3-masted, iron steamer 'Glenocum' which was deliberately beached after hitting a rock in 1883. Built in 1875 at the shipyard of T. Grendon & Co., Drogheda, Ireland, the 'Glenocum' was owned by The Belfast Steamship Company and propelled by a 75-horsepower, 2-cylinder steam-engine. According to the 1881 edition of Lloyds Register, the 'Glenocum' was 146 feet 5 inches long, with a beam of 22 feet 4 inches. Having measured this wreck from the prominent bow to the sternpost, I came to a total of 147 feet 8 inches which, allowing for minor errors, is virtually the same as the 'Glenocum'. Other divers have suggested that this wreck is that of the 'Priscilla', but the only local reference to a steamer of this name gives an overall length of 120', which is much too short for this wreck.

Lloyd's List of 25th May, 1883, reported that the 'Glenocum' was ashore and full of water. By the 28th, the Liverpool Salvage Association had refloated the ship, but then had to beach her again at Aberdaron in the hope of removing the cargo and repairing the ship. Operations continued all summer to recover most of the cargo of iron bars, along with the ship's anchors, chains and fittings. By September 20th, 246 tons of cargo had been removed, but all hope of saving the ship had been lost and work was abandoned. The wreck and remaining fittings were sold for £70.

Aberdaron

'Glenocum' - north west transit

The left half of a 'Scotch boiler'

The 'Glenocum' provides an excellent introduction to wreck diving, being shallow, out of the main current and close to the shore. The prominent bows are intact and point seawards (south), indicating that the ship probably dropped anchor before grounding. This is the deepest part of the wreck, where even at high-water the maximum depth will be less than 10 metres. The deck is completely missing, so there are no passageways or holds to explore other than the forepeak, but the single 4-metre high 'Scotch' (tubular) boiler remains upright and intact, with dense kelp growing on its upper surface. The twin stoke-doors face towards the stern, a design feature of a small vessel in which the jobs of engineer and stoker could be combined. The hull has collapsed outwards so that the iron hull-plates now lie almost horizontal, creating large gaps that provide a safe haven for large shoals of pout. Take a good torch to look at the pout, the prawns in the fireboxes and the conger that usually peers out of the hole in the top of the boiler or hides in one of the boiler pipes. Be aware that the conger (nicknamed 'Dinky') does object to divers hammering away at his home inside one of the copper pipes, and will come out to chase off the noisy intruder!

In addition to the shoals of pout already mentioned, pipefish and small two-spotted gobies hide among the wreckage and thick kelp, while large ballan wrasse will follow a diver around the wreck in the hope that he or she will dislodge an easy meal.

Lobster-pots are usually set around the wreck, but large spiny spider-crabs and small squat-lobsters are common.

The bay is popular with water-skiers and dinghy-sailors, so always display the 'A' flag when divers are in the water. North-westerly to north-easterly winds leave the bay calm and sheltered, providing ideal conditions for launching and diving. A south-westerly gale soon stirs up the

'Glenocum' - north east transit

seabed, while heavy rain will turn Aberdaron Bay from blue to brown. Don't despair, the underwater visibility soon returns to normal once the weather improves.

In calm weather, the site makes an excellent night-dive after having located and buoyed the wreck during daylight. Note that during the evening, Aberdaron slipway may be blocked by cars until their owners leave the local pubs at closing time.

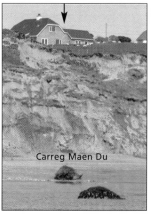

Carreg Maen Du

Location: I always use the transits to find this wreck, as the boiler is the only prominent feature that appears on the echo-sounder. As this is only about 3 metres wide, it is difficult to pick up on the sounder, but there is usually a marker-buoy or lobster-pot buoy close by to give a reference point. Motor towards Aberdaron using the north-western transit, with the left hand dormer-window lined up with the end of the church, and drop the shot-weight when Carreg Maen Du lines up with the middle of the new bungalow on the cliff top. Carreg Maen Du is the large rock on the beach at the high-water mark. This rock does not become submerged, even at high water on a spring-tide.

Why do I believe in using the 'kill switch' or 'dead-men's handle'? Returning to Aberdaron beach in two inflatables with tiller steering, we encountered heavy surf close inshore. The first boat went into the waves and almost overturned, throwing the coxswain into the water. The 'dead-men's handle' was fitted to his wrist, so the engine stopped immediately. The same thing happened to the second boat, but there wasn't a 'dead-men's handle' fitted to this engine and everyone aboard was thrown into the water. With no-one holding the tiller, the engine spun over to full lock and carried on running, making the boat circle among the four people in the water. Luckily, everyone managed to keep clear of the spinning propeller until one brave person clambered back onboard to stop the engine.

Always use the dead-men's handle! It seems a contradiction in terms, but the 'kill switch' can actually save your life.

4.21 - Caravan Rock

Latitude	52° 46.975'N	Longitude	004° 43.770'W
Position Fix	Differential - GPS	Datum	WGS84

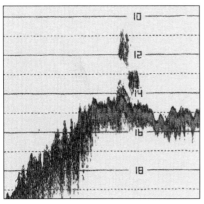

'Caravan Rock' echo-sounder trace (metres)

Towards the southwest corner of Aberdaron Bay and about 300 metres north-east of Pen-y-Cil, there is a submerged rock about the size of a large static caravan. It lies on the edge of the underwater shelf in Aberdaron Bay, just before the seabed drops away into Bardsey Sound. Giving an echo-sounder trace just like a small wreck, this rock has vertical sides about 4 or 5 metres high, with a flat top measuring about 6 metres by 8 metres. The base of the rock is slowly being eroded by the current and it will probably topple over in a few hundred thousand years or so. The top is covered in kelp at a depth of about 9 metres at low-tide, while the surrounding seabed is at 14 metres and littered with large boulders.

Some divers have described the site as 'eerie' or 'unnatural', probably because the rock looks totally out of place, but this is a rather enjoyable site with lots of marine-life. Rock-cook, corkwing and ballan wrasse, two-spotted gobies and pollack all hide under and around the rock, while dead-men's fingers will be seen clinging to the vertical sides.

Slack-water occurs around half an hour to an hour before high-water at Liverpool, but there is some shelter behind the rock when actually diving. If you still have a reasonable amount of air left after a dive at Bardsey, this is a pleasant site to finish it off.

4.22 - Pen-y-Cil Headland and unidentified wreck

Latitude	52° 46.860'N	Longitude	004° 43.955'W
Position Fix	Differential - GPS	Datum	WGS84

Pen-y-Cil headland showing the overfalls

The headland at Pen-y-Cil has steep underwater cliffs that drop off rapidly to nearly 30 metres. Strong currents sweep the site, resulting in sand-blasted rocks, smooth cliffs and little silt. Dives need to be timed for slack-water as overfalls form off the point, with the most danger occurring between five hours and two hours before high-water at Liverpool. When passing Pen-y-Cil, avoid these overfalls by either going well offshore or by keeping close to the cliffs. Always keep a lookout for lobster-pot buoys in this area. Slack-water is around one hour before high-water at Liverpool and one hour before low-water at Liverpool, but it is advisable to arrive on site early and wait for the current to ease off.

The wreck of an old wooden ship lies close to the base of the cliff at Pen-y-Cil, with its cargo of roofing slates neatly stacked on the seabed at a depth of 27 metres. Other slates and two badly corroded, 2-metre long, admiralty-pattern anchors lie close by, but very little remains of the vessel itself.

The headland is a popular site for anglers, so watch out for their lines as well as the lobster-pot buoys.

4.23 - Underwater Cave system

Latitude	52° 46.930'N	Longitude	004° 44.065'W
Position Fix	Differential - GPS	Datum	WGS84

Underwater cave system near Pen-y-Cil

This under-water cave system has three entry or exit points, all close to Pen-y-Cil, where it gives an interesting second dive in 12 to 14 metres of water. Being close to Pen-y-Cil headland, there can be strong currents inside the cave as well as along the outer cliff face. When there is such a current, take great care inside the tunnels, and especially in the side passage with its narrow, inclined exit point. The main tunnel is only about 20 to 25 metres long, but torches are advisable even though the natural light is not totally lost. Artificial light will bring out the true colour of the anemones, sea-squirts and other marine-life covering the rock walls. Take a look at the small crevice in the roof of the cave, near the main entrance.

Despite the strong currents, there is quite a collection of spiny spider-crabs, pipefish, crabs and lobsters living inside the caves. Look for the large prawns tucked away under the boulders at the smaller exit.

Anchor in the sheltered area in front of the main entrance shown in the photograph, but watch out for the white rock which dries out as the tide falls. Swim over to the entrance and submerge in the gully, where the roof of the cave will be found only a few metres under the surface. Note that while divers are in the cave system, boat coxswains should patrol all three of the access points to the cave system, as the under-water currents can cause unexpected changes to the dive-plan. If divers surface on the far side of the rocky outcrop, they could be out of sight of the boat.

4.24 - Parwyd

Latitude	52° 47.045'N	Longitude	004° 44.320'W
Position Fix	Differential - GPS	Datum	WGS84

Parwyd is a narrow, south-facing bay with spectacular cliffs rising almost vertically from sea-level to a height of about 90 metres. These cliffs are home to peregrine falcons, choughs and seagulls, while large hares are often seen bounding along the neighbouring grassy slopes. This inlet gives a calm, sheltered anchorage, located out of the main tide-race through Bardsey Sound. The middle of the bay drops to a depth of about 15 metres where there are large areas of flat sand and weed-covered, broken rock. The edges of the bay are more interesting, with many large boulders having fallen from the cliffs above. Just outside the bay, one huge rock the size of a small house rests on several others to create a haven for marine-life. The mouth of the bay then falls away gradually into Bardsey Sound, eventually reaching a depth of nearly 30 metres.

On one dive, the base of an old brandy bottle was found here, but it is probable that other divers had recovered it from the 'Horse-Brass Wreck' on Bardsey Island (see dive 5.4) and subsequently discarded it.

4.25 - Carreg Ddu

Latitude	52° 46.875'N	Longitude	004° 44.690'W
Position Fix	Differential - GPS	Datum	WGS84

'Carreg Ddu' with Bardsey Island in the background

Surrounded by deep water, Carreg Ddu is a barren, rocky islet about 200 metres off the north coast of Bardsey Sound. Although the rock never becomes totally submerged, it is frequently covered in spray during bad weather. Very strong currents run along the sides of Carreg Ddu and at full flow it is possible to see a difference in the level of the sea as the tide races over the small outcrops alongside the main islet. At this time, the surrounding area boils with whirlpools, eddies, undertows and overfalls. Never underestimate the power of the tide in Bardsey Sound.

Marine-life around Carreg Ddu is extremely prolific. Dead-men's fingers, anemones, sea-firs, mussels and other species thrive on the bed-rock and boulders. Wrasse and pollack are the most noticeable fish, but look out for the large bull-huss that tuck themselves into small caves, presumably to shelter from the current.

Dive at slack-water, preferably on neap-tides, but boats should avoid anchoring because of the strong currents. Arrive on site at least one and a half hours before high-water at Liverpool, and wait for the current to ease off. Slack-water lasts only a short time, so divers should be dropped off in the sheltered areas at either the east or west point of the rock so they can drift alongside the rock as the tide turns. SMBs are strongly recommended. At the eastern point of Carreg Ddu, the rocks drop vertically to about 10 metres, before sloping away to around 25 metres. Most dives around here will be in a maximum of 25 to 30 metres, although one pair of divers did record 36 metres after drifting away from Carreg Ddu.

A badly corroded aluminium mast, with part of the sail still attached, lies against the east side of the rock at a depth of around 12 to 15 metres. This mast has been snapped in two, but I am unaware of any other modern wreckage against the rock. Nearby, at a depth of around 10 metres, there is a 1.8 metre long admiralty-pattern anchor with an iron stock which dates from a different era to the mast. There is no chain attached to the anchor, and the folding stock has

been set into its normal operating position, so this anchor was probably lost while in use, rather than being from a wrecked vessel.

The site has been fished for lobsters and crabs for many years, so loose ropes and the remains of old lobster-pots are found all around the rock. Netting for fish has also taken place here, as both stone and lead net-weights have been recovered. See photo.

4.26 - Porth Felen

Latitude	52° 47.320'N	Longitude	004° 45.220'W
Position Fix	Differential - GPS	Datum	WGS84

Porth Felen is a wide, shallow bay which provides shelter from north-westerly winds and the strong tidal streams in Bardsey Sound. The position given is roughly in the middle of the bay, which provides an ideal site for a second dive or for training drills. Around the edges of the bay, rocky cliffs drop off sharply to a depth of around 10 metres before flattening out at around 15 metres on to large areas of sand with the odd rock.

The east side of the bay, close to the shore, is rather interesting, with many large boulders and small cliff faces. Sponges, anemones, sea-firs and sea-mats carpet the rock surfaces. This area also has many wrasse, pipefish and a shoal of large pollack, with lots of spider-crabs, brittle stars and sand-eels further out in the middle of the bay. The western side of Porth Felen affords more shelter from the wind, but take care not to stray out of the bay into the strong currents of Bardsey Sound.

There are at least two admiralty pattern anchors lying on the sand, possibly the result of sailing ships seeking shelter here or waiting for the tide to turn, but I have not found any other signs of wreckage. Alternatively, a ship may have lost these anchors when replenishing its water supply from the nearby waterfall. In 1974, divers located and recovered the stock from a Roman anchor at Porth Felen. Made of lead, it weighed 71.5 kilograms, measured 1.18 metres long, and is now on display at the National Museum for Wales in Cardiff. One of the oldest maritime artefacts ever found in Wales, it is believed to date from before the birth of Christ, but, despite detailed searches, no other signs of an ancient wreck have been found or reported. Maritime Wales, Volume One (see bibliography) contains further details. Having searched the area with an underwater metal-detector, my only discoveries have been lost fishing weights and several spark plugs!

4.27 - Trwyn-y-Gwydel

Latitude	52° 47.250'N	Longitude	004° 45.325'W
Position Fix	Differential - GPS	Datum	WGS84

This is the western point of Porth Felen where the rocks drop off rapidly to more than 30 metres. The site provides a nice dive at slack-water but has very strong currents at other times. Many dead-men's fingers grow on the near-vertical cliff faces, with a large shoal of pollack sheltering out of the current. Just off the rocks and clear of the thick kelp, there is a length of heavy wire rope, about 20 metres long, with an eye spliced into each end. One eye has split, perhaps suggesting that it broke while one vessel was being towed by another in a position close to the shore, but, to my knowledge, no further wreckage has been found here.

4.28 - St. Mary's Well

Latitude	52° 47.485'N	Longitude	004° 45.700'W
Position Fix	Differential - GPS	Datum	WGS84

This is another shallow bay which can provide shelter from northerly winds and the strong tidal streams in Bardsey Sound. Approaching the site from Aberdaron, beware of the rock immediately to the east of the bay. This dries out as the tide falls to create a nasty hazard. St. Mary's Well gets its name from a spring and small waterfall in the corner of the bay that create a small freshwater pool as the tide falls.

There is a small underwater cave almost underneath the spring, at a depth of only around 3 metres. A narrow crevice in the cliffs on the west side of the bay is worth exploring, being about 3 metres wide and around 6 metres deep. Moving away from the cliffs, but still within the bay, the seabed drops to 15 metres where hundreds of sand-eels dart in and out of the clean sand. Look out for thornback rays on the sand, and 15-spined sticklebacks hidden in the weed.

The foundations of an ancient church can be found in the bracken above this bay, where in ancient times pilgrims would pray before setting out on the dangerous journey to Bardsey Island. It has been suggested that the pilgrims may have thrown offerings into the sea at this spot before sailing. Certainly, there are well-worn steps leading down to the water's edge, but my own underwater searches have uncovered only lost fishing weights and empty beer cans.

Outside the bay, the seabed drops away rapidly into Bardsey Sound, with its strong tides. Much of the seabed at 30 metres or more has been swept clean by the currents to give large, barren areas.

The strange-shaped rock on the hillside above the bay is called Maen Melyn (Yellow Rock), but is often referred to as 'Toad Rock' as it looks just like a giant amphibian about to leap off the cliff. When you next visit St. Mary's Well, can you think of a better name or description?

Maen Melyn (Toad rock)

4.29 - Un-named Bay

Latitude	52° 47.620'N	Longitude	004° 45.880'W
Position Fix	Differential - GPS	Datum	WGS84

The small bay between St. Mary's Well and Braich-y-Pwll provides another sheltered mooring and dive-site along this rocky coast. From the surface to a depth of about 8 metres, the steep-sided rocks are covered in dense kelp. This clears in middle of the bay where there is a maximum depth of about 15 metres. There are many large boulders, some of which have been worn smooth by current and wave action.

Close to the western point of the bay (52° 47.610' N 004° 46.025' W), there is a 2.5 metre long, admiralty-pattern anchor lying against the sheer rocks, in about 14 metres of water. It has one fluke missing and does not have an anchor ring or chain attached. Despite being so close to the rocks, no other pieces of wreckage have been noticed, although other large anchors and old bottles have been reported further out from the cliffs in 30 metres of water.

Dive only within the confines of the bay, as further out the seabed drops off rapidly to around 30 metres where there is flat shingle swept clean by the incredibly strong and confused currents. At certain times of the tide, a massive whirlpool appears, running southwards offshore and northwards close to the rocks, so always check the compass rather than relying on the expected direction of the current.

4.30 - Braich-y-Pwll

Latitude	52° 47.865'N	Longitude	004° 46.090'W
Position Fix	Differential - GPS	Datum	WGS84

Overfalls at Braich-y-Pwll

This is the most westerly headland on the Llŷn Peninsula and has incredibly strong currents, overfalls and whirlpools, so is best avoided on spring-tides. You can hear the roar of these overfalls from the cliff-top above. Diving off the point requires good planning and boat-cover, but there is usually a little shelter from the current on one side of the headland or the other. Watch out for semi-submerged lobster-pot buoys and fishing lines.

Away from the cliffs, the current has sandblasted all the rocks smooth and clean, in places resembling an underwater desert or a scene from an alien planet. This is certainly the place for you if you like diving in a tumble-dryer, but do take care. I have surfaced here in a whirlpool, spinning round and round during the ascent, making a controlled ascent or decompression stop almost impossible. Slack-water is about 2 hours before high-water at Liverpool, and once the tide turns, the current increases rapidly, so you will go with the flow whether you like it or not. Be careful!

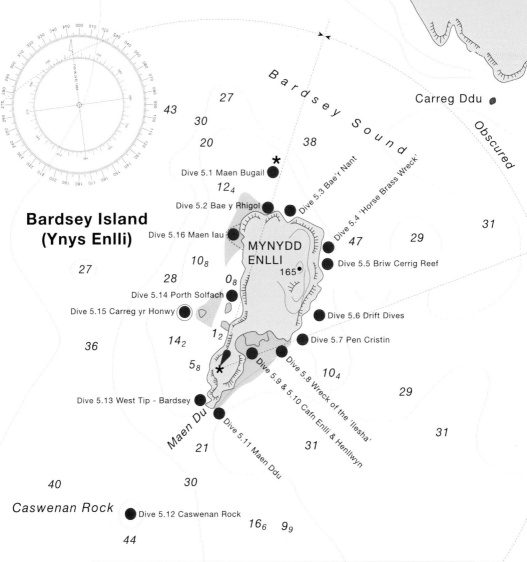

Bardsey Island
(Ynys Enlli)

MYNYDD ENLLI

Bardsey Sound

Carreg Ddu

Obscured

43
27
30
20
38
31

Dive 5.1 Maen Bugail ✱

12₄
Dive 5.2 Bae y Rhigol

Dive 5.3 Bae'r Nant
Dive 5.4 'Horse Brass Wreck'

Dive 5.16 Maen Iau

47
29

Dive 5.5 Briw Cerrig Reef

165

27
10₈
0₈
28

Dive 5.14 Porth Solfach
Dive 5.15 Carreg yr Honwy

Dive 5.6 Drift Dives

14₂
1₂

Dive 5.7 Pen Cristin

36
5₈ ✱

10₄

Dive 5.13 West Tip - Bardsey

Dive 5.8 Wreck of the 'Ilesha'
Dive 5.9 & 5.10 Cafn Enlli & Henllwyn

29

31

Maen Du

21
Dive 5.11 Maen Ddu
31

30

40

Caswenan Rock

Dive 5.12 Caswenan Rock
16₆   9₉

44

Bardsey Island from the mainland

● Boat Dive

Not to be used for Navigation

CHAPTER FIVE

Bardsey Island (Ynys Enlli)

'The British name of the island is Ynys Enlli, or The Island In The Currents, from the fierce current which rages particularly between it and the mainland. The Saxons named it Bardseye, probably from the bards who retired there, preferring solitude to the company of invading foreigners'.

Thomas Pennant, 1781

General Description

Bardsey Island or Ynys Enlli lies about two miles south-west of Pen-y-Cil and 1.75 miles south-south-west of Braich-y-Pwll, the extreme tip of the Llŷn Peninsula. A trip right round the island, starting from Aberdaron, is about 11 miles - but take plenty of fuel as this is not the place to run dry! Bardsey is the third largest island off the coast of North Wales after Anglesey and Holy Island, measuring about 1.75 miles from north to south and 0.75 miles maximum from east to west. The highest point on Bardsey is at 167 metres, giving superb views across Bardsey Sound towards Aberdaron, eastwards to Harlech, southwards as far as Pembroke, and westwards to Ireland.

The island has been owned by the Bardsey Island Trust since 1979 and was declared a National Nature Reserve in 1986. The prominent red and white square tower of the lighthouse was built near the south tip of the island by Trinity House and became operational in 1821. Until 1988, it was occasionally possible to be given a guided tour of the 45 metre-high structure, but automation removed the need for resident keepers. It is now unmanned, except for maintenance purposes.

For anyone interested in this area, it is worth checking the Bardsey Island Internet web-site on www.bardsey-island.co.uk. There are several magnificent photographs, providing many happy memories of warm summer days during those cold winter evenings.

The island is a very important breeding and resting site for birds, so please do not disturb either the birds or the visiting ornithologists. The north of the island is the site of a 13th century abbey as well as a more modern church. Bardsey is reputedly the burial place of 20,000 saints, but there is some doubt as to whether this figure is correct. Perhaps the number was translated wrongly, or was it simply a bug in Windows AD 10.66? In those days of religious pilgrimages, the Pope had asserted that three trips to Bardsey were equivalent to one trip to Rome, but who knows which was the easier journey? Bardsey Sound is a wild place even in a modern RIB, let alone in a small, wooden sailing boat. After the abbey fell into disuse, the island became a base for Irish Sea pirates. Ogof Lladron on the south-west coast translates into English as 'Pirate's Cave'.

You can get information about the island from the Bardsey Trust shop in Aberdaron or from a small bookshop on the island, near the abbey. There are basic toilet facilities close to the Abbey, but this entails a three-quarter mile walk from the Bardsey slipway.

Bardsey has deep water off the north, east and south coasts, with a depth of 50 metres only about 100 metres away from the island's north-east point. Unfortunately, the western coast is shallow, with several reefs which lie awash at low tide. Since the prevailing winds blow from the south-west, most of the recorded shipwrecks are on the west coast under a dense covering of kelp. Those who have dived in shallow water on the island's west coast have found many isolated pieces of wreckage but, to my knowledge, no complete vessels have been discovered.

For further information: call at the Bardsey Trust shop in Aberdaron (Tel 01758 760667)

or contact :- The Bardsey Island Trust Officer, Coed Anna, Nanhoron, Pwllheli LL54 6AB

Essential Information:-

- The shortest route to Bardsey is from Aberdaron, but there are major problems launching here. Otherwise, use Abersoch, Porth Colmon or Porth Ysgaden.

- There are very strong currents with heavy overfalls in Bardsey Sound and off the south point of Bardsey, so avoid the exposed sites on spring-tides. Many sites, such as Caswenan Rock and Maen Bugail, can be dived only at slack-water on neap-tides.

- Further offshore, there are overfalls on the Devil's Ridge, Devil's Tail and Bastram Shoal.

- Large whirlpools and back-eddies exist at various states of the tide, causing the current to run in the opposite direction to what might be expected.

- Beware of the under-current off the north-east point of the island (see details under 'Horse-Brass Wreck').

- Slack-water does not coincide with either local high-water or low-water, but occurs approximately mid-way between the two.

- This is a national nature reserve, so do not disturb the wildlife.

- Fog banks may suddenly appear in Bardsey Sound, reducing surface visibility to as little as 50 metres. The island has its own mini-climate, so sunshine in Abersoch does not always mean sunshine on Bardsey.

- There is a close season for taking scallops (July 1st until December 31st).

- Lobster fishing is a well-established local industry. Watch out for pot-buoys and floating lines.

- The gate to the main slipway in Abersoch is locked at 8pm.

- The car park at Aberdaron usually closes at 7pm.

- Please pay the landing fee (£2.00 per person) if you go ashore on Bardsey Island.

- Take care when approaching either of the landing places on Bardsey, as there are several drying rocks close by. The main landing place on Bardsey is about two-thirds of the way down the eastern side of the island, where there is a concrete slipway running out into a narrow gully. Drying rocks close to this gully can easily damage a hull or propeller. To avoid them, motor directly towards the slipway while keeping a close watch on the echo-sounder. This gully is quite wide at high-water, but at low-water it becomes only just wide enough for one boat.

- At least one unexploded sea-mine from the Second World War has been found here.

- If you go wandering about the island, keep to the marked paths and be careful not to block the slipway or leave your boat stranded high and dry as the tide recedes.

- Charts required – 'Cardigan Bay North' (Number 1971).

- Maps – Ordnance Survey Explorer Map number 12 (Lleyn Peninsula West).

- Bardsey Island is accessible only by boat, so all sites have been treated as boat-dives.

Boat Dives - Where to Dive

5.1 - Maen Bugail (Shepherds Rock)

Latitude	52° 46.390'N	Longitude	004° 47.330'W
Position Fix	Differential - GPS	Datum	WGS84

Maen Bugail is an isolated rock about 600 metres off the north coast of Bardsey Island. Sometimes referred to as 'Mind Boggles', it dries out by 4.1 metres. Despite the horrendous tide-rip, this is an excellent dive-site, but only for experienced divers and competent coxswains. Although the rock is usually visible above water, it is awash at high-water on spring-tides, posing an unexpected danger to passing vessels. The surrounding seabed drops off rapidly to more than 30 metres where anchors and small amounts of wreckage have been reported.

Do not attempt to dive here on a spring-tide. Low-water slack on a neap-tide occurs between 30 and 60 minutes before low-water at Liverpool, but dives can take place well before this by sheltering in the lee of the rock. I have managed to marshal two consecutive 50-minute dives in the period leading up to slack-water. Avoid anchoring at this site and beware of the overfalls that build up close to the rock when the current changes direction after low-water and starts to run to the north-west. Delayed surface marker-buoys are essential, and should be deployed before leaving the shelter of the rock as divers can easily drift off without being noticed. Fixed SMBs tend to drift out into the current while you are diving. This creates a constant pull, making underwater progress rather difficult.

The rock surface is covered in marine-life, while the reef attracts conger, spur-dog, wrasse and a shoal of well over one hundred pollack, making the site popular with angling boats. Individual large pollack are also present. The underwater scenery consists of vertical cliffs, crevices and a variety of boulders, several of which are as big as a house. One massive boulder rests on top of

other smaller boulders, enabling an adventurous diver to swim underneath. Crevices around these boulders go back up to 10 metres. Torches are useful to illuminate the anemones and dead-men's fingers covering the rock-walls. Slightly west of Maen Bugail, there is another submerged rock with vertical sides and a flat top at a depth of about 20 metres.

Maen Bugail

5.2 - Bae y Rhigol

Latitude	52° 46.120'N	Longitude	004° 47.470'W	
Position Fix	Differential - GPS	Datum	WGS84	

This is a small, shallow bay which gives some shelter from the tidal stream through Bardsey Sound. As such, it is only really suitable for a second dive, but stay inside the bay to avoid strong currents and deep water. Old bottles and marmalade-jars have been found here.

5.3 - Bae'r Nant

Latitude	52° 46.045'N	Longitude	004° 47.205'W	
Position Fix	Differential - GPS	Datum	WGS84	

This is another small bay on the north side of Bardsey where there is also some shelter from wind and tide, but beware of deep water and the strong tidal flow in Bardsey Sound. Take care to avoid the large rock that dries out as the tide falls. The narrow gully in the corner of this bay has a crevice into which a large boulder has fallen, creating an underwater cave, so it is worth taking a torch to explore here. The sandy floor of the cave is only about 4 metres deep and at times is covered with dead kelp. Outside the cave, the seabed is only 6 to 8 metres deep and is mainly covered in sand, but there are many isolated rocky patches. Among these rocks and about 15 metres from the shore, there is at least one area of ferrous concretion, either from a wreck or simply the remains of a large mooring weight or anchor. The bay has probably been used in the past as a convenient sheltered mooring, as Victorian marmalade jars have been recovered here - presumably having been thrown overboard when empty or broken. Fish life is prolific, with wrasse, pollack and large shoals of sand-eels in evidence. The rocks to the west of the bay are covered in kelp, but those on the eastern side have been swept clean by the current to produce vertical walls. These drop away to a depth of about 10 metres, where they are undercut with several horizontal crevices.

5.4 - Wreck of an unknown sailing vessel (Horse-brass wreck)

Name	Unknown	Type	Sailing vessel	
Date Lost	Mid 19th century	Location	Bardsey Island	
Cause	Weather?	How Lost	Ran ashore	
Hull	Wood	Weight	Unknown	
Cargo	General cargo	Access	Boat only	
Latitude	52° 45.815'N	Longitude	004° 46.785'W	
Position Fix	Differential-GPS	Datum	WGS84	
Seabed	5 to 10 metres	Wreck Height	0.5 metres	
Charted as	Uncharted			
Slipway (1)	Aberdaron	Distance	3.5 miles	
Slipway (2)	Abersoch	Distance	13 miles	
Tidal Data	Strong currents - See text			

This unidentified wreck lies very close to the rocks in a sheltered bay on the north-east coast of Bardsey. Much of the wreck is covered in thick kelp, so it is very easy to swim over the site without seeing any indication of a shipwreck. The vessel has not yet been positively identified, and it is possible that more than one vessel has been wrecked here. It is known as the 'Horse-Brass' wreck since many equestrian items have been recovered here.

The wreck is of a copper-sheathed, wooden sailing vessel. It was wrecked after Queen Victoria came to the throne in 1839, since some items of cargo are marked 'VR'. The vessel appears to have run straight into the island, as two Admiralty-pattern anchors lie at a depth of around 5 metres and only a few metres from the cliffs. However, the rudder-pintles were found nearby, so these anchors may have been the kedge (stern) anchors with the main bower anchors lying elsewhere.

Many small items of wreckage and cargo are to be found within 15 metres of the cliff face, lying scattered between large boulders and hidden under a thick covering of kelp. An underwater metal-detector with a small probe is useful to locate these items, but most detectors tend to give a constant reading all over the site. Digging for these artefacts always attracts several large wrasse, intent on grabbing any morsel of food which becomes exposed. Ornate horse-bits, brass buckles, decorative stars for leather straps and at least two different types of stirrup have been found, while more mundane items including belt-buckles, buttons, stoneware jars, brass barrel-taps, bobbin-ends and dozens of bone or wood knife-handles lie scattered around the seabed. Hundreds of copper sheathing nails will be found, with most still retaining their sharp points. Take care if digging among the debris; they hurt!

A knife handle

Further away from the cliffs, dozens of broken bottles and several metal bars will be found in about 8 to 12 metres of water. These bottles are all made from a very dark glass and, strangely, there appear to be far more bottle-bases than necks. I understand that when the wreck was first discovered, the sextant and several pewter plates were found. French and Spanish coins have also been recovered.

Close to the cliffs, there are many large boulders sitting on the seabed. These must have tumbled from the cliffs above. Where they have fallen close together, there are narrow gullies, undercuts and small caves to explore. Moving further out into Bardsey Sound, the seabed has been swept clean by the current and quickly drops away on a 45 degree slope to a depth of 48 metres. The only items of interest on this slope are a small amount of wreckage at 20 metres, and several massive boulders. These rocks are distinct from the ones in the shallows as they have the appearance of Swiss cheese, presumably having been eroded by the strong currents.

Despite lying in a small, shallow and apparently tranquil bay, this site should only be dived at slack-water, as a fierce current can sweep over the wreck and has been known to drag divers down into the depths of Bardsey Sound. At least two divers have experienced this down-current, unintentionally hitting a depth of 40 metres before regaining control of their buoyancy and returning to the surface. Spring-tides are especially dangerous and, as with all sites around Bardsey Sound, slack-water does not coincide with high or low-water at Bardsey.

The 'Horse brass wreck' transits

The wreck can best be dived at around 4 to 5 hours after high-water at Liverpool. There is a short period of slack at high-water Liverpool, but after this time, the current picks up rapidly, causing anchored boats to suddenly swing round. Any diver still in the water will have difficulty swimming back to the boat and could be swept away round the corner, out of sight of the coxswain.

The main part of the wreck lies close inshore, underneath the steep hillside on the north-east side of Bardsey Island. The diver (above) is directly over the anchors. As the sun tracks across the sky the site will be in shadow, so it is better to avoid diving here in the late afternoon.

For those not interested in shipwrecks, the site is rich in marine-life. Conger eels live in clefts in the cliffs, and seals hunt in the bay. Pollack, wrasse, octopus and cuttle-fish will be seen underwater, while above the surface the sky is filled with guillemots, razorbills, puffins and cormorants.

Location: Having launched at Aberdaron or Abersoch, head for the pronounced 'V' mark on the hillside at the north-east corner of Bardsey Island. As you approach the island, you will see a jumble of massive boulders at the foot of the hillside to the right of the 'V'. To the right of the prominent rock, shown in the photograph, there is currently an old wooden pallet that has been there since at least 1990. The wood will eventually rot away, but if you look carefully, you can also see what appears to be a series of steps cut into the rock near the high-water mark. These may be a natural feature, or may have been cut to help salvage work on the wreck. Anchor about 15 metres off shore.

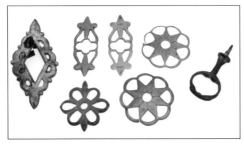

'Horse Brass Wreck' finds

5.5 - Briw Cerrig Reef

Latitude	52° 45.660'N	Longitude	004° 46.730'W
Position Fix	Differential - GPS	Datum	WGS84

Slightly south of the 'Horse-brass' wreck, a shallow reef projects eastward from the island before the seabed plunges into Bardsey Sound to a depth of more than 40 metres. Several large boulders rest on this reef and become exposed as the tide falls, creating a danger to navigation. About 50 metres north of the reef, there is a badly corroded 1.5 metre-long anchor in 12 metres of water. Other divers have reported at least one more anchor here, so there may be yet another wreck close to this reef or this could be the main anchor from the Horse-Brass wreck.

5.6 - Coastline to the north of Pen Cristin

Latitude (1)	52° 45.500'N	Longitude (1)	004° 46.855'W
Latitude (2)	52° 45.250'N	Longitude (2)	004° 47.100'W
Position Fix	Differential-GPS	Datum	WGS84

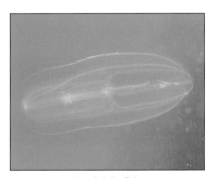

Comb jelly-fish

Long, fast drift-dives are possible all along the north-east coast of Bardsey, keeping close inshore but clear of the dense kelp, which grows to a depth of about 10 metres. Surface marker-buoys and good boat-cover are essential, but beware of the many lobster-pot buoys found here. Down to around 20 metres, the terrain is varied, with small vertical cliffs, deep crevices and piles of fallen boulders. Other areas are less interesting scree-slopes, but cuckoo wrasse, pollack and octopus are usually seen around the seabed. On occasions, divers have observed comb-jellyfish near the surface.

5.7 - Pen Cristin

Latitude	52° 45.155'N	Longitude	004° 47.165'W
Position Fix	Differential - GPS	Datum	WGS84

Pen Cristin is a rocky headland about halfway down the east coast of Bardsey Island, where the seabed rapidly drops off to a depth of more than 20 metres, with several interesting underwater gullies and crevices.

On the ebb tide, it is worth drifting south with the current along the edge of the island. By keeping close inshore, it is possible to turn the corner into a bay where there will be little or no current. Large pollack often hover in the sheltered water close to the point, so if you enjoy the taste of fresh fish, take a fishing rod or hand-line.

5.8 - Wreck of the 'Ilesha', off Pen Cristin

Name	Ilesha	Type	Motor vessel
Date Lost	8/8/1915	Location	Bardsey Island
Cause	Ran ashore	How Lost	Foundered
Hull	Steel	Weight	109 tons (gross)
Cargo	In ballast	Access	Boat only
Latitude	52° 45.095'N	Longitude	004° 47.260'W
Position Fix	Differential-GPS	Datum	WGS84
Seabed	22 metres	Wreck Height	2.5 metres
Charted as	Uncharted		
Slipway (1)	Aberdaron	Distance	4 miles
Slipway (2)	Abersoch	Distance	13.5 miles
Tidal Data	Some current - See text.		

Transit A

The 'Ilesha' transits

White rock A

There is an uncharted wreck lying broken up on a sandy seabed, off the east coast of Bardsey and approximately 200 metres south of Pen Cristin. This is the remains of a twin-screw vessel, built during 1914 by Isaac J. Abdela & Mitchell, of Queensferry, North Wales, and originally named 'Kingsholm'. The ship was sold to Butler & Co. of Bristol for service in the Bristol Channel, but it was later purchased by Elder, Dempster & Co. and renamed 'Ilesha'. Sent for service in West Africa, the ship developed problems with its starboard engine off South Wales and headed back towards the safety of the St. Tudwal's Islands. Less than 24 hours later, the port engine failed in a position less than 3 miles off Bardsey. The ship did have a set of sails in case of emergency, but when the wind dropped she was abandoned and drifted onto the rocks on the west side of Bardsey Island. There was still hope of recovering the situation, so the salvage steamer 'Lady of the Isles' was sent to assist, using divers to blast away a channel into deeper water. This was successful, but while the 'Ilesha' was being taken round to the east side of Bardsey for further repairs, she suddenly foundered in 11 fathoms (20 metres) of water. Apart from cutting away the protruding foremast, the wreck was left alone until revisited by divers in the 1980s.

Other vessels built by Abdella & Mitchell had their Bolinder's engines replaced fairly early in their working life, possibly because of a known design fault. If these engines were known to be unreliable, why was such a vessel, less than 30 metres long, being sent all the way to West Africa?

The vessel lies approximately east - west, with the bows at the east in around 23 metres of water, slightly deeper than the stern. The rounded stern rail lies on the seabed, close to the sternpost, twin-propellers and the rudder. Although made of iron, the port propeller is still easily recognised but the starboard one is very badly corroded. Moving forward from the sternpost, the two engines can be seen among a tangled mass of winches, ribs, riveted hull-plates, hand-wheels, bitts and other unidentified machinery. The forward section of the vessel has totally collapsed, with many ribs and plates still visible, but the bow has either broken off or is covered with sand and gravel.

Large ballan wrasse will be seen swimming around the wreck, while the cavities under the hull provide a home for crabs and the odd lobster.

Pen Cristin

Transit B

Directions: Head southwards down the east coast of Bardsey with the steep hillside to your right until you reach Pen Cristin point. Once the slipway and lighthouse are in sight, continue south for another 150 metres, slow down and turn right, heading westwards towards the island. Look for the westerly transit A (the pole and the left-hand edge of the white rock A), and motor towards them while checking the northerly transit B. The prominent white rock B on the mainland cliffs should be just visible beyond Pen Cristin. The highest part is the sternpost and rudder assembly, standing proud of the seabed by about 2 to 3 metres. With some difficulty, it can be picked up by an echo-sounder. Otherwise, use a GPS or magnetometer. Unless the surface visibility is poor, I use the transits alone to find the wreck.

Transit B

White rock B

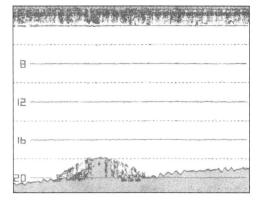

A Bolinder engine at the Ellesmere Port Boat Museum.

The 'Ilesha' was named after a Nigerian town, and the wreck has been positively identified by its maker's name-plate. Its twin, two-stroke oil engines were an early version of this type of propulsion, having been built by Bolinders Ltd. of Stockholm. Before the engine could be started, a cast-iron dome on each cylinder head needed to be warmed up by means of a blowlamp. A wonderfully-restored example of a Bolinder engine can be seen at Ellesmere Port Boat Museum.

Broken crockery has been found scattered around this wreck and in the bay to the south. These plates have a blue printed pattern on a white background, and are marked 'B.B. & Co, Patent Ironstone Pottery'. The 'Encyclopaedia of British Pottery & Porcelain' lists this mark as that of Baker, Bevans & Irwin (Glamorgan Pottery, Swansea), who produced dishes and plates from 1813 to 1838. This factory did produce dedicated 'ship-plates', but the crockery probably does not come from the wreck of the 'Ilesha', which did not sink until 1915. Therefore, the remains of another vessel may lie close to this wreck, perhaps making an echo-sounder and magnetometer search worthwhile.

Lying off the east coast of Bardsey, the wreck has some protection from the prevailing winds. Although it is out of the main tide-race flowing past Pen Cristin, the current can be quite strong on spring-tides. I usually dive the wreck about one hour before high-water or low-water at Liverpool. Unfortunately, the area around the wreck can be rather silty, so it is best dived by only a small group. Alternatively, choose a time when there is some current to wash away any sediment.

5.9 - Ridge of rocks running out from the slipway at Cafn Enlli

Latitude	52° 45.125'N	Longitude	004° 47.495'W
Position Fix	Differential - GPS	Datum	WGS84

Bardsey slipway

Cafn Enlli is the main landing area on Bardsey, with a concrete slipway leading to the narrowest point of the island. A long ridge of rocks, submerged for much of the time, runs due east from a point immediately south of the slipway. This ridge presents a danger to any boats heading to or from the Bardsey landing site, so keep a careful watch on the echo-sounder. Large sheets of fibre-glass on the seabed show that it can still claim victims.

A large red mooring buoy on a single-fluke mooring anchor usually marks the east-most point of this ridge (at 52° 45.105'N 004° 47.480'W). Anyone diving here needs to have adequate boat-cover and marker-buoys, since the mooring buoy is used by the Bardsey Island ferry-boat. A second admiralty-pattern anchor with an iron stock lies close by in 15 metres of water, probably from an older mooring. I understand that a large, stone anchor has also been seen in this area. The ridge provides a useful dive-site for training purposes, being out of the main current and having a maximum depth of less than 20 metres. There are large boulders,

Candy-striped flatworm

vertical walls, crevices and overhangs. The seabed can be a little silty close inshore, but further out - where there is a current - there is very little loose sediment. Note that at certain states of the ebb-tide, the current near the buoy goes to the north when the main current further out is actually running to the south, so divers need to rely on the compass rather than navigating by the direction of the current.

As the east side of Bardsey is home to a large seal population, expect to be buzzed by one or more of them during your dive. I have often had a fleeting glimpse of one underwater, and they do seem to be becoming bolder, but avoid scaring them off the rocks and into the water. As always, thick kelp close inshore causes problems, but towards the east end of the reef there are clear, vertical cliffs inhabited by a large shoal of pollack. Other marine-life is rather colourful, often with many candy-striped flatworms and gaudy cuckoo-wrasse living on this reef.

5.10 - Henllwyn

Latitude	52° 45.100'N	Longitude	004° 47.610'W		
Position Fix	Differential - GPS	Datum	WGS84		

This sheltered bay is located south-east of the slipway and is only 6 to 8 metres deep. The seabed consists of thick kelp with areas of flat sand and bootlace weed, and it is worth a rummage under the kelp to see the stratified rock formations. The nooks and crannies in the rocks provide a haven for lobsters, crabs and squat lobsters. Large pollack and wrasse are common, as well as thousands of two-spotted gobies and sand-eels. The area is sheltered from the south, east and north. As it lies out of the main tidal stream, it can be dived almost any time. At low-water, dozens of seals will be seen resting on the rocks.

5.11 - Maen Ddu (South Tip of Bardsey)

Latitude	52° 44.670'N	Longitude	004° 48.170'W
Position Fix	Differential - GPS	Datum	WGS84

The southern-most tip of the island is marked by a distinctive black rock known as Maen Ddu. To the east of Maen Ddu, strong currents run in a north-south direction to produce heavy overfalls, so any diving here must be timed for slack-water. Be on site at least an hour before high-water at Liverpool and wait for the current to ease off.

The seabed drops off rapidly to more than 20 metres, with deep gullies and smooth rock providing a very pleasant underwater terrain with much marine-life. Beware of the drying rock just out from the cliffs. An old anchor and a long length of chain lie about 200 metres south of the point. Although I can't confirm any wreckage, there are reports of cannon-balls being found here.

Bardsey Lighthouse

5.12 - Caswenan Rock

Latitude	52° 43.970'N	Longitude	004° 49.290'W
Position Fix	Differential - GPS	Datum	WGS84

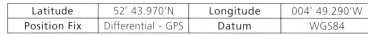

'Caswenan' echo-sounder traces - note expanded scale. (metres)

Just under a mile south-west of Bardsey Lighthouse - and reputedly named after King Arthur's ship - Caswenan Rock is one of my favourite dive-sites around North Wales. Caswenan is for experienced divers only and should be attempted only on those rare occasions when good weather coincides with slack-water and neap-tides. It helps if you have a non-diving boatman available, since there is normally only enough slack-water time for one wave of divers - especially if decompression stops are needed. Alternatively, charter a hard-boat or RIB to ensure that everyone who wants to dive can do so. Caswenan Rock is a small, isolated rock that does not dry out at low-water, being charted as Rk 17.8. At low-water on a neap-tide, it rises from more than 45 metres to 23 metres. Overfalls or whirlpools usually mark it, but due to the strong currents these areas of disturbed water will be some distance from the actual rock. Even on neap-tides, the currents will pull a marker-buoy underwater or drag the shot-weight off the top of the rock, resulting in a 45 metre dive instead of a 23 metre one. A wise dive-marshal will arrive on site early, locate the rock by GPS, but wait until slack-water approaches before

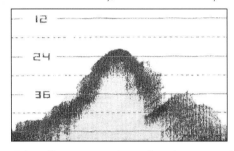

dropping the shot-weight. Even then, the rounded shape of the rock often causes the shot-weight to roll off into deeper water.

The main peak of the rock is dome-shaped, with several deep fissures at the top. See echo-sounder trace. The rock is smooth and rounded, and has several near-vertical walls which drop away steeply to a seabed covered in large boulders.

Other divers report the rock to be saucer-shaped, but this is probably the second peak (at 52° 43.935'N and 004° 49.300'W), slightly to the south and about 4 or 5 metres deeper. The echo-sounder trace also shows a third peak, but this is at a depth of more than 30 metres.

With the rock being so deep, there is no weed growth on it. The clean rock faces are covered in mussels, anemones, sea-firs and sea-mats. Large pollack hover out of the main current, making the site popular with angling-boats which drift across the area, leaving mackerel traces, fishing weights and mono-filament line snagged on the rock. There are also many lost anchors, shot-weights, lumps of concrete and even old computer power-supplies scattered around Caswenan Rock.

Location: Use the GPS position given above, taking care to avoid the overfalls off the south tip of Bardsey. Check the echo-sounder to ensure that you are on the shallowest peak in the vicinity.

Timing: Good timing is essential when diving Caswenan. If you are late, dive elsewhere, as the current runs like the proverbial train. Dive only at low-water slack on a neap-tide. arriving on site well over an hour before low-water at Liverpool, as the tidal flow is starting to slacken. The current will start to ease at one hour before low-water at Liverpool, with slack being around 30 minutes before low-water at Liverpool. However, these timings have been known to vary slightly, so arrive early, and be ready to dive as soon as conditions allow.

King Arthur (as is reported) had a ship called Gaswenan cast away there. Hence the place is called Gorffrydau Caswenan.

From the Lewis Morris chart of Bardsey

'Publish'd According to Act of Parliament Sept. 29. 1748'

5.13 - West of the South Tip of Bardsey

Latitude	52° 44.780'N	Longitude	004° 48.260'W
Position Fix	Differential - GPS	Datum	WGS84

To the west and south-west of Maen Ddu, the seabed is carpeted with thick kelp down to a depth of about 10 metres. Beyond this, down to about 20 metres, it changes to a series of gullies cut into the bare volcanic rock, with small vertical walls, deep crevices and clean, sandy patches. A number of roofing slates can be found on the seabed, about 300 metres to the west of Maen Ddu, possibly from the vessel which lost its anchor there. If this is the case, perhaps the main area of wreckage lies even further to the west, the ship having hit Bardsey Island and drifted with the tide in a sinking state. Close inshore and out of the current, the seabed has a thin layer of silt. Further offshore, strong currents sweep the seabed clean.

Nice drift-dives can be enjoyed in this area, where a diver can repeatedly drop into the gullies and canyons to explore the rocky crevices and overhangs. The area is peppered with lobster-pots, so take care as you drift along.

West Coast of Bardsey

The seabed on the west coast of Bardsey is much shallower than that to the east. As the prevailing winds are from the west, most of the ships wrecked on the island must surely lie along this coast. However, little wreckage has been discovered as the sea is shallow and the seabed is covered in a thick layer of kelp, hiding any evidence. Being largely unexplored by divers, the area must be well worth a magnetometer search. Certainly, large anchors have been seen while drift-diving. These would probably have been dropped in a final, desperate effort to keep a ship off the rocks.

5.14 - Gybie and Porth Solfach

Latitude	52° 45.435'N	Longitude	004° 47.900'W
Position Fix	Differential - GPS	Datum	WGS84

The small rocks known as Gybie lie between Carreg Honwy and Porth Solfach on Bardsey Island. Although the seabed is shallow and covered in boot-lace weed, the site is out of the current, making it useful for a second dive or for training drills. The seabed is covered in kelp close inshore, but there are some interesting rocks for snorkelling - perhaps in the company of the local seals.

Although this is the only place on the west coast of Bardsey where one can easily get ashore, boats should avoid Porth Solfach if ornithologists are occupying the bird-hide on the beach. If you do approach this kelp-covered beach, beware of several half-submerged rocks.

5.15 - Carreg yr Honwy

Latitude (North)	52° 45.465'N	Longitude (N)	004° 48.160'W
Latitude (South)	52° 45.340'N	Longitude (S)	004° 48.270'W
Position Fix	Differential-GPS	Datum	WGS84

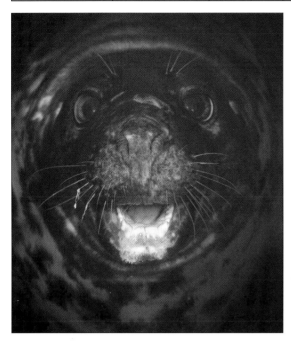

Carreg yr Honwy is a small, barren islet about 500 metres west of Bardsey Island. It provides a resting home for a large group of seals. Please do not disturb these mammals, observing only from a distance. The seabed to the east and north of the islet is shallow and covered in dense kelp, with very strong currents making the area unsuitable for diving. The western side of the reef is better as the rocks quickly drop off to 15 metres.

Long drift-dives, covering up to a mile, may be undertaken further to the west in around 20 metres of water where the seabed comprises broken rock with areas of sand and gravel. Occasionally, crayfish will be found in the summer months.

5.16 - Maen Iau (Jupiter Rock)

Latitude	52° 45.915'N	Longitude	004° 47.915'W
Position Fix	Differential - GPS	Datum	WGS84

Charted as a drying rock (*), this kelp-covered rock lies about 150 metres west of the north-west coast of Bardsey Island. At high-water there is 3 or 4 metres of water over Maen Iau, but at low-water on a spring-tide, the tip of the rock breaks the surface and creates a major hazard to navigation. This is not the place to damage your propeller or skeg, so keep well clear at low-water! Although only a small amount of rock becomes exposed at this time, the reef is quite extensive, dropping off to a flat seabed at a depth of only 10 metres.

Strong currents and overfalls occur in this area but to the west of Maen Iau, long drift-dives are again possible over ridges of broken, volcanic rock. Stay shallower than 20 metres for a more enjoyable dive. If you do drift along this stretch of coast, make sure you end your dive before reaching the overfalls at the north or south of the island, as your support-boat may not be able to follow your marker-buoy through the rough water. There is at least one magnetic anomaly near Maen Iau which may be worth investigating, perhaps suggesting that an undived wreck or a large anchor lies close by.

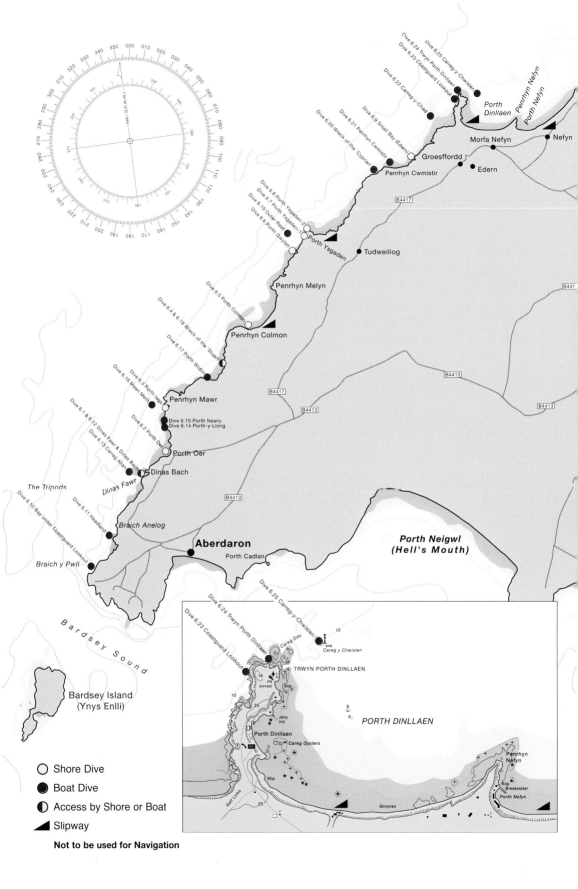

Dive 6.25 Carreg y Chwislen
Dive 6.24 Trwyn Porth Dinllaen
Dive 6.23 Coastguard Lookout
Dive 6.22 Carreg-y-Chad
Dive 6.9 Small Bay (Edern)
Dive 6.21 Penrhyn Cwmistir
Dive 6.20 Wreck of the Cyprian

Porth
Dinllaen

Penrhyn Nefyn
Porth Nefyn

Morfa Nefyn
Nefyn
Groesffordd
Edern
Penrhyn Cwmistir

B4417

Dive 6.8 Porth Ysgaden-2
Dive 6.7 Porth Ysgaden-1
Dive 6.19 Outer Reef
Dive 6.6 Porth Gwylan

Porth Ysgaden
Tudweiliog

B441

Penrhyn Melyn

Dive 6.5 Porth Colmon

Dive 6.4 & 6.18 Wreck of the Stuart
Penrhyn Colmon

Dive 6.17 Porth Widlin
Dive 6.3 Porth Iago
Dive 6.16 Maen Mellt

B4417
B4413

B4413

Penrhyn Mawr

Dive 6.1 & 6.12 Dinas Fawr & Dinas Bach
Dive 6.15 Porth Newry
Dive 6.14 Porth-y-Llong
Dive 6.2 Porth Oer
Dive 6.13 Careg Allan

Porth Oer

Dinas Bach

B4413

The Tripods
Dinas Fawr

Dive 6.10 Bay under Coastguard Lookout
Dive 6.11 Headland
Braich Anelog

Aberdaron
Porth Cadlan

Porth Neigwl
(Hell's Mouth)

Braich y Pwll

B a r d s e y   S o u n d

Bardsey Island
(Ynys Enlli)

Dive 6.25 Carreg-y-Chwislen
Dive 6.24 Trwyn Porth Dinllaen
Dive 6.23 Coastguard Lookout

Careg Ddu
10
BRB
Careg y Chwislen

TRWYN PORTH DINLLAEN
26
(occas)
FR
Slip

10
25

Jetty
(ru)

PORTH DINLLAEN

6

Penrhyn Nefyn

Porth Dinllaen
Careg Oysters
WC

Slip
Breakwater
Porth Nefyn

Slip

Golf Links
25
Groynes

○ Shore Dive
● Boat Dive
◑ Access by Shore or Boat
◤ Slipway

Not to be used for Navigation

CHAPTER SIX

Braich-y-Pwll to Nefyn

'Amongst these are Porth Towyn, Porth Colman, Porth Gwylan and Porth Ysgadan. Near the last, about thirty years ago, a rock which towered a great height out of the sea was suddenly missed, after a horrible night of thunder and lightning, was supposed to have been struck down by the resistless bolt'.

Thomas Pennant, 1781

General Description

This coastline has high, rocky cliffs, narrow inlets cut into the sharp volcanic rock, and several small, sandy beaches such as Porth Iago, Porth Oer, Traeth Benllech, Porth Ysgaden and Porth Towyn. Being quiet and isolated, the area abounds with wildlife. Watch out for buzzards soaring high above the cliffs. This is the southern part of Caernarfon Bay, where there have been confirmed sightings of basking sharks, blue sharks, thresher sharks, porbeagle sharks and mako sharks.

Essential Information:-

- This area has several good sites suitable for snorkelling or shore-dives.
- Launching sites are available at Porth Colmon, Porth Ysgaden and Morfa Nefyn.
- There are very heavy overfalls at Braich-y-Pwll, the Tripods, Braich Anelog and Penrhyn Mawr.
- Strong currents are found all along this coast.
- There are isolated drying-reefs at Carreg-y-Trai (Porth Oer) and Maen Mellt.
- Obey the speed limits off the beaches at Morfa Nefyn.
- The close season for scallops does not apply north of Braich-y-Pwll.
- Charts required – 'Cardigan Bay North' (Number 1971) and 'Plans on the Llŷn Peninsula' (Number 1512).
- Maps – Ordnance Survey Explorer Map number 12 (Lleyn Peninsula West).

Shore Dives or Snorkelling Sites

6.1 - Dinas Fawr and Dinas Bach

Latitude	52° 49.780'N	Longitude	004° 44.185'W
O.S. Reference	SH	157E	294N

Dinas Bach

Dinas Fawr and Dinas Bach are two rocky promontories, surrounded by fairly shallow water and thick kelp. The area between them is shallow, sandy and sheltered from the current.

It is possible to park at the National Trust car park at Carreg, near Porth Oer and climb down to the small sandy beach at Dinas Bach but there is a 70 metre difference in vertical height and the last few metres are over steep, sharp rocks. This would be very difficult with full diving equipment and is not recommended. The site can be used for snorkelling, providing you keep within the confines of the two promontories.

Path to Dinas Bach

Directions: You first need to find the small village of Pen-y-Groeslon, about 3 miles north-east of Aberdaron. There are two alternatives:

1. From Nefyn, take the B4417 south-west, passing through Edern and Tudweiliog. Continue until you reach the 'T' junction at Pen-y-Groeslon. Turn right on to the B4413 for Aberdaron.

2. From Pwllheli, take the A499 for Abersoch and turn right at Llanbedrog onto the B4413, heading for Aberdaron. Pass through the villages of Mynytho, Botwnnog and Sarn Meyllteyrn before reaching Pen-y-Groeslon.

Having reached Pen-y-Groeslon, follow the B4413 for Aberdaron, immediately passing the 'Eifionydd Groeslon' farm supplies. Half a mile from Pen-y-Groeslon, just as the road bends to the left, take the turning on the right for Porth Oer/Whisling Sands. Zero the milage trip meter on the car. Follow this road, passing the turning for Porth Oer. After 3.1 miles, turn into Carreg car park on the right (at 52° 49.610'N 004° 43.720'W, SH 162E 291N) and park at the top end of the car park. Walk through the gate and continue straight on over the hill. The path eventually leads down between two fences to the cliff top, turn right and follow the path, then scramble down the cliff to the water's edge. See the photos of Dinas Bach and the path opposite.

6.2 - Porth Oer (Whistling Sands)

Latitude	52° 50.080'N	Longitude	004° 43.495'W
O.S. Reference	SH	164E	299N

Porth Oer is a westerly-facing, sandy beach. It is about 350 metres wide, with access down a long, steep hill, but vehicles are not allowed down to the beach and must be left in the car park. The beach is known to tourists as 'Whistling Sands' because of the strange noise made by anyone sliding their shoes along the dry sand. Owned by the National Trust, the car park (at 52° 49.910'N 004° 43.415'W / SH 165E 296N) is free to their members, or £2.00 per day to non-members. Boats cannot be launched here. The beach is very popular with families and sun-worshippers during the summer months. A café sells ice-cream, cakes, hot drinks and beach-ware such as surfboards. This café was closed for several years but reopened in the summer of 2002.

The site is sheltered from the south and east, providing an easy, shallow dive off a gently sloping beach. Avoid diving during or after a period of westerly winds, as the underwater visibility will be poor. The central part of the bay is mainly flat sand with little marine-life. The better diving or snorkelling site is found around the rocks to the left and out to the small, drying-reef of Carreg-y-Trai. Take care to avoid this hazard if you approach Porth Oer by boat. Even after a long swim, depths will only be around 6 to 8 metres, with underwater gullies up to 3 metres high. Here, the sharp rocks have been smoothed and rounded by the storms. Currents close inshore are fairly weak, but once you venture away from the rocks, they are much stronger where the ebb-tide could carry a diver south-westward along the coast and away from any easy exit point.

There is a newspaper report of nine vessels coming ashore here in a single night - the 29th of October 1859. Most were probably refloated, but a search close inshore among the thick kelp may provide some evidence of wreckage. This storm became known as the 'Royal Charter Gale' when more than 400 people were lost at Moelfre on the east coast of Anglesey.

This is a typical surf beach, with a sandy seabed and rocky boundaries. Shoals of sand-eels are found on the sand, with wrasse, pollack and dogfish among the rocks and kelp.

The main disadvantage of diving from this beach is the long climb back up the hill carrying full diving gear, so it is probably better just to snorkel around the rocks. If you do decide to dive here, a single 10-litre cylinder is all that is required, being much easier to carry back up the hill than a twin-set.

Directions: From Pen-y-Groeslon (see page 84), follow the B4413 for Aberdaron, passing the 'Eifionydd Groeslon' farm supplies. Half a mile from Pen-y-Groeslon, just as the road bends to the left, take the turning on the right, sign-posted Porth Oer/Whistling sands. Follow this road for 2.8 miles, and turn right to the car-park at Porth Oer. See your Ordnance Survey map for further details.

6.3 - Porth Iago

Latitude	52° 51.105′N	Longitude	004° 43.290′W
O.S. Reference	SH	168E	318N

Porth Iago consists of a shallow, sandy beach at the base of high cliffs. Access to the shore is down a steep path from a car park and Caravan Club campsite. The land is privately owned and parking costs £2.00 (in 2002) at the farm. The beach makes the site ideal for those divers with young families, but take care as the cliffs are dangerous and unfenced in places.

It is possible to carry diving gear down to the beach but the return trip is only for the energetic diver. It is, however, a good snorkelling site. As the bay faces south-west, it is badly affected by surf when strong winds blow from this direction, but is otherwise well sheltered. Beware of being caught in the strong current that runs outside the bay, as exit from the water is possible only at Porth Iago beach. There is a reef in the middle of the bay which is fringed with kelp and surrounded by flat sand. The cliffs are popular with anglers who are often seen catching wrasse and pollack from the rocks.

A report from the Hydrographic Office says that timbers, pottery and an anchor were found during a shore dive in 1979. Subsequent dives failed to relocate the wreck, so it is probable that the debris is covered or uncovered by sand movement from year to year. This wreck may be the 249-ton, Scottish brig 'Luther' which was wrecked in a storm on 21st January 1884 when transporting coal and general cargo from Troon to Newfoundland. The captain, three seamen and a boy were drowned.

Directions:. See previous directions for Pen-y-Groeslon, then follow the B4413 for Aberdaron, immediately passing the 'Eifionydd Groeslon' farm supplies. As the road bends to the left, take the turning on the right, sign-posted Porth Oer/Whistling sands. From here, take the second lane on the right and follow this narrow lane through the sharp left-hand bend to the T-junction. Turn left then immediately right. The road and track to Porth Iago are signposted from here.

6.4 - Wreck of the 'Stuart' at Porth Ty-Mawr

Latitude	52° 51.870'N	Longitude	004° 41.580'W
O.S. Reference	SH	188E	332N

For full details of this wreck, see the information later in this chapter under 'Boat-dives'. The wreck lies nearly a mile along the cliff top path from the car park at Porth Colmon, so this would be a long and difficult walk in full diving gear. Those who have done so, do not recommend the trek. However, it does make an interesting snorkelling site, with much wreckage and fish life to be seen in shallow water.

Directions: Park at Porth Colmon (see following dive-site) and walk to the left (south-west) following the cliff-top path for nearly a mile, until you reach a sign-post marked 'Porth Colmon, Porth Widlin' (at 52° 51.960'N 004° 41.505'W / SH 188E 333N). Clamber down the bank, cross the stream and climb over the fence at the stile. Don't climb back up the bank, but follow the fence towards the group of yellow rocks above the wreck at position 52° 51.915'N 004° 41.540'W / SH 189E 332N. The wreck lies immediately south of the yellow rocks, with parts of the mast and hull visible on the rocks once the tide begins to fall. Access is much easier at local high-water, about 2 hours before Liverpool, but even then, take care clambering down the rocks to the water's edge.

6.5 - Porth Colmon

Latitude	52° 52.510'N	Longitude	004° 41.020'W
O.S. Reference	SH	194E	343N

Porth Colmon has parking for about ten cars, but do not block the entrance to the house or slipway. There is access to the sea from the beach or rocks, but the water is shallow and - on the lowest of spring-tides - kelp actually breaks the surface about 300 metres offshore. The site is best dived at high-water, as at low-tide there is a large area of dead kelp on the beach by the slipway. This layer of weed may be half a metre thick. At one time, a drain running into the bay produced a foul-smelling concoction bad enough to make anyone sea-sick before actually stepping into a boat, but this problem has improved in recent years.

Even without the smell, Porth Colmon is not an immediately impressive dive-site, since the bay consists of a dense kelp forest with only a few sandy patches. The only way to view the sea life is to delve among the kelp and study the small fish and crustaceans that inhabit this underwater jungle. Once you do this, there is a surprising amount of animal and plant life to be seen. Surface marker-buoys and buddy-lines are difficult to use in this situation since they quickly become entangled in the kelp, but some sort of surface cover is essential as the bay is popular with pleasure-craft and lobster-boats. There are many lobster-pots here, so watch out for half-submerged lines and buoys.

Old newspaper accounts have recorded many sailing vessels being wrecked in this area. There are more modern reports of several ships' winches being seen at low-water. Having searched along the rocks on a very low tide, I have seen only one windlass, partially buried on the beach and close to the slipway, but other artefacts may still lie hidden among the kelp.

Directions: Take the B4417 southwest from Morfa Nefyn, passing through Edern and Tudweiliog, then climb up the hill with a nasty 'S' bend. Pass the signs for Llangwnnadl and the Carrog Guest House before turning right, sign-posted Porth Colmon and Llangwnnadl. Pass the church on the right before stopping at the crossroads junction. Carry straight on, down a narrow, twisty lane to the slipway and car park at Porth Colmon (See photo Section-2).

6.6 - Porth Gwylan

Latitude	52° 53.980'N	Longitude	004° 39.185'W
O.S. Reference	SH	126E	369N

Porth Gwylan at high water

This is a small, sheltered cove which can be reached on foot from the car park at Porth Ysgaden. Porth Gwylan faces north-west and has a ridge of rocks running out to sea, so this area is more sheltered than Porth Ysgaden during south-westerly winds. Best dived at high-water (2 hours before high-water at Liverpool) the cove is like a small salt-water swimming pool. At low-water, several rocks dry out to restrict access to and from the open sea.

As Porth Gwylan is only a few metres deep at high-water, it provides a good snorkelling or training site in a restricted area, with little current and no passing boat traffic. Once at the dive-site, access is fairly easy from a shingle beach. Wrasse, pollack and shoals of sand-eels will be seen, while small conger eels hide among the rocks. There is less life outside the bay. Once you've got clear of the kelp, the seabed is mostly flat sand at a maximum depth of about 8 metres. Seals swim inside the cove and in a sea-cave just outside the bay. This cave has a vertical shaft which emerges inside Porth Gwylan, about 8 metres above the beach. Visitors are often mystified when they hear the call of a bull seal apparently coming from halfway up a cliff-face, not realising that the animal is actually on the seaward side of the rocks and the sound is being funnelled upwards through the cave.

On 4th January 1848, the barque 'Christian' was carrying rum and sugar from Demerara to Liverpool when she was abandoned at sea. She ran ashore at Porth Gwylan and was dashed to pieces, but not before local people had been aboard to relieve her of her sails and cargo, including '5 hogsheads of rum' - a hogshead being about 50 gallons. It must have been good quality rum, as someone later raided the local customs store and drained yet another hogshead. See the extract from the local newspaper.

Directions: See the notes on page 90 for directions to Porth Ysgaden. From the car park, go through the gate near the top of the slipway and walk about 500 metres south-west along the coastal footpath towards Porth Colmon. Go through the swing-gate and bear right down a short track and a flight of concrete steps to the shingle beach at Porth Gwylan.

Porth Dynllaen - On Tuesday last the barque Cristian, William Stirling master, bound from Demerara to Liverpool with a cargo of rum and sugar came on the rocks at a place called Porthgwylan, about three miles southwards of this place. She had been abandoned at sea. She was taken possession of by people from the neighbourhood who succeeded in getting all her sails up the cliffs and about 5 hogsheads* of rum was brought to shore. We have since learnt that she has gone to pieces. Agents for the Receiver of Droits, the officers of the Customs and Lloyd's Agent immediately repaired to the spot.

Carnarvon and Denbigh Herald, 8th January 1848

On the night of the 13th instance or early on the following morning some person or persons bored the floor of the custom house at this place by which means they succeeded in emptying a hogshead* of rum which was placed there to await its shipment to Liverpool.

Carnarvon and Denbigh Herald, 22nd January 1848

*Hogshead = 50 Gallons

6.7 - Porth Ysgaden (Shore Dive from the Beach)

Latitude	52° 54.260'N	Longitude	004° 38.925'W
O.S. Reference	SH	219E	375N

Porth Ysgaden beach

Probably the most popular diving area along this stretch of coast, Porth Ysgaden is easily recognised from a distance by a derelict house and chimney on the headland. Port Ysgaden, (The Bay of Herrings) provides a shallow, sheltered beach suitable for novices, but divers must be aware that the bay is popular with dive boats, water-skiers and lobster boats. Shore cover and marker-buoys are essential when diving off the 75-metre wide beach, and watch out for mooring-ropes and lobster-pot lines. The bay faces south-west, so a strong wind from this direction quickly stirs up the sand to give poor visibility.

An interesting, shallow shore-dive can be undertaken from the beach by keeping to the rocks along the northern side of the bay. This area never has any current, making it a good site for novices. There are many crevices and small caves along this edge, all full of life. I have seen a dozen prawns and a goby in one small cave at a depth of less than 5 metres, making this an ideal location for the underwater photographer. Ling, plaice, wrasse, leopard-spotted gobies, pollack, sea-hares, spiny spider-crabs, edible-crabs and small lobsters provide an ideal introduction to marine-life. The middle of Porth Ysgaden bay has a large area of flat sand with some kelp and bootlace weed, whilst the rocks against the cliffs are covered in dense kelp. About 50 metres off the point, there is a 1-metre long, admiralty-pattern anchor, stuck at the bottom of a deep crevice.

Directions: Take the B4417 south-west from Morfa Nefyn and pass through the village of Tudweiliog. After leaving the 30mph area, pass a parking area on the left before turning right at the sign for 'Penrallt Coastal Campsite'. After a short distance, where the main road goes sharp left, carry straight on into a narrow lane marked 'Beach/Camping'.

Pass a house called 'Minafon', currently painted cream and blue with an anchor motif on the chimney. The main road then curves to the right, but take the narrower lane straight on. As the Tarmac lane goes sharp left, carry straight on into a narrow dirt-track which leads to Porth Ysgaden.

6.8 - Porth Ysgaden (Shore Dive from the Rocks)

Latitude	52° 54.370'N	Longitude	004° 38.915'W
O.S. Reference	SH	219E	377N

The outer edge of the rocks at Porth Ysgaden is a more interesting dive-site, as long as you accept that entry to the water from the rocks is rather difficult, and exit over them is virtually impossible. There is a small patch of shingle at the above GPS position which, at high-water

Porth Ysgaden (the shingle patch)

only, makes entry and exit much easier than clambering over the sharp rocks. This area is not suitable for novices, and dives should not be attempted if there is a swell.

Several vessels have been wrecked at Porth Ysgaden. Lots of copper sheathing has been found close inshore among the dense kelp, where there are many vertical walls up to 3 metres high. When analysed, this proved to be copper rather than muntz metal, suggesting a wreck that occurred before the mid 1800s. Certainly, there is a great deal of hidden wreckage close to the rocks in around 8 metres of water. An underwater metal-detector has picked up many large objects buried under the sand, while anchors, anchor chains, winches and gear wheels have all been seen within 100 metres of the shore in around

12 metres of water. Some divers have reported finding iron cannon and cannon balls, but have been unable to relocate them the following year - presumably due to the artefacts being reburied by winter gales or hidden by kelp. Others divers have recovered shards of pottery.

Marine-life coats the rock surfaces under the kelp in the shallows. Further out where there is no kelp, the seabed changes from sand and rock to soft boulder-clay, which looks just like soft putty. Here, at around 16 metres, you will find vast mussel-beds with dozens of predatory starfish grazing on them. Apart from the usual pollack, wrasse and dogfish, you may see bull-huss, spur-dog, octopus, sea-hares and the occasional free-swimming conger eel.

As the current runs roughly parallel to the shore, drift-diving with the tide is easier, especially as there are exit points in either direction. The strong currents mean that drift-dives should be timed only either side of slack-water and not at full flood or ebb-tide. Head south or south-east to get back to the exit point at Port Ysgaden beach. If you really get your tidal predictions wrong and drift a long way to the south-west, then exit at Porth Gwylan (dive 6.6) and walk back from here. If you drift to the north-east, leave the water at the next bay (Porth Llydan) and walk back over the headland.

Directions to the shingle patch: Dive at local high-water only, starting your dive around 2.5 hours before high-water at Liverpool. Assemble your kit and carry it to the gate by the notice-board. This gate is very difficult to negotiate in full diving gear, so pass the cylinders over the gate before kitting up fully. Head towards the derelict building, but beware of the barbed-wire fence next to the path (it hurts!). Pass the derelict building on the headland and follow the cliff-top for about 50 metres to the right, looking for an area of shingle at the water's edge (see photo). Take care going down the slope if the grass is wet.

6.9 - Small bay, located off Groesffordd and Edern

Latitude	52° 55.705'N	Longitude	004° 35.415'W
O.S. Reference	SH	259E	400N

This is a small, shallow, and secluded north-westerly facing shingle bay which gives shore access suitable for snorkelling or training dives. There is little current and access is fairly easy at all states of the tide. Close inshore, large pollack will be seen hovering over the kelp beds, with dozens of dozy dogfish on the sand further out.

Directions: Take the B4417 from Morfa Nefyn, heading south-west towards Tudweiliog and Aberdaron. Pass the 'Ship' public house in Edern and, as you climb the hill, turn right by the Post Office into a narrow country lane. Pass the speed de-restriction sign and a farm called 'Bryn Gwydd'. Park by a public footpath sign on the right (at 52° 55.585'N 004° 35.120'W / SH 262E 398N). There is only enough parking space for one vehicle without obstructing the farm gate. Follow the path for about 400 metres to the small bay. Bring a trolley with large, pneumatic wheels to transport heavy equipment to and from the beach.

Boat Dives - Where to Dive

6.10 - Bay underneath Coastguard Lookout

Latitude	52° 47.890'N	Longitude	004° 45.920'W
Position Fix	Differential - GPS	Datum	WGS84

This is a fairly shallow, sheltered bay under the coastguard lookout on Mynydd Mawr, the most westerly hilltop on the Llŷn Peninsula. To reach this site from Abersoch or Aberdaron, you need to brave the strong currents and overfalls off Braich–y-Pwll. Coastguards have reported that derelict cars have been dumped into the sea from the cliffs above. To my knowledge, none has ever been seen by divers, although a wartime sea-mine and a large anchor have been found here. Fortunately, cars can no longer be driven off the cliffs as access is now blocked by a row of large boulders.

6.11 - Headland between Coastguard Lookout and Anelog

Latitude	52° 48.555'N	Longitude	004° 45.240'W
Position Fix	Differential - GPS	Datum	WGS84

Down to about 15 metres, the seabed comprises large boulders covered in dense kelp. Deeper than this, there are many exposed boulders, with overhangs and gullies interspersed with large, flat areas of coarse sand. Most crabs found here are small. The fish are mainly dogfish and conger. Sunstars are common. Strong currents occur out from the cliffs, but there is some shelter either side of the headland.

6.12 - Dinas Fawr and Dinas Bach

Latitude	52° 49.770'N	Longitude	004° 44.300'W
Position Fix	Differential - GPS	Datum	WGS84

Dinas Fawr and Dinas Bach are two rocky promontories surrounded by fairly shallow water and thick kelp. Dinas Fawr is the more southerly of the pair. The area between them forms a shallow, sandy bay sheltered from the current. From a boat, fast drift-dives are possible on the seawards side of either landmark, where the seabed is a mixture of sand and rock. (See photo page 84)

Dive 6.13 - Carreg Allen

Latitude	52° 49.815'N	Longitude	004° 44.550'W
Position Fix	Differential - GPS	Datum	WGS84

This submerged reef is about a quarter of a mile west of Dinas Bach where it is charted at 2.4 metres. During the summer months, there is usually at least one lobster-pot buoy marking the rock.

Partially covered in kelp, the reef has at least two peaks. The surrounding area is mainly flat sand, with some interesting areas of rock. This site is very exposed to the current, but the area can be used for a drift-dive of up to a mile at a maximum depth of around 18 metres.

6.14 - Porth-y-Llong

Latitude	52° 50.630'N	Longitude	004° 43.530'W	
Position Fix	Differential - GPS	Datum	WGS84	

This small, enclosed bay drops off to flat sand at a depth on high-water of only 6 metres. Being named 'Ship Bay', one might have expected to find some evidence of wreckage, especially as there is a report of a Dutch convoy going aground at Porth Llong in 1641. Despite a thorough search, nothing more than a collection of empty aluminium beer-cans has been found, although a further visit may be more successful. The bay has little current, so can be used for a second dive or as a site for novice divers.

6.15 - Porth Llwynog, Porth Newry and the wreck of the sailing ship 'Newry'

Name	Newry	Type	Sailing Vessel	
Date Lost	16/3/1830	Location	Porth Newry	
Cause	Weather	How Lost	Ran ashore	
Hull	Wood	Weight	500 tons	
Cargo	Passengers	Access	Boat	
Latitude	52° 50.755'N	Longitude	004° 43.575'W	
Position Fix	Differential-GPS	Datum	WGS84	
Seabed	6 metres	Wreck Height	0.5 metres	
Charted as	Uncharted			
Slipway (1)	Porth Colmon	Distance	3 miles	
Slipway (2)	Porth Ysgaden	Distance	5.5 miles	
Tidal Data	Little current			

Porth Newry was named after the 500-ton wooden sailing-ship 'Newry' which ran ashore when outward-bound from Warren Point (Northern Ireland) to Quebec with 400 emigrants. Most of those aboard managed to escape by climbing on to the rocks via the mast before the vessel broke up two days later. Part of the ship must have remained on the jagged rocks, as it was later sold at auction and presumably salvaged.

Mast bands and parrels

This is a shallow, sandy bay with many pollack and a few bass, presumably feeding off the large shoal of sand-eels which sweeps the area. There is little current in a maximum depth of only 6 metres. Underwater visibility can be more than 10 metres in settled weather but the site is very exposed to south-westerly winds which create a considerable underwater surge and poor visibility.

Several angled rocks form a short underwater tunnel with a sandy seabed. A metal-detector gives many readings here, but the only items that could be exposed have proved to be ferrous rods and bars. A large iron ring lies just off the rocks at a depth of about 4 metres on high-water. Measuring about 75 centimetres (2' 6") in diameter and about 25 centimetres (10") wide, this is possibly a mast-band. A smaller, more badly worn, iron ring lies close by. None of these items proves whether these are actually the remains of the 'Newry', but a cave in the cliffs above water is marked on the Ordnance Survey map as 'Ogof Newry'.

Most Calamitous Shipwreck - In our last, we gave such particulars as had then reached us of the melancholy loss in Carnarvon Bay of the 'Newry', Captain Crosbie, outward bound from Ireland to Quebec, with 400 passengers, mostly Irish emigrants on board. The number of lives lost was stated to be two hundred, but we are glad to see that the North Wales Chronicle estimates it at between 40 and 50 and this statement is corroborated by a letter in the Liverpool papers from the Captain to his owners, giving the particulars of this melancholy catastrophe.

After the vessel had struck, by the most fatiguing and dangerous exertion, nearly 300 of the passengers were enabled to land, many of them in a state of nudity and others with blankets round them, having been in their berths and most of them sea-sick at the time the vessel struck. 'At this trying moment (says the Liverpool Journal, on the authority of Captain Crosby) we regret that the crew acted in a manner derogatory to the character of British Sailors. With a selfish and cowardly inhumanity, they quitted the wreck and refused to lend the Captain any further assistance. The first and second mate (the latter is Captain Crosbie's son) and the carpenter, however, stood by him in this emergency and the two last, having got onto a rock, they made preparations for getting the passengers ashore. In a state of exposure and exhaustion, they continued their exertions for the preservation of the passengers until four o'clock in the morning when David Griffiths, a seaman in the neighbourhood, assisted by Owen Jones and other persons, succeeded in rescuing between forty and fifty men, women and children, from their perilous situation on the wreck.

The vessel broke up on Sunday and what remained of the wreck was sold by auction on Monday. Fourteen dead bodies were found amongst the broken timber and on the rocks, all of which were decently interred. The conduct of the inhabitants towards the destitute survivors has been beyond all praise.

Chester Chronicle - Friday 30th April 1830

6.16 - Maen Mellt

Latitude	52° 51.020'N	Longitude	004° 43.930'W
Position Fix	Differential - GPS	Datum	WGS84

Maen Mellt rock at low water

The isolated rock of Maen Mellt (Lightning Stone) lies about 400 metres off the cliffs at Porth Iago, where it rises about 6 metres above the low-water mark. This is the visible part of a long reef that runs south-west to north-east, roughly parallel to the coastline. Cormorants use the rock as a convenient resting point, and the fishy smell of their droppings carries for some distance downwind. The side of the rock nearest the coast has near-vertical sides which drop off to around 18 metres, but beware of several drying rocks immediately to the south. On the seaward side and as the tide falls, a narrow gully becomes exposed between the main rock and a smaller, outlying rock.

The rock has claimed at least four ships over the years:

- The 80-foot long schooner 'Royal Charter' was lost on 3rd March, 1881, after striking Maen Mellt. This 119-ton vessel was built locally at Porthmadog in 1858, and was in ballast from Dublin to Porthmadog when it was wrecked. All hands were saved.

- The 36-ton Caernarfon sloop 'Ann' was lost at Maen Mellt on 11th June, 1864.

- The Lovely, a small sloop which was wrecked in the early 1800s.

- The 213-ton 'Atlantic' is believed to have been lost here in 1793.

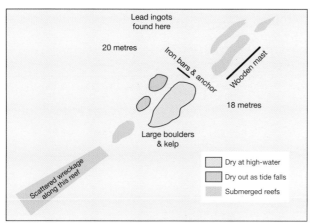

Plan of wreckage around. Maen Mellt

Ivory chips from Maen Mellt

The rock and surrounding seabed was surveyed in 1968, when 46 lead ingots (each weighing about 90kg), nearly 150kg of copper sheathing, and 30 small elephant tusks were all declared to the Receiver of Wreck. See 'Maritime Wales' Volume One (1976) for a more detailed account. An iron anchor, reputed to be from the 'Lovely', is now on display near the bridge in the centre of Aberdaron.

Many items of wreckage remain around Maen Mellt, with a wooden mast lying off the north-east point. Chips of ivory have been found in the gully on the seaward side, and more wreckage has been reported to the north of the rock. I understand that a small tusk was recovered in recent years,

The iron anchor from the 'Lovely'

and that a windlass has been seen on the site. Old fishing-net weights made of lead have been found here, distinctly different in shape from the modern angler's weights.

Strong currents run past Maen Mellt, with only a little shelter to be found. The north-east point gives some shelter when the current is flowing to the north-east, but emerging from the lee of the rock is like opening a window during a howling gale. Speaking from bitter experience, surface marker-buoys (fixed or delayed) should always be used, as the current can carry divers a considerable distance from the rock in a very short time. Unless a long, fast drift-dive is envisaged, divers need to be on site more than 2 hours before high-water at Liverpool and wait for the current to slacken.

Many bright blue, male cuckoo-wrasse will be seen around the edges of the rock, while the surrounding seabed has large numbers of dogfish and plaice.

6.17 - Porth Widlin

Latitude	52° 51.575'N	Longitude	004° 42.140'W	
Position Fix	Differential - GPS	Datum	WGS84	

This is one of the few sites along this coast with some shelter from southerly winds. The rock and thick kelp close inshore change to flat, coarse sand at a depth of about 10 metres. There are many pollack and dogfish here, but shellfish are few and far between. Seals are often seen resting on a small reef that dries out at low-water.

6.18 - Wreck of the 'Stuart' at Porth Ty-Mawr

Name	Stuart	Type	Sailing Vessel	
Date Lost	6/4/1901	Location	Porth Ty-Mawr	
Cause	Poor visibility	How Lost	Ran ashore	
Hull	Iron	Weight	912 tons (gross)	
Cargo	General cargo	Access	Boat	
Latitude	52° 51.870'N	Longitude	004° 41.580'W	
Position Fix	Differential-GPS	Datum	WGS84	
Seabed	1 to 6 metres	Wreck Height	1.5 metres	
Charted as	Uncharted			
Slipway (1)	Porth Colmon	Distance	1 mile	
Slipway (2)	Porth Ysgaden	Distance	3 miles	
Tidal Data	Little current			

Footpath sign directly above top of rock

Transit for the 'Stuart' at Porth Ty-Mawr
The wreck lies only 20 metres from the rocks

Outward bound for New Zealand, the iron-built barque 'Stuart' was completely wrecked in shallow water at Porth Ty-Mawr on the 6th of April, 1901. The wreck became known as the 'Whisky Wreck' because of its cargo, but the cases of spirits were recovered soon after the vessel ran ashore - initially by local 'salvors', then later by professional contractors. Early hopes of salvage were high, and a steamer was sent to remove as much of the cargo as possible. A large quantity of earthenware was recovered before strong winds forced recovery operations to cease. Other goods were saved, including six pianos. Contemporary reports from the Liverpool Salvage Company say that a large boulder forced its way through the ship's hull before the vessel split into three pieces, causing some of the remaining cargo to be washed out and scattered along the coastline.

 The barque also carried pottery, plates and glass Codd (pop-alley) bottles. These green bottles have a marble in the neck and are marked 'Gifford Plowman & Co, Napier', presumably being exported empty for use in Napier, New Zealand. Dated 1901, they were made in St. Helens, Lancashire, by Cannington, Shaw & Co.

Porth Ty-Mawr lies less than a mile south of the slipway at Porth Colmon. The wreck has been dived from the shore, but this entails a long and difficult walk along the narrow path from Porth Colmon, followed by a clamber over sharp rocks. Better to use a boat, as the wreck site is easily located by heading for a light-coloured group of rocks. These are prominently visible from well out to sea, and Porth Ty-Mawr is the bay immediately to the south of them.

Old photographs show the vessel high and dry at low-water, lying almost broadside on to the shore-line. The wreck is easily found, since iron ribs and sections of riveted plate can be seen from a boat at low-water, about 30 metres from the shore. Indeed, parts of the wreck dry out on spring-tides to create a hazard to any approaching boat. In this shallow location, it would be expected that all items of value would have been recovered at the time of wrecking, yet a dive in July 2000 produced several complete Codd bottles and two small stoneware jars, which probably contained writing ink. An intact 'dead-eye' was also recovered.

The 'Stuart' lies roughly parallel to the shore, with the bow on the rocks at the north, and the stern on flat sand to the south. The ship's ribs have collapsed outwards and now stand only about 1.5 metres proud of the seabed. They do show on an echo-sounder, but care must be taken at low-water as they are shallow enough to easily damage a hull or propeller. At this time, the water is too shallow for diving, being only just over one metre deep at the wreck site. Gaps between the iron ribs are full of sand, but they may be worth excavating as they still hold complete bottles and pieces of crockery. Intact items of pottery, recovered from the 'Stuart', may be seen in Nefyn Maritime Museum.

Porth Ty-Mawr is a shallow, exposed bay which should be avoided in south-westerly, westerly or northerly winds when there will be high surf and poor visibility. In calm weather, a massive shoal of sand-eels sweeps the bay, followed by some very well-fed pollack. Whenever a diver disturbs the seabed, wrasse appear from nowhere to follow him or her round the wreck like hungry dogs, hoping for an easy meal.

The wreck of the 'Stuart'   Photo Gwynedd Archive Services

A 'dead-eye'

6.19 - Porth Ysgaden Outer Reef

Latitude	52° 54.300'N	Longitude	004° 39.655'W
Position Fix	Differential - GPS	Datum	WGS84

About 500 metres off Porth Ysgaden, a series of two-metre high rocky ridges runs roughly parallel to the coastline. These underwater reefs can be picked up with an echo-sounder by running directly out from the shore, but the easiest way to locate them is to look for the line of lobster-pot buoys usually found here. The GPS position given is a typical starting point for a drift-dive, but once you pick up the reef on the echo-sounder, similar dives can be undertaken either to the north-east or south-west. The reef is mostly covered with a soft layer of matted material, probably due to the millions of mussels which cling to the underlying rock. Boulders of varying sizes are scattered around the site, providing shelter for a wealth of marine-life including goldsinnys, dogfish, wrasse, octopus, sea urchins and crabs. Anyone not diving should try their hand at angling, as boats have occasionally been surrounded by small fry leaping out of the water, presumably to escape the pursuing mackerel.

Depths are normally around 18 to 25 metres, but it is possible to hit 30 metres further out. Slack-water is around two hours before high-water at Liverpool, and four hours after high-water at Liverpool.

6.20 - Wreck of the steam-ship 'Cyprian'

Name	Cyprian	Type	Steamer
Date Lost	13/10/1881	Location	Penrhyn Cwmistir
Cause	Engine failure	How Lost	Ran ashore
Hull	Iron	Weight	1,433 tons (gross)
Cargo	General cargo	Access	Boat only
Latitude	52° 55.480'N	Longitude	004° 36.890'W
Position Fix	Differential-GPS	Datum	WGS84
Seabed	7 metres	Wreck Height	1.5 metres
Charted as	Uncharted		
Slipway (1)	Porth Ysgaden	Distance	2 miles
Slipway (2)	Morfa Nefyn	Distance	3.5 miles
Tidal Data	Strong currents - see text		

The iron steam-ship 'Cyprian' was built in 1874 by Bowdler, Chaffer & Co. of Liverpool, and by 1881 was owned by F. Leyland & Co., also of Liverpool. Carrying a general cargo, mainly manufactured cotton goods, the vessel was wrecked on the North Llŷn coast during a hurricane. A large proportion of those aboard were killed when they were dashed upon the rocks, and are now buried in a grave at Edern Old Church.

Gravestone at Edern Old Church

The Hurricane. Disasters at sea. Wreck of a Liverpool steamer.

Great loss of life.
The loss of the Cyprian. A terrible battle with the waves

Accounts are now being received of the terrible results of Friday's hurricane on the coasts. The number of vessels lost, large and small, is at present absolutely unknown. October would seem to be a fateful month as regards ship disasters on the Welsh coast. It was in October that the Royal Charter was dashed to pieces on the coast of Anglesey and her freight of souls left to perish in the lashed waters of the Irish Sea and it is in October that the Cyprian belonging to Messrs. F. Leyland and Co. of this city has foundered almost in the same waters and with similar fatal consequences. Leaving the Mersey on Thursday with everything in shipshape order the Cyprian passed Holyhead at 3:30am on Friday, bound with a general cargo for Gibraltar, Genoa, and Trieste.

She was a steam-ship of 941 registered tonnage and of 170 horsepower and was built in Seacombe in 1874. She was schooner-rigged and carried a complement of 27 men, including captain and officers. When passing the extreme point of Anglesey, her machinery failed her in consequence of a tube breaking. In order to repair this damage it was necessary to extinguish one of her furnaces. This was done but during the mending operations, the water burst into the engine room and extinguished the fires in the other furnace. The vessel was completely left to the mercy of the elements, which just then ran the very height of their fury, the sea rising in great mountainous volumes and the wind blowing a perfect hurricane. About 4 o'clock in the afternoon,

Steam-valve from the Cyprian

Cogdell, the donkey-engineman went into the engine-room and found that the furnace bars were about a foot under water. In a short time afterwards the ill-fated steamer dashed against Carregwhislan rocks at Rhosgor, and in 10 minutes had left not a single vestige of herself on the surface of the waters. The crew jumped overboard, the captain and one of the officers being the last to leave. A touching incident occurred when these unfortunate men were struggling for the shore. The captain, seeing a stowaway boy in peril of drowning, threw him the life belt to which he himself was clinging at the same time crying out 'Take this my boy. I shall be able to swim to shore'. The lad was saved, but the captain perished. Out of the 28 hands, only eight succeeded in reaching land, the rest being either drowned or dashed against the rocks and killed. Indeed, the appearances of the recovered bodies showed unmistakably that there had been a hard fight for life.

It was curious that all the corpses were fearfully bruised about the eyes, which may be accounted for by collision with the sharp-pointed rocks which jut out into the sea at the point where the vessel foundered. Up to 4 o'clock yesterday, 13 of the bodies had been recovered, out of which four only could be identified. The rescued men were loud in their praises of the farmers in the neighbourhoods of the disaster for the kindness which they received at their hands.

The 'Cyprian' has been a popular dive-site for many years and the wreck can be found close inshore, about 2 miles north-east of Porth Ysgaden and 2.5 miles south-west of Porth Dinllaen headland. Most references say the ship was wrecked at Penrhyn Cwmistir headland, but it actually lies off the smaller headland just south-west of Penrhyn Cwmistir. The badly smashed main part of the vessel can be found in 5 to 7 metres of water, very close to the rocky shore.

Other parts of the vessel lie scattered in a small bay that is less exposed to the current. This wreckage consists of riveted iron plates, iron ribs, bitts and the remains of two boilers. During the summer months, the wreck becomes covered in kelp and other seaweeds, making identification of individual items more difficult. Broken crockery with various markings can be found among the kelp, both on the wreck and along the shoreline. The bell and other artefacts were removed some time ago, but one report suggests that a porthole has recently been recovered. Other items recovered from the 'Cyprian' may be seen in the Nefyn Maritime Museum.

As with most wreck-sites, there is an abundance of marine-life, including conger, sandeels and wrasse. Large pollack will be seen above the kelp, while dozens of sea-hares live among the kelp-fronds and holdfasts or on the red seaweeds. Seals are often seen underwater.

Timing: Strong currents will be encountered at full flood or ebb, but slack-water is about 2 to 2.5 hours before high-water at Liverpool and about 4 hours after high-water at Liverpool.

Wreck site

Directions: Launch at Porth Ysgaden and head north-east along the coast, passing the sandy bay of Porth Towyn. The main hull of the 'Cyprian' lies very close to the shore, immediately off the first headland, about 2 miles from Porth Ysgaden. Look for the prominent post on the skyline, as shown in the transit, then align this post until it is roughly midway between the two prominent gates (circled), lower down the hillside. The 'Cyprian' is located within 20 metres of the nearest rocks.

The 'Cyprian' transit

6.21 - Penrhyn Cwmistir

Latitude	52° 55.590'N	Longitude	004° 36.460'W
Position Fix	Differential - GPS	Datum	WGS84

Long drift-dives are possible along this coastline in less than 10 metres of water, with the strongest currents being encountered off Penrhyn Cwmistir headland. Thick kelp close inshore rapidly gives way to a mixed seabed of sand, bedrock and boulders. These areas of bedrock are more interesting as they have many cracks and crevices to shelter any 'bugs and beasties'.

6.22 - Carreg-y-Chad

Latitude	52° 56.535'N	Longitude	004° 34.905'W
Position Fix	Differential - GPS	Datum	WGS84

This submerged reef is charted as Rk 1.6 and, at high-water, rises from a depth of about 12 metres to 5 or 6 metres below the surface. Located nearly three quarters of a mile south-west of Porth Dinllaen headland, it has several peaks and is usually marked by at least one lobster-pot. As it is about a quarter of a mile offshore, the current can be quite strong, so dive at slack-water (just over 2 hours before high-water at Liverpool) or enjoy a fast drift-dive over the reef.

6.23 - Rock face under disused coastguard lookout

Latitude	52° 56.830'N	Longitude	004° 34.090'W
Position Fix	Differential - GPS	Datum	WGS84

This is a nice, easy dive-site, tucked close inshore against a rock wall underneath the disused coastguard lookout on Porth Dinllaen headland. The rocks drop off rapidly to around 10 metres. Before local high-water, there is some current, but once the tide starts to ebb to the south-west, the headland provides some shelter from the flow - as long as you keep close to the rocks. High-water at Porth Dinllaen is around 2 hours before high-water at Liverpool. The site is also exposed to westerly winds, but the cliffs give some protection from easterly and southerly winds.

The local golf course is close by, so expect to find a few golf balls while diving. Look out for the large mussel beds and the dozens of spiny starfish that feast on this carpet of fresh meat.

6.24 - Trwyn Porth Dinllaen and Carreg Ddu

Latitude	52° 56.950'N	Longitude	004° 33.935'W
Position Fix	Differential - GPS	Datum	WGS84

During strong south-westerly winds, Porth Dinllaen headland and its outlying rocks could be one of the few accessible dive-sites on the whole Llŷn peninsula. The launching site at Morfa Nefyn (Porth Dinllaen) is totally sheltered from the east, south and west, while the headland provides a haven as long as you keep tucked in among the rocks or close under the cliffs.

The shoreline is rocky, dropping away to a sand and gravel seabed in 5 to 10 metres of water. Very strong currents will be found away from the rocks, especially after local high-water. Large mussel beds, spiny starfish, golf balls, blue pottery and odd pieces of aluminium will all be seen, the metallic parts possibly being the remains of an aircraft.

6.25 - Carreg-y-Chwislen

Latitude	52° 56.990'N	Longitude	004° 33.540'W
Position Fix	Differential - GPS	Datum	WGS84

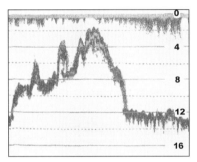

Echo sounder trace (metres)
on Carreg-y-Chwislen

'Isolated Danger' marker on Carreg-y-Chwislen

About 400 metres off the point at the western end of Porth Dinllaen bay, there is a large, kelp-covered rock roughly 120 metres in diameter. It is prominently marked by an 'Isolated Danger' pillar, and rises from flat sand at 15 metres to only 2 metres below the surface. This allows a diver with a good-sized air cylinder to circumnavigate the rock in a single dive.

Marine-life is plentiful, with many shoals of fish, squat-lobsters and spider-crabs. Some of the larger rocky clefts provide homes for conger eels. The deeper rock faces are clear of kelp, providing a habitat for plumose anemones. Strong currents will be encountered here, with slack-water being about two to three hours before high-water at Liverpool. Fortunately, the sheltered side of the rock does give a diver some respite from the tide-race.

Juvenile plumose anemone

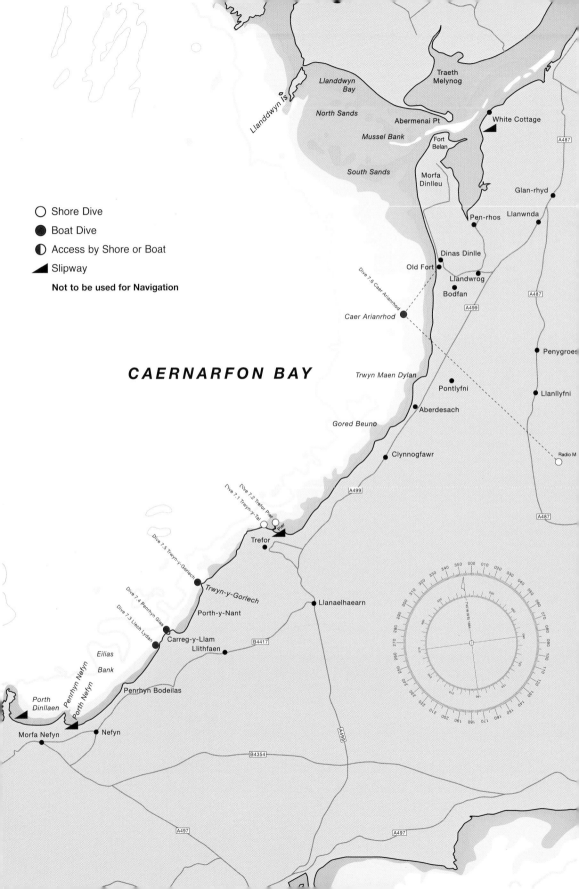

○ Shore Dive

● Boat Dive

◐ Access by Shore or Boat

◣ Slipway

Not to be used for Navigation

CAERNARFON BAY

Llanddwyn Is

Llanddwyn Bay

North Sands

Traeth Melynog

Abermenai Pt

White Cottage

Mussel Bank

Fort Belan

South Sands

Morfa Dinlleu

Glan-rhyd

A487

Pen-rhos

Llanwnda

Dinas Dinlle

Old Fort

Dive 7.6 Caer Arianrhod

Llandwrog

Bodfan

A487

Caer Arianrhod

A499

Trwyn Maen Dylan

Penygroes

Pontlyfni

Llanllyfni

Aberdesach

Gored Beuno

Clynnogfawr

A499

Radio M

Dive 7.2 Trefor Pier

Dive 7.1 Trwyny-Tal

A499

Trefor

Dive 7.5 Trwyn-y-Gorlech

Llanaelhaearn

Trwyn-y-Gorlech

Porth-y-Nant

Dive 7.4 Penrhyn Glas

Dive 7.3 Llech Lydan

Carreg-y-Llam

B4417

Llithfaen

Eilias Bank

Penrhyn Nefyn

Porth Dinllaen

Porth Nefyn

Penrhyn Bodeilas

Morfa Nefyn

Nefyn

B4354

A499

A497

A497

CHAPTER SEVEN

Nefyn to Fort Belan (Caernarfon)

'A vessel was washed ashore near Llyngele, Clynnog, about noon on Wednesday. She turned out to be the schooner 'Kate' of Trentwood, Miller, master, laden with coal from Swansea to Belfast. The schooner 'Henry' of Liverpool, Jones, master, laden with culm from Briton Ferry, came ashore near Ty Mawr, about 11 o'clock on Wednesday night. The crews of both vessels were saved. A flat*, carrying stones from Llaneillaiarn, is also ashore. A considerable amount of wreckage is afloat in Carnarvon Bay'.

Carnarvon & Denbigh Herald, Saturday 15th October, 1870

* flat – small sailing vessel.

General Description

Despite some really impressive rocky cliffs, this stretch of coastline offers few good dive-sites, being fairly shallow and sandy. One exception is Trefor pier, which is extremely popular because of its wide variety of marine-life and ease of access. This site is particularly suitable for newcomers to diving.

Essential Information:-

- Apart from Trefor, there are no suitable shore dives along this stretch of coast.
- Use the slipways at Trefor or Nefyn for boat-dives.
- There are strong currents off all the rocky headlands.
- The isolated reefs of Gored Bueno and Caer Arianrhod partially dry out at low-water springs.
- There are extensive sandbanks between Fort Belan and Llanddwyn Island, with the wreck of the Grampian Castle appearing close to the channel as the tide falls.
- Obey the speed limits off the beaches.
- The close season for scallops does not apply north of Braich-y-Pwll.
- Chart required – 'Caernarvon Bay' (Number 1970).
- Maps – Ordnance Survey Explorer Maps number 12 (Lleyn Peninsula West) & 13 (Lleyn Peninsula East).

Shore Dives or Snorkelling Sites

7.1 - Trwyn-y-Tal

Latitude	52° 59.940'N	Longitude	004° 25.440'W
O.S. Reference	SH	373E	474N

If, on arriving at Trefor Pier (see the next dive-site) you find it already awash with divers, then this is a nearby alternative. Trwyn-y-Tal headland is located to the left (west) of Trefor Pier.

The site is best dived in southerly or easterly winds and should be avoided if the air-stream is from the south-west, west or north-west. Access to the sea is much easier at high-water, as the shore consists of a shingle and cobble bank which is difficult to cross in full diving gear. The seabed slopes away gradually, causing problems when entering or leaving the sea, especially if any swell is running. The cliffs are a popular venue for anglers, so beware of their lines and the many metres of discarded fishing-line strewn about the seabed. This area is mostly covered with boulders and kelp, with some sandy patches further out, at a maximum high-water depth of around 10 metres.

My most vivid memory of the marine-life here is of a rather large bull-huss and a shoal of over 200 pollack, but many other dogfish, plaice and wrasse will be encountered. The rocks have a scattering of dead-men's fingers, indicating that strong currents are found here. On the areas of sand, divers have seen large shoals of cuttlefish or squid.

High-water is about 2 hours earlier than at Liverpool, but once the tide starts to ebb, strong currents off Trwyn-y-Tal headland could prevent a diver from swimming back to his or her entry point. Try to finish your dive before local high-water, so check your tide tables beforehand unless you are willing to risk a long walk back along the cliff-top.

An old concrete jetty juts out from the cliffs at the left (western) side of the bay, where strong currents will be encountered on the ebb-tide. Divers must take care in this area, as the jetty has several protruding iron-bars that could easily cause injury.

Directions: Take the A487, sign posted Porthmadog, for Pwllheli. Pass through Bontnewydd and past the 'Dinas' Garage. Turn right at the 1st roundabout, then straight on at the 2nd, following the A499 for Pwllheli before turning on to the A499 at the second roundabout. After you have passed the Glynllifon Country Park on the left you will progress through Pontllyfni, Aberdesach, Clynnog Fawr and Gyrn Goch before turning right for Trefor / Plas yr Eifl Hotel. Immediately after the 30 mph sign, take the first right, signposted 'To the Beach', and drive between the bungalows down a very narrow, steep, twisting road. Beware: the local kids have been known to turn the signpost so that it points in the wrong direction. The road runs alongside the beach to a small harbour, protected by a breakwater. Leave any heavy diving gear by the gate in the wall (at 52° 59.940'N 004° 25.440'W / SH 373E 474N) to the left of the breakwater, then park back in the main car park. Squeeze past the side of the gate and kit up before walking to the small bridge about 200 metres to the left. Enter the water on the other side of the bridge.

7.2 - Trefor Pier

Latitude	52° 59.975'N	Longitude	004° 25.320'W
O.S. Reference	SH	375E	475N

Trefor Pier is the most popular dive-site along this coast, where it provides an excellent location for novices, photographers and marine-life enthusiasts alike.

This wooden pier was built in 1912 at the end of the existing stone breakwater, and was used for exporting granite from the quarries visible on the hillside above Trefor. It closed to commercial traffic in 1971. Sheltered from southerly winds but exposed to westerly winds, the pier is about 75 metres long and 8 metres wide. It runs out to sea in a northerly direction, with 20 vertical legs along each side and a single line of them down the centre.

Underwater visibility can be 10 metres or more but varies considerably, depending on weather conditions and the time of year. South-westerly to north-easterly winds usually cause poor visibility, while heavy rain creates a runoff from the quarry workings on the hillside above Trefor, again affecting visibility. On arrival, however, if the water appears to be murky against the breakwater, don't abort the dive until you have fully checked out the site by walking the length of the pier. There may be only one or two metres visibility against the breakwater, but four or five metres further out. As this is a small but very popular dive-site, it is best visited at quiet times, preferably avoiding weekends in mid-summer.

Trefor Pier at low water

The best dives are at local high-water, which is about two hours earlier than high-water at Liverpool. On spring-tides, there will be a maximum depth of about 7 or 8 metres under the pier, but on low-water, only about 4 metres. As this is a popular angling venue, it is essential to stay underneath the pier to avoid the fishing lines. Also take care to avoid the lost fishing-hooks and knives lying on the seabed under the pier.

For such a small area, the marine-life is diverse and plentiful, but only for those divers prepared to look carefully. Freshwater eels, octopus, lobsters, edible-crabs, pipefish, swimming crabs, squat lobsters, spiny spider-crabs, dragonets, tiny flatfish, dogfish, bib, sea-scorpions, two-spotted gobies, sand gobies, pollack, corkwing wrasse and ballan wrasse have all been seen on a single dive. Plumose anemones and dead-men's fingers grow on the wooden supports, while every single crack in the breakwater wall seems to have its own resident prawn or tompot blenny. Kelp and bootlace weed grow on the supporting legs and on the many wooden beams and blocks of cut stone which litter the seabed.

Carcasses of dead fish are often seen, presumably having been caught and thrown back by the anglers on the pier. Watch carefully, as the fish, crabs and lobsters all congregate to feed off this unexpected bonus. Another way to create a mini feeding-frenzy is to simply waft away the sand and watch how the fish move in, hoping for an easy meal.

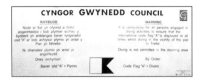

Parking is not permitted alongside the pier, but diving gear may be unloaded near the breakwater and vehicles left in the main car park where there are basic toilet facilities and an emergency telephone. Notices state that diving is not permitted among the boat-moorings, and that the 'A-flag' should be flown while divers are in the water. Just where and how the flag is to be flown while you are under the pier is not stated.

This is an excellent place for a night-dive, but again stay within the confines of the pier as anglers also enjoy their sport during the hours of darkness. There are picnic tables close by, so after the dive, why not have a barbeque as well?

Directions: See directions for the previous dive-site. The pier runs northwards from the end of the breakwater.

Access: Remember that Trefor is a working port, so there is boat traffic in and out of the harbour. Enter the water from the breakwater steps and stay on the surface until you reach the security of the pier, taking care to avoid the small diesel slicks occasionally seen here. Submerge and surface only underneath the security of the pier. Note that the steps towards the end of the breakwater do not reach the waterline.

View along Trefor pier

Boat Dives - Where to Dive

7.3 - Llech Lydan

Latitude	52° 57.795'N	Longitude	004° 29.180'W
Position Fix	Differential - GPS	Datum	WGS84

This small, rocky outcrop forms an island at high-water and can provide a little shelter in south-westerly winds. Unfortunately, even at high-water, the sea is not much deeper than 5 metres, and the slightest swell produces very poor underwater visibility.

7.4 - Penrhyn Glas

Latitude	52° 57.980'N	Longitude	004° 28.940'W
Position Fix	Differential - GPS	Datum	WGS84

These magnificent cliffs rise more than 100 metres above sea-level. At the base of the cliffs, the sea is only 4 to 8 metres deep where the bare rock is partially covered with jewel and snakelocks anemones. Strong currents run along the cliff face, so long drift-dives can be undertaken if required, but further offshore the seabed is mainly sandy.

The cliffs provide nesting sites for many cormorants, guillemots and terns, so take care not to disturb them during the breeding season.

7.5 - Trwyn-y-Gorlech

Latitude	52° 58.900'N	Longitude	004° 27.840'W
Position Fix	Differential - GPS	Datum	WGS84

This is another spectacular vertical cliff-face which rises steeply from sea level to a height of more than 250 metres, but as with other sites along this part of the coast, the diving is not brilliant. The sea at the base of the cliffs is only about 6 metres deep where the flat, sandy seabed is interspersed with large rocks. A small cave at the south-west of the cliff-face is usually full of dead seaweed. Quite strong currents will be found out from the cliffs, but they are more sedate close inshore where the rocks are covered with large anemones.

Although several metal bars have been found here on the seabed, they probably don't belong to a shipwreck, although further investigation may prove otherwise.

7.6 - Caer Arianrhod

Latitude	53° 03.980'N	Longitude	004° 21.310'W
Position Fix	Differential - GPS	Datum	WGS84

With such an inspiring name, the Castle of the Silver Wheel (Caer – Castle, Arian – Silver, Rhod - Wheel) has to be dived at least once, if only to search for the silver wheel. It is impossible to discern any pattern while diving, but some reports say there is a complete circle of white stones, while others say it is only a semi-circle. Located half a mile offshore, this is a shallow but quite extensive reef, which partially dries out on the lowest of spring-tides to reveal several large boulders standing proud of a rock and boulder-strewn seabed.

Several theories have been put forward about the origins of the reef, including the view that Caer Arianrhod is all that remains of a site of human habitation that became submerged as sea levels rose. I have found no sign of any man-made structure and a more likely theory is that it was formed by glacial action at the end of the ice-age. Others probably know better, and further information or investigation may prove otherwise. The reef is best dived around local high-water, about 2 hours before high-tide at Liverpool, when there will be only 4 or 5 metres of water covering the reef. The flat sand surrounding the reef is only 2 or 3 metres deeper.

The boulders and rocks have all been worn smooth by the action of the sea and the whole reef is covered with a layer of kelp, bootlace weed and small mussels to provide a home for the many small corkwing wrasse. On sighting a diver, these fish rush up to him or her before suddenly taking fright and darting into the security of the kelp forest. This is quite unusual, and I haven't noticed this behaviour anywhere else.

The current over the reef can be fairly strong. This makes the site suitable for a long, shallow drift-dive after having undertaken a deeper dive such as the wreck of the 'Segontium' (see Chapter 10). Caer Arianrhod lies about 4.5 miles north-east of Trefor slipway and about 6 miles from Ty Calch (White Cottage) in the Menai Strait. If you launch at Ty Calch, don't be tempted to take the direct line from Fort Belan to the site as you will probably run aground on the South Bank of Caernarfon Bar. Keep to the channel as far as Llanddwyn Island before heading south to the GPS position given.

If you don't have a GPS receiver to locate the reef, use the following compass bearings:

• Approximately 140' magnetic to the large T.V. aerial on the skyline.

• Approximately 40' magnetic to the high point on the ancient hill-fort at Dinas Dinlle.

• See Chart on page 104.

Octopus beneath Trefor Pier

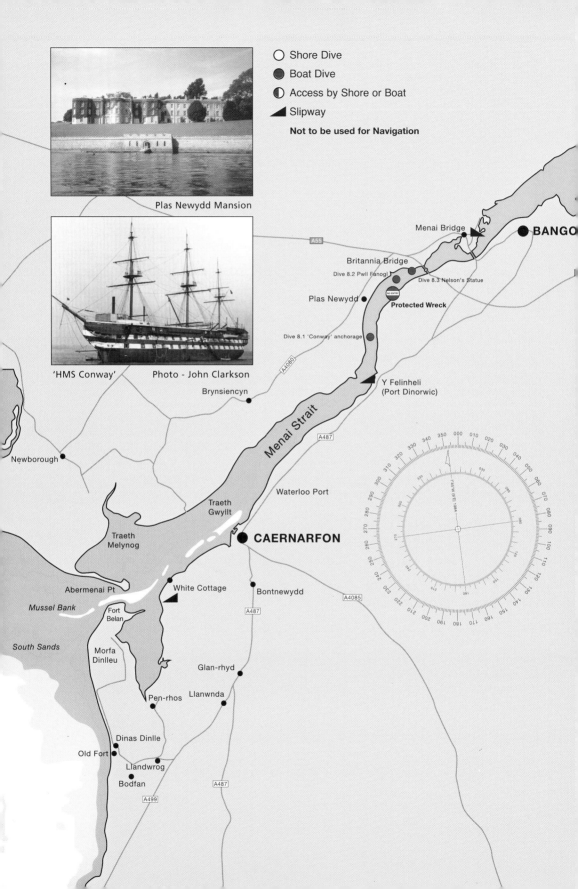

Plas Newydd Mansion

'HMS Conway'   Photo - John Clarkson

○ Shore Dive
● Boat Dive
◐ Access by Shore or Boat
◣ Slipway
Not to be used for Navigation

Menai Bridge

● **BANGO**

Britannia Bridge

Dive 8.2 Pwll Fanogl

Dive 8.3 Nelson's Statue

Plas Newydd ●

NO ENTRY

Protected Wreck

Dive 8.1 'Conway' anchorage

Y Felinheli
(Port Dinorwic)

Brynsiencyn

Menai Strait

A55

A4080

A487

Newborough

Waterloo Port

Traeth
Gwyllt

Traeth
Melynog

CAERNARFON

Abermenai Pt

White Cottage

Bontnewydd

A4085

Mussel Bank

Fort
Belan

A487

South Sands

Morfa
Dinlleu

Glan-rhyd

Pen-rhos   Llanwnda

Dinas Dinlle

Old Fort

Llandwrog

Bodfan

A487

A499

The Menai Strait
(Western part – Fort Belan to Britannia Bridge)

'One of the most treacherous stretches of sea in the world'.

Admiral Horatio Nelson (describing the Menai Strait)

General Description

The Menai Strait separates the Isle of Anglesey from the mainland. It consists of a narrow channel about 18 miles long, and varies in width from almost 4 miles at Puffin Island in the north-east to only about 400 metres at Fort Belan in the south-west. Several theories have been put forward as to how the Menai Strait was formed. Current theory suggests that a melting ice-sheet formed a river which found a route through an existing geological fault, to create the Menai Strait.

The buoyage system through the Strait is unusual and can cause confusion, especially around the Caernarfon area. For navigational purposes, Caernarfon harbour is regarded as the 'head of

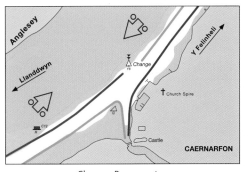

Change Buoy routes

The Change Buoy

navigation' for the whole of the Menai Strait. Vessels approaching Caernarfon harbour from either the south-west or the north-east follow the normal navigation rules of red to port (left), green to starboard (right) all the way to the quayside by the castle. Confusion arises for those boats that are simply passing the entrance to Caernarfon harbour, as they sail or motor along the length of the Menai Strait. There is a south-cardinal buoy moored off Caernarfon, towards the Anglesey side of the strait. Look for the church in Caernarfon with a very prominent steeple and the buoy is moored (at 53° 08.800'N, 004° 16.770'W) on the opposite (northern) side of the channel. The buoy is painted in the normal colours of yellow over black to indicate a south-cardinal marker, but the most significant - and not immediately obvious - piece of navigational information is the word 'CHANGE' written on the buoy. This position, the 'CHANGE' buoy, is where the two routes into Caernarfon meet. Unfortunately, this south-cardinal buoy appears simply to be a warning indicator for the sandbanks and, as the wording on it is not always visible, boat-handlers may not immediately recognise its additional significance, that of 'Changing over' the direction of buoyage.

Suppose we launch our boat at Y Felinheli (Port Dinorwic) slipway and wish to dive at Llanddwyn Island. Initially, we will be travelling in a south-westerly direction towards Caernarfon, with red to port (left) and green to starboard (right). Once we reach the 'CHANGE' buoy, we will pass the entrance to Caernarfon harbour. From now on, our south-westerly passage will be away from the 'head of navigation', so it will be red to starboard (right), green to port (left). The same rules apply as we approach and pass the 'CHANGE' buoy on our return from Llanddwyn. Ignore this navigational oddity at your peril, as you could easily run on to a sandbank as you pass one or more channel-buoys on the wrong side!

In short, don't forget to CHANGE at Caernarfon.

The Menai Strait has the advantage of being well sheltered from the wind, providing a large expanse of relatively calm water when weather conditions are too severe to take a boat on the open sea. However, localised rough seas and overfalls are present, especially when wind and tide are in opposite directions. Take great care when taking a boat through the narrow channels at Belan, the Swellies or Penmon, near Puffin Island.

Essential Information:-

- Slipways are available at Menai Bridge, Y Felinheli (Port Dinorwic), and Ty-Calch (White Cottage, between Caernarfon and Fort Belan).

- The direction of buoyage changes at 53° 08.800'N, 004° 16.770'W, just north of Caernarfon (see the previous note and diagram).

- Very strong currents exist in the Menai Strait, so take great care when planning a dive here. Avoid spring-tides.

- Tidal diamonds on chart 1464 (Menai Strait) refer to Holyhead, not Liverpool.

- The area is very busy during the summer months, especially during yachting galas.

- This is a narrow channel, frequently used by large sailing yachts which have to tack to and fro across the Strait. The 'A' flag should be prominently displayed when divers are in the water, otherwise the yachts will assume that they have right of way and expect the dive-boat to sheer off.

- There is a Protected Wreck on the mainland side of the strait at Pwll Fanogl.

- There are several areas of the Menai Strait where a 5-knot speed-limit is enforced. For details, see the notice boards at Caernarfon and Y Felinheli (Port Dinorwic) or obtain a full list of the bylaws from the Caernarfon Harbour Trust office on the quayside at Caernarfon.

- Chart required – 'Menai Strait' (Number 1464).

- Maps – Ordnance Survey Explorer map 263 (Anglesey East).

Shore Dives or Snorkelling Sites

Snorkelling in this area is not advised because of the strong currents and limited visibility, while access for shore-dives is not particularly easy.

Boat Dives - Where to Dive

8.1 - Former anchorage site of the training ship 'Conway'

Latitude (1)	53° 11.940'N	Longitude (1)	004° 12.605'W
Latitude (2)	53° 11.940'N	Longitude (2)	004° 12.870'W
Position Fix	Differential-GPS	Datum	WGS84

The 'Conway' was an old wooden warship, released by the Admiralty in 1876 for use as a training ship at Liverpool. Moved to the Menai Strait during the Second World War, she was initially moored off Bangor before being relocated to a position between Y Felinheli (Port Dinorwic) and Plas Newydd. For further details of the 'Conway' and where to find the remains of the vessel, see Chapter 9.

The 'Conway' anchor and chain. East side of strait.

To maintain the ship's position despite the strong current at Y Felinheli, a network of chains and large anchors was laid in a diagonal cross, with a central chain leading up to a mooring buoy. This buoy has now gone, but the massive ground-chains still stretch across the Menai Strait and can usually be followed from one shoreline to the other, although in places they disappear under the seabed. The chain leading from the seabed to the surface now lies in a tangled heap on the bottom of the strait. One of the Conway's 5-ton anchors is displayed outside the Caernarfon Maritime Museum, and another lies outside the Merseyside Maritime Museum in Liverpool.

At low tide, the chains can be seen emerging from the water at the following positions:-

East side of Strait . . . . . . 53° 11.940' N   004° 12.605' W

West side of Strait . . . . . 53° 11.940' N   004° 12.870' W

This dive-site is normally used as a back-up site when other areas are inaccessible because of bad weather. Divers can enter the water at either side of the Strait and attempt to follow the chains, or simply use the area for long drift-dives using SMBs. Low-water slack is about 4 hours 30 minutes to 5 hours after high-water at Liverpool. Before this time, the current runs towards Caernarfon before reversing its direction and flowing towards Bangor. The seabed is rather flat and comprised of coarse gravel, with only a few rocky areas. Apart from the usual assortment of crabs and small fish, a number of large whelks can be seen. The depth gradually drops off to around 18 metres. Divers have reported finding broken pottery, which may date from the time when the Conway was moored here. Alternatively, it could simply be rubbish discarded by passing vessels.

The nearest slipway is at Y Felinheli (Port Dinorwic), with others at Menai Bridge and Ty-Calch (Caernarfon).

Directions: The site lies about a quarter of a mile south of the magnificent mansion of Plas Newydd, and is easily identified at low-water when the anchors and short lengths of chain dry out. The anchor on the mainland (east) side of the strait is easier to see and has the upper fluke bent over, presumably to reduce the potential damage to passing boats. On the present-day chart, the area is marked as 'Foul Ground', but a more detailed plan is shown on the older charts, one of which may also be inspected in the Caernarfon Maritime Museum.

8.2 - Pwll Fanogl

Latitude	53° 12.735'N	Longitude	004° 11.975'W
Position Fix	Differential - GPS	Datum	WGS84

Pwll Fanogl

Pwll Fanogl is a broad curve in the Menai Strait between Y Felinheli (Port Dinorwic) and the Britannia Bridge. It is the deepest part of the Strait between Caernarfon and Beaumaris, with a maximum depth of nearly 30 metres at the quoted GPS position. There is a Historic Wreck marked on chart 1464 (Menai Strait), lying close to the eastern (mainland) side of the channel. These are the remains of an ancient wooden vessel and its cargo of slates, believed to have been lost before the middle of the 16th century. Diving is not permitted in the restricted area, so avoid the mainland side of the strait, as the current could easily take a diver over the site.

Slack-water at Pwll Fanogl is rather limited, so drift-diving with boat cover is the preferred method. As you can drift more than a mile in 20 minutes, this area is for experienced divers only. The visibility can be quite poor, so make sure you have a good torch and buddy-line. As with all areas in the Menai Strait, currents are strong, with the chart showing 5 knots on spring-tides and 3.5 knots on neaps. Slack water is around 1 hour 45 minutes before high-water at Liverpool and three hours before low water at Liverpool.

Old lobster-pots may be encountered in places. Some of these lost pots may still be linked together, so take care not to become entangled in any of the horizontal ropes as you drift along with a SMB. On a windy day, there are always several angling-boats either moored in the middle of the strait or drifting with the tide.

Directions: Launch at Menai Bridge (Porth Aethwy) slipway, clear the green post and pass under the Menai Suspension Bridge, keeping to the centre of the Strait. Pass the white cottage on the mainland side before moving towards the mainland side of the Strait, with the Swelly Rock pillar to your right. Hug the left bank and pass under the southern (mainland) span of the Britannia Bridge and the electricity power-cables. Pwll Fanogl is the large area of the strait to the west of the Britannia Bridge.

8.3 - Nelson's Statue

Latitude	53° 12.950'N	Longitude	004° 11.595'W
Position Fix	Differential - GPS	Datum	WGS84

Nelson's statue

Easily located, this site lies directly under a statue of Admiral Horatio Nelson. Strong currents are found here, so only dive this site on a neap-tide. At times, a back eddy causes confusion with the underwater navigation, so rely on your compass rather than the expected direction of the current as you could have drifted into this back-eddy. If the current proves too strong, simply go with the flow - but make sure you have a surface marker-buoy deployed to allow the dive-boat to follow.

The quality of the dive-site varies considerably depending on whether you are diving to the east or to the west of the statue. On the western (Caernarfon) side of the statue, the seabed is fairly flat and comprised of coarse sand and gravel, with only a few rocks and boulders. Dogfish are in abundance, while the hundreds of *myxicola infundibulum* burrowing worms instantly retract once they sense an intruder to their patch of ground. The seabed drops away slowly to 20 metres or more, but the whole area is rather featureless. No wonder Nelson turned his blind right-eye in this direction.

His good eye gazes out over a much more interesting dive-site, the area to the east, between the statue and Britannia Bridge. Here, the seabed is bedrock and boulders which drop off to a little over 10 metres. The whole area is totally covered in layers of soft sponges, where lots of velvet swimming-crabs and undersized edible crabs will be seen. Even if you could legally take these, you would need at least a dozen of them to make a single crab-sandwich. Look out for the tiny spider-crabs with their coating of camouflage. Again, dogfish are in abundance, but this time there are more wrasse, pipe-fish, two-spotted gobies, dragonettes and the occasional bass. Many sponge-covered wine-bottles litter the area and in the spring-time, note the strings of sea-slug eggs.

Timing: The site is best dived at low-water slack on a neap-tide, around 3 hours before low-water at Liverpool.

Directions: Follow the directions given above for Pwll Fanogl, where the prominent statue of Lord Nelson gazes over the Menai Strait from the high-water mark on the northern (Anglesey) side of the channel. The second statue on the far skyline is that of Lord Uxbridge, who lost a leg while leading the cavalry at the Battle of Waterloo. The owner of Plas Newydd mansion, he later became the Marquis of Anglesey.

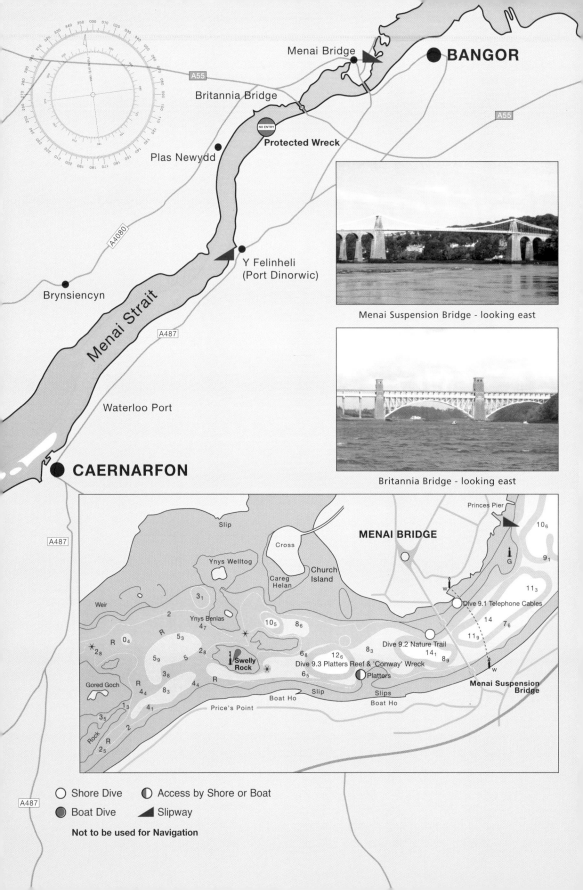

Menai Suspension Bridge - looking east

Britannia Bridge - looking east

BANGOR

Menai Bridge

A55

Britannia Bridge

Plas Newydd

Protected Wreck

NO ENTRY

Y Felinheli
(Port Dinorwic)

Brynsiencyn

Menai Strait

A4080

A487

Waterloo Port

CAERNARFON

A487

A55

MENAI BRIDGE

Princes Pier

10_6

9_1

G

11_3

Dive 9.1 Telephone Cables

14

7_6

11_9

Menai Suspension Bridge

Slip

Cross

Ynys Welltog

Careg Helan

Church Island

Weir

3_1

2

Ynys Benlas

4_7

10_5

8_6

Dive 9.2 Nature Trail

14_1

8_9

8_3

R

0_4

5_3

2_8

2_8

5_9

5

Swelly Rock

6_8

12_6

Dive 9.3 Platters Reef & 'Conway' Wreck

6_5

Platters

Gored Goch

4_4

8_3

3_8

4_4

R

Slip

Slips

Boat Ho

Boat Ho

1_3

4_1

Price's Point

3_5

2

Rock

R

2_5

A487

○ Shore Dive   ◑ Access by Shore or Boat

● Boat Dive   ◣ Slipway

Not to be used for Navigation

CHAPTER NINE

The Swellies or Pwll Ceris (Menai Strait)

This is a dangerous part of the straits of Menai, an arm of the sea between Anglesey and Caernarvonshire. It is called by the Welsh, Pwll Keris, a name borrowed (it is likely) from the Roman Charybdis, such another dangerous place as this on the coast of Sicily. The opposition of rocks and islands and the narrowness of the channel, occasions great overfalls, violent currents and whirlpools here, while the tide of flood or ebb makes strong.

And it is not to be meddled with, but upon slack tide.

Lewis Morris, 1748

General Description

Those unfamiliar with the area should note the following place names:-

- Menai Bridge. This is the town of Menai Bridge, or in Welsh, Porth Aethwy.

- Menai Suspension Bridge. Opened in 1830, this is the original, narrow bridge over the Menai Strait.

- Britannia Bridge. This carries the railway and the A55 expressway over the Menai Strait. It opened to rail traffic in 1850 and was rebuilt to carry additional road traffic after a fire in 1970.

This chapter refers to that part of the Menai Strait between the Britannia Bridge to the west and the Menai Suspension Bridge to the east, but I have also included the telephone cables immediately north-east of the suspension bridge. The two bridges are about one mile apart, while this part of the Strait varies in width from about 180 metres to 500 metres.

There are several dive-sites here, each providing some interest for wreck divers, marine biologists and photographers. Because of the strong currents, the whole area is unsuitable for novices. Being sheltered from the wind, the area can be dived throughout the year as long as the tides are favourable, so the Swellies are often visited when bad weather has made an inland slate quarry the only other viable dive-site.

For those unfamiliar with local conditions, dive-sites have been organised in order of increasing difficulty rather than geographically. Anyone new to the area should gain experience and confidence by diving the Telephone Cables and the Nature Trail, before attempting a 'boomerang' dive to the wreck of the 'Conway' and back again. A 'boomerang' dive is my description for a drift-dive where the change in direction of the current on either side of slack-water is used to bring the diver back to his or her original starting point. By studying the tides, I have undertaken drift-dives of more than two hours in the Swellies, and still returned to shore at my entry point. Obviously, these longer dives can be undertaken only with an ample air-supply, during the warmer months of the year.

The water throughout the Menai Strait is usually very turbid, so light does not penetrate to any great depth. This lack of light, along with the strong currents, ensures that kelp and other seaweeds do not grow deeper than a few metres below the low-water mark. Although the underwater visibility is often poor, it is usually adequate from July until Christmas. I have successfully dived the Menai Strait in every single month of the year. In recent years, a project by Hyder (Welsh Water) has improved the local sewage outfall system, so that effluents are now treated before being discharged into the Strait. The old sewage outfall between the two bridges is no longer used, so there has been a vast improvement in the local water quality and marine-life. Until recently, vast mussel beds existed between the two bridges, but in recent years, divers have noticed that these mussel beds seem to be disappearing, leaving just bare rock.

The most amazing sight I have witnessed here was when a helicopter from 22 Squadron at RAF Valley flew underneath both bridges to transport a 'bent' diver from Dorothea Quarry to the recompression chamber on the Wirral. Fortunately, they don't have to do this too often, but why didn't I have a camera ready?

Essential Information:-

- Do Not dive here on spring-tides.

- Very strong currents will be encountered in the Swellies. Chart number 1464 shows a tidal flow of 8 knots on spring-tides and 5 knots on neaps. Get your timings wrong and you'll feel like you're diving inside a washing machine.

- Ensure that you have enough air for the dive and that your diving-suit is warm enough for the prevailing conditions and the expected duration of the dive. You may not be able to leave the water until after slack-water, when the current will bring you back to the entry point.

- The description 'slack-water' does not truly apply to the Swellies. There are always back-eddies and counter-currents, as the current decreases in strength before totally reversing its direction. Timings given in this chapter will vary slightly depending on the tide height, time of day and prevailing weather conditions.

- Slack-water DOES NOT correspond with either local high-water or local low-water. As the tide-level drops from high-water, the current will be running to the west (i.e. towards Caernarfon). A short period of slack-water will occur at the suspension bridge approximately 2 hours and 45 minutes before low-water at Liverpool; then the current will run to the east, towards Bangor. Despite the fact that slack-water has been and gone, the tide-level will continue to fall for well over an hour.

- Note that all observations in this book are based on Liverpool tide-tables.

- There is very little slack at high-water. Better to dive at slack-water as the tide is falling, but even then there will always be some water movement.

- Timing is critical. If you are late and miss slack-water, dive elsewhere.

- This is a narrow channel with considerable boat traffic that has no room to manoeuvre. Yachts running under engine power may have insufficient thrust to avoid surfaced divers, so do not come up in the main shipping channel.

- The channel between the two bridges is not buoyed. The only channel-marker is a pillar on Swelly Rock with a south-cardinal top-mark.

- Ynys Gored Goch, the main island between the two bridges, has several radiating underwater walls. These were built as fish-traps, but could prove lethal to divers.

- There are several unmarked rocks lying either just beneath the surface or drying out as the tide falls. Over the years, a number of yachts and speedboats have run on to these obstructions. If you are using a boat, consult the chart beforehand and take one with you.

- The area is very popular with anglers. During fishing competitions there may be more than 100 anglers lined up on the shoreline, so dive elsewhere at this time. Angling boats often anchor here.

- Rough water occurs under the Menai Suspension Bridge when wind and tide are in opposite directions.

- Underwater visibility is usually poor and dark, so always take a good torch when diving here. I have had some excellent night-dives around lunch-time!

- The underwater visibility varies according to the present and recent weather conditions. North-easterly winds tend to stir up the sandbanks around Puffin Island, causing poor visibility at Menai Bridge for some time afterwards. Check the weather forecast for several days before your planned dive.

- There is only a limited amount of parking underneath the Suspension Bridge on the Anglesey side of the Strait. Traffic Wardens visit the area, so beware of parking on the yellow lines. Do not block access to any of the houses.

- At the time of writing, the Menai Strait is a candidate Special Area of Conservation.

- The nearest slipways are at Menai Bridge town and Y Felinheli (Port Dinorwic).

- Chart required –'Menai Strait' (Number 1464).

- Maps – Ordnance Survey Explorer map 263 (Anglesey East).

Sagartia elegans anemone on wreck of HMS Conway

Shore Dives

9.1 - The Telephone Cables

Latitude	53° 13.290'N	Longitude	004° 09.785'W
O.S. Reference	SH	556E	716N

'The starting point'

Several old telephone cables cross the bed of the Menai Strait, about 150 metres north-east of the suspension bridge. The point at which the cables come ashore is clearly marked by a yellow and red pole, topped by a yellow diamond. This is probably the easiest dive in this location but, as with all dives here, should be attempted only on a neap-tide. It is then possible to cross the Strait and come back again by following the cables. Do not disturb the marine-life growing on or around them, as they have been used for a long-term study of the local underwater habitat.

At least one of the cables is broken and does not continue all the way to the far side, so take a compass in case of navigational difficulties. From the entry point to the far marker post, the bearing is about 160 degrees magnetic, but note that compasses can be affected by the huge ferrous mass of the bridge. Close to the Anglesey shore, the cables are partly obscured by a tangle of weed, but this growth quickly gives way to coarse sand and then to bare rock as the midway point of the strait is approached. A maximum depth of around 19 metres will be found at low-water slack.

There is an incredible amount of marine-life around this area, most of which is described in the next dive, the Nature Trail. Don't assume the best marine-life is in deeper water, as there is plenty to see close inshore. I always spend the last 10 minutes of a dive delving among the weed in the shallows to check out the prawns, crabs and the occasional 15-spined stickleback.

The easiest access to the cables is from the Anglesey shore, where a gap in the wall leads to a grass-covered area with narrow steps down to a muddy beach. As shown in the photo, the cables start about 2 metres from the seaward end of the quay wall, but this picture was taken at low-water, which is later than slack-water. Diving normally commences when the water is level with the corner of the wall.

Timing: If you require a half-hour dive with little current, enter the water on a neap-tide at 3 hours before low-water at Liverpool. If you have enough air for a one-hour dive, start the dive at 3 hours and 15 minutes before low-water at Liverpool. As you begin your dive, the current will be running westwards, towards the Menai Suspension Bridge and Caernarfon. By the end of the dive it will be running towards Bangor, but be aware of a counter-current that runs close inshore at this time.

Slack-water as the tide is rising occurs around two hours before high-water at Liverpool, but is of a very limited duration and best avoided. Although I have dived at this time, the dive has always been curtailed to avoid a long walk home from Caernarfon or beyond.

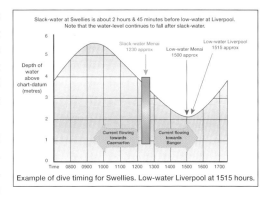

Slack-water at Swellies is about 2 hours & 45 minutes before low-water at Liverpool. Note that the water-level continues to fall after slack-water.

Slack-water Menai 1230 approx
Low-water Menai 1500 approx
Low-water Liverpool 1515 approx

Depth of water above chart-datum (metres)

Current flowing towards Caernarfon
Current flowing towards Bangor

Time 0800 0900 1000 1100 1200 1300 1400 1500 1600 1700

Example of dive timing for Swellies. Low-water Liverpool at 1515 hours.

Directions: Take the A55 from Conwy and cross the Britannia Bridge, taking exit 8A, signposted 'Menai Bridge, Porth Aethwy, Plas Newydd, Sea Zoo'. Immediately turn right at the 'T' junction. After about a mile, go straight on at the roundabout and down the hill into Menai Bridge town centre. At the crossroads, go straight across between the Bulkeley Arms and the Post Office into Water Street. Pass the 'Liverpool Arms' public house, the 'William Roberts' wood-yard and the slipway. If possible, park underneath the Menai Suspension Bridge, but spaces are limited. Otherwise, unload the diving gear and park elsewhere. After kitting up, walk 50 metres back towards the slipway until you reach a gap in the wall. This leads to a grassy bank with narrow steps down to the beach.

'Confrontation on the Cables'

9.2 - The Nature Trail under the Menai Suspension Bridge

Latitude	53° 13.275'N	Longitude	004° 09.885'W
O.S. Reference	SH	555E	716N

The entry point for the Nature Trail is on a small island known as 'Craig-y-Moch' (Pig Rock), which carries the largest pillar on the Anglesey side of the Suspension Bridge. This dive starts with a sharp, vertical drop, then slopes away to around 19 metres at low-water on a neap-tide. It is another enjoyable dive-site, but again I can only recommend diving here at low-water slack on a neap-tide, because of the extremely strong currents under the bridge.

There are two possible exit points. The first is at the same place as you entered the water, but this means a difficult scramble back up the steep bank. The other option is to drift north-eastwards after slack-water, keeping close to the Anglesey shore. Eventually, you will come to the Telephone Cables that will guide you back to a sand and mud beach and a much easier exit. Note that once the tide has started to run to the north-east, a large back-eddy forms in the lee of the bridge supports.

If you drift under the bridge to exit by the Telephone Cables, watch out for fishing-lines cast out by anglers on the grassy bank. You can usually pick up a few fishing weights on a dive here, so why not pass them back to the fishermen as a peace offering for disturbing their sport?

The Menai Strait absolutely crawls with marine-life. At times, it seems impossible for a diver to put a hand down without touching one creature or another. In the shallower areas, the rocks are almost totally covered in sponges and anemones. The most commonly-seen fish are two-spotted gobies, short-spined sea scorpions and butterfish, but in good visibility try looking upwards as large shoals of mullet congregate on the surface, close to the bridge support-pillars. Expect to see pollack, whiting, bass, conger, edible-crabs and small lobsters. On night-dives, 15-spined sticklebacks and even a salmon have been silhouetted in a torch beam.

Two-spotted goby

All sorts of junk will be found on the seabed under the bridge, presumably thrown off the roadway. One small area has a large number of keys, coin-slot tokens, part of a gaming machine, and several live .22 bullets. Goodness knows what story lies behind that collection. Perhaps an armed robbery by a one-armed bandit?

Several divers have reported a 2-metre long Admiralty-pattern anchor lying directly under the bridge, but others, including myself, say it lies west of the bridge. Other divers dispute the overall size of the anchor, but perhaps there are two, three or even more lying under or around the suspension bridge.

Even in the winter months, the Nature Trail can make an excellent night dive, but check out the underwater visibility in daylight beforehand. The bridge is normally floodlit, making life easier for divers, but this also allows a small number of herons to fly around and hunt here during the hours of darkness. This is the only place where I have ever heard herons calling out at night. A good torch and a backup light are essential, but occasionally try switching the torch off and moving your hands around to disturb the water, watching closely for the blue sparkling light caused by bio-luminescence. Don't try this unless you have a spare torch, as this is the most likely time to blow the bulb.

Timing: As for diving the Telephone Cables. If you require a half-hour dive with little current, enter the water on a neap-tide at 3 hours before low-water Liverpool. If you have enough air for a one-hour dive, start the dive at 3 hours and 15 minutes before low-water at Liverpool. As you start the dive, the current will be running towards Britannia Bridge, and at the end of the dive it will be running towards Bangor. High-water slack is very limited, so diving is not recommended at this time. If the dive was begun late, the current will take you westwards towards Swelly Rock, away from any easy exit point - and guaranteeing a long walk back to the car.

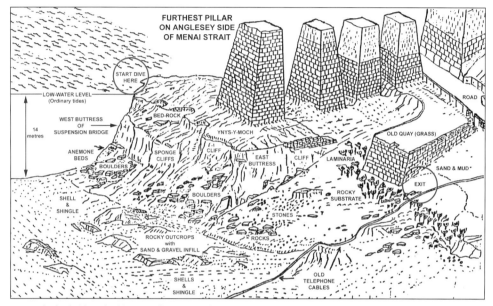

Beneath the bridge, looking south-westwards   Reproduced by kind permission of Dr. Cecil Jones

Start of Nature trail (arrowed). Looking eastwards

Directions: Follow the directions above (Telephone Cables) and park under the Menai Suspension Bridge. Walk 50 metres westwards up the hill with a strong length of rope. Go through the gap in the wall and tie the rope around the tree about 10 metres ahead of you. The rope will assist you when clambering up or down the loose bank. Having kitted up, use the rope to go down the bank on to the rocky beach. You now need to paddle, wade, stumble and trip-up as you make your way out to the furthest of the four pillars which support this side of the bridge. If your timing is correct, the current should be running from left to right (i.e. towards Caernarfon) and the tide level will be falling. Start your dive at the far right-hand corner of Ynys-y-Moch, the island on which the furthest and largest pillar stands.

9.3 - The Platters Reef and the wreck of the 'Conway'

Name	Conway	Type	Warship
Date Lost	14/4/1953	Location	Platters Rock
Cause	Hit reef	How Lost	Caught fire 16/10/1956
Hull	Wood	Weight	4,375 tons
Cargo	Ballast	Access	Boat or Shore
Latitude	53° 13.140'N	Longitude	004°10.045'W
Position Fix	Differential-GPS	Datum	WGS84
Seabed	5 to 10 metres	Wreck Height	1 metre
Charted as	Uncharted		
Slipway (1)	Menai Bridge	Distance	0.5 miles
Tidal Data	Very strong currents - see text		

HMS Conway on the Platters Reef   Photo: 'Friends of HMS Conway'

The Platters is an isolated reef that juts out from the southern shore of the strait, about half a mile west of the Menai Suspension Bridge. Normally covered by the tide, it appears only at low-water on a spring-tide when two separate peaks can be seen.

At low-water on a neap-tide, there are only a few metres of water over the shallowest areas and it is possible to stand up, chest-deep, on the Platters Reef nearly half-way across the strait. But do take care, as water-skiers, jet-skis and fishing boats zoom around the area. When diving, I have seen mackerel feathers dangling only inches from my face-mask, so use a surface-marker buoy or keep your head down!

The Mercantile Marine Service Association of Liverpool was formed in 1857 to educate and train boys for the Merchant Navy and, in 1858, accepted an offer from the Admiralty for the use of the small frigate, 'HMS Conway', as a training base. By 1859, the 'Conway' was moored in the Mersey with accommodation for 120 boys. By 1861, the vessel was proving to be too small, so another warship - 'HMS Winchester' - became the 'Conway'. By 1876, however, the training ship needed replacing for a third time - so 'HMS Nile' was offered to the Association by the Admiralty.

Work had begun on HMS Nile at Devonport in October, 1827. She was originally built as a 92-gun, two-decked, wooden sailing-ship of 4,375 tons, and was launched in June, 1839. Her total cost as a fully-armed warship, including guns and rigging, was £86,197. Already somewhat dated in design, the vessel was placed in the Reserve Fleet until 1852, when she was fitted with a steam engine and propeller. To reduce drag, the ship had a novel mechanism to raise the propeller out of the water when under sail alone.

Finally, in 1854, the ship was commissioned into the Royal Navy, just in time for service against the Russians during the Crimean War. In 1854 and 1855, 'HMS Nile' served with the Baltic Fleet where she went into action to capture and destroy a large number of enemy boats and supplies. By 1856, an armistice had been signed to end the war, so the 'Nile' was formally paid-off in 1857.

The boilers and screw were removed from 'HMS Nile' before the ship was towed from Devonport to the Mersey in June, 1876. Re-named 'Conway', she remained off Rock Ferry until May, 1941, when the danger from German air raids forced her to be moved to Bangor, in the Menai Strait. After the war, in 1949, she was taken westwards through the Swellies, the narrowest part of the Menai Strait, to a new set of moorings off Plas Newydd, north of Port Dinorwic (see the previous chapter for the location of the moorings). The ships' history and an account of life aboard the vessels can be found in the book 'The Conway' by John Masefield. See the bibliography for details.

In April, 1953, it was decided to tow the ship back eastwards through the Strait, for a re-fit in Birkenhead. Two tugs were employed for the tow through the restricted channel of the Swellies but, at a critical moment, a tow-line snapped - allowing the hulk to drift on to the Platters reef where she broke her back as the tide ebbed. The ship was declared a constructive loss and during demolition on 16th October 1956, she was accidentally set on fire and totally destroyed.

Most of the wreck lies on top of the reef at a depth of only 5 to 10 metres, where divers will find solid oak timbers and iron knees, but only a few baulks of timber will be found below this depth. She is now completely flattened because of the very strong currents, but the wreck remains a very interesting dive since there are many copper bars, nails, rivets and clench-ring washers to be found. These items are usually stamped with the broad-arrow mark indicating Government property, and occasionally with the size of the item. Presumably, in the 1820s, possession of a copper bar with the broad-arrow mark would have guaranteed an instant one-way ticket to Australia.

Should you recover any of these copper bars, do not clean them with a wire brush in a confined space as the dust produced can cause an adverse respiratory effect. I speak from bitter experience, having nearly choked myself with the dust. If you do want to clean a copper bar, work outside, use a dust mask and keep the bar wet.

Ceramic tiles marked 'Ruabon, North Wales' are often found scattered on and around the reef, and are believed to have originated from the 'Conway'. Old iron cannon were used to ballast the ship, and the badly corroded remains of one of them still lie alongside the reef. When the ship caught fire, many wooden beams, planks and other timbers were scattered over the area. The exposed baulks of wood have rotted away, but those buried in the sand and gravel are still as hard as new.

In September, 1993, one of the masts from the 'Conway' was refurbished and erected at Birkenhead Docks as a memorial 'To the many thousands of cadets trained to command, not forgetting those who lost their lives at sea'. Artefacts from the 'Conway',

including items recovered from the site by divers, are now buried in a 'time-capsule' underneath this memorial. One of the ship's massive anchors can be seen at the entrance to the Merseyside Maritime Museum, and another 5-ton anchor lies on the quayside in Caernarfon.

The seabed immediately west of the wreck is mainly gravel, and less interesting. Even without the wreck, the Platters Reef is an excellent dive, extending eastwards from the wreck of the 'Conway' almost as far as the white bungalow (see transit and chart). There are vertical rock faces up to 2 metres high, with many overhangs, gullies and small caves. One of these caves extends back for about 2 metres before it narrows to the width of a large conger eel. There is also a good variety of life to be found in the vicinity: sponges, anemones, sea-firs, butter-fish, gobies etc. Shoals of pollack, mullet, bass and whitebait cruise leisurely around the reef, while it is virtually impossible to touch bare rock because of the carpet of marine-life. Velvet swimming-crabs are common, and have a habit of launching themselves off rock faces to land on any passing diver, thereby hitching a lift. Colourful sea-slugs and their egg strings are often seen early in the year. There is less marine-life deeper than 10 metres, mainly due to the strong current which sweeps through the middle of the Strait.

The wreck of the Conway lies immediately off these tree roots

Underwater visibility is normally poor and a good torch is recommended, although 3 to 4 metres is probable from July to early October, and visibility can be as good as 10 metres during a settled period in mid-summer.

It is essential to judge slack-water correctly, as the tide runs at up to 5 or 6 knots even on a neap-tide (see photo). The best dives are to be had on low-water slack, which is earlier than actual low-water at Menai Bridge. As with other sites here, although the current changes direction either side of low-water slack, the tide-level continues to drop after this time. See previous diagram on page 123.

To dive the wreck from the shore.

I believe the best and easiest dives are made from the shore, combining the Platters Reef and the 'Conway' in one go. Car parking and toilets are available immediately adjacent to the southern end of the Menai Suspension Bridge (at 53° 13.110'N 004° 09.710'W / SH 557E 713N) and there is even a covered area for changing into your diving-suit when it is raining! Access to the shore is via a large grey gate which leads down a steep path and a series of steps to the base of the bridge but the path can be difficult going down and extremely tiring on the return journey. On a rainy day, the path can be very slippery. The gate is usually locked, so pass your gear over the fence before squeezing past the right-hand gate-post.

Allow yourself plenty of time to reach the water's edge from the car-park, especially as the walk along the shore is difficult and slippery. For a one-hour dive, enter the water on a neap-tide, three hours and 15 minutes before low-water at Liverpool. The current will still be running westwards, towards Caernarfon, but some slack water will be found in the lee of the Platters reef. This means you can drift with the current away from the suspension bridge, enjoy slack-water on the wreck and then drift back to your point of entry as the tide changes. This is the lazy diver's way to travel effortlessly to the dive-site and back again, which I call a 'boomerang' dive. If your timing is correct, and you have enough air, the current will bring you back underwater towards the Suspension Bridge. If you run short on air, surface and drift back with the tide to the Suspension Bridge, or walk along the wrack-covered shore. On the best neap-tides, by starting earlier and with a good air-supply, it is possible to spend more than 90 minutes underwater. The hardest part is at the end of the dive, with the steep climb back up to the car.

To dive the wreck by boat.

Launch at Menai Bridge slipway and motor under the Suspension Bridge along the far side of the Strait. Pass the white bungalow near the water's edge, then look for the prominent tree roots just above the high-water mark while keeping an eye on the echo-sounder. The water over the Platters Reef is very shallow, so be careful not to damage your skeg or propeller. At least one complete out-drive assembly still lies here on the seabed. Pull into the shore (at 53° 13.115'N 004° 10.050'W / SH 553E 713N) close to these tree roots, about half-way between the white bungalow and the red-brick boat-house on the point.

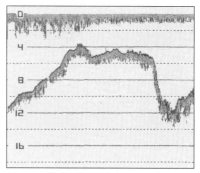

Platters Reef echo sounder trace (metres)

If you scramble ashore, you may be able to see pieces of scattered wreckage on the bank, including a group of four large bolts lying partially hidden among the weed.

Slack-water on a neap-tide will be about 2 hours 45 minutes before low-water at Liverpool. Before this time, the general direction of the current will be westwards towards Caernarfon, and afterwards towards Bangor. To confuse matters, a large whirlpool forms immediately to the west of the wreck, so divers need to rely on the compass and not the direction of the current. Even on neap-tides, there is not really enough time to have two waves of divers on the wreck, because of the short period of slack-water, so it is preferable to take a non-diving boat-handler to look after the boat. He or she should be aware that the tide level will still be falling after slack, and that the boat may be left high and dry if moored too close to the shore.

Swelly Rock, close to the wreck

Platters Reef at low water on a spring tide | Inset: A deck-light recovered from this area

HMS Conway aground on Platters Reef | Photo: 'Friends of HMS Conway'

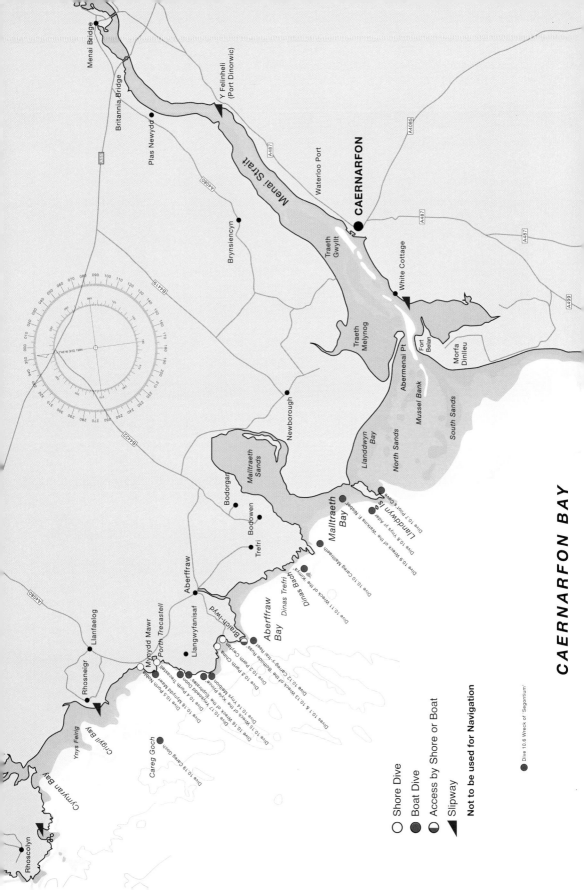

CAERNARFON BAY

Dive 10.6 Wreck of 'Segontium'

Shore Dive ○
Boat Dive ●
Access by Shore or Boat ◑
Slipway ▼

Not to be used for Navigation

Menal Bridge

Britannia Bridge

Plas Newydd

A55

A4080

Y Felinheli
(Port Dinorwic)

Waterloo Port

CAERNARFON

A4085

A487

A487

A499

White Cottage

Fort Belan

Morfa Dinlleu

Abermenai Pt

South Sands

Mussel Bank

North Sands

Traeth Melynog

Traeth Gwyllt

Menai Strait

Brynsiencyn

B4419

B4422

Newborough

Llanddwyn
Bay

Malltraeth
Sands

Bodorgan

Bodowen

Trefri

Aberffraw

A4080

Lanfaelog

Rhosneigr

Mynydd Mawr

Porth Trecastell

Llangwyfanisaf

Braich-lwyd

Aberffraw
Bay

Dinas Trefri

Dinas Bach

Malltraeth
Bay

Llanddwyn Is.

Dive 10.7 Plas's Cove
Dive 10.8 Wreck of the 'Watkins F. Nisbet'
Dive 10.9 Wreck or Ynys yr Adar
Dive 10.10 Careg Malltraeth
Dive 10.11 Wreck of the 'Kimya'
Dive 10.12 Careg-y-trai Reef
Dives 10.14 & 10.13 Wreck of the Euphrates
Dive 10.3 Porth Cwyfan
Dive 10.15 Wreck of the 'Kyle Mellbron'
Dive 10.16 Wreck of the 'Elspeth'
Dive 10.17 Wreck or the 'Place'
Dive 10.4 Porth Trecastell
Dive 10.5 Porth Nobla

Ynys Feirig

Crigyll Bay

Careg Goch

Dive 10.19 Careg Goch

Cymyran Bay

Rhoscolyn

CHAPTER TEN

Fort Belan to Rhosneigr

On Wednesday afternoon, the brig 'Eliza' of Waterford, bound from Cardiff to Liverpool with a cargo of steam coal, was observed off Llanddwyn having carried away her foremast and all of her sails. Early on Thursday morning, the City of Dublin Co's steamer 'Fairy', Captain Evans, entered the bay and proceeded to the assistance of the distressed vessel, but on coming within hail, it was found that the Captain had landed at Holyhead to engage a steamer and in his absence, the mate refused to accept the services of the 'Fairy' which remained within a cable's length of the vessel during the whole day. In the afternoon, the 'Eliza' struck on a small rock close to the Gaseg on the west of Malltraeth River. She soon filled and between 4 and 5 sunk, her masts being above water. The Captain did not make his appearance and all the crew landed meanwhile in safety. Had the proffered assistance of the 'Fairy' been accepted, the vessel and cargo would have been safe in Carnarvon Harbour.

Carnarvon & Denbigh Herald, 8/2/1854

General Description

The coastline along the west coast of Anglesey consists of low, rocky cliffs with clean, sandy beaches. Vast, drying sandbanks will be found around the southern approaches to the Menai Strait and in the river estuaries at Malltraeth and Aberffraw.

Essential Information:-

- The nearest slipways are at White Cottage, Rhosneigr and Rhoscolyn, but the area can be reached from Trefor or Trearddur Bay.

- There is very little shelter during south-westerly winds.

- There are heavy overfalls and strong currents at the entrance to the Menai Strait.

- Dive boats launched in the Menai Strait must keep to the narrow channel between Fort Belan and Llanddwyn Island. Note the the direction of buoyage, as described in Chapter 8.

- The wreck of the 'Grampian Castle' lies close to the channel between Fort Belan and Llanddwyn Island (at GPS position 53° 07.300'N 004° 22.965'W) where it dries out almost completely at low-water. Despite the danger, it is not individually buoyed and makes a dangerous obstruction for the unwary coxswain who strays out of the main channel.

- The channel buoys between Fort Belan and Llanddwyn have been known to drag out of position during stormy weather.

- Charts required – 'Menai Strait' (Number 1464) and 'Caernarvon Bay' (Number 1970).

- Maps – Ordnance Survey Explorer map number 262 (Anglesey West).

Shore Dives or Snorkelling Sites

10.1 - Wreck of the German steamship 'Bothilde Russ'

Name	Bothilde Russ	Type	Steamer
Date Lost	20/1/1903	Location	Aberffraw
Cause	Weather	How Lost	Blown ashore
Hull	Iron	Weight	1,190 tons (gross)
Cargo	Ballast	Access	Boat or Shore
Latitude	53° 10.715'N	Longitude	004° 29.380'W
Position Fix	Differential-GPS	Datum	WGS84
Seabed	5 to 10 metres	Wreck Height	3 to 4 metres
Charted as	Uncharted		
Slipway (1)	Ty-Calch	Distance	8 miles
Slipway (2)	Trearddur Bay	Distance	8 miles
Tidal Data	Little current		

Most divers refer to this iron wreck as the decommissioned warship 'Enterprise', but from my own observations I believe the wreck is actually that of the German steamship 'Bothilde Russ'.

This 1,190 gross ton, Hamburg-registered steamer was in ballast from Liverpool to Cardiff when it stranded under the cliffs at Aberffraw Point during a south-westerly force 9 gale. Lloyds List of 21st January, 1903, reported that the ship had gone ashore the previous night and that the Lifesaving Apparatus had been used to land the crew. There was still a strong south-westerly wind and the situation was becoming critical, with the boilers having shifted out of position and the funnel washed overboard. Already, the local Lloyd's representatives were saying there was a poor prospect of salvaging the vessel. Their fears were correct, and a month later they reported that the wreck had split apart and broken up.

Much iron wreckage lies badly smashed in a gully close to the rocks at Trwyn y Wylan (see photo above), at a depth of only 5 to 10 metres, where it is usually visible when snorkelling.

Two large boilers provide homes for prawns, lobsters, wrasse, conger and squat-lobsters, being located in only 6 metres of water and about 20 metres from the cliffs. These are tubular Scotch-pattern boilers, lying about 10 metres apart and measuring 3 to 4 metres in diameter. The fire-doors have broken off and lie alongside the furnaces. At low-water on a spring-tide, it is possible for a diver to stand only waist-deep on one of the boilers. Nearby, there is a large stockless-anchor, a capstan, an auxiliary-boiler and the remains of a steam-winch. Many riveted rib-frames, attached to pieces of hull-plate, lie scattered around the site, but most of the hull is badly broken up and covered with boulders and kelp. The surrounding area is mainly kelp-covered rock, which gradually gives way to a flat, sandy and rocky seabed where there are many lobster-pots. Large wrasse and pollack are usually seen slowly gliding over the wreck, and anglers often cast from the shore. These fishermen have lost a large amount of equipment on the wreck, so beware of hooks and monofilament fishing-line lying about.

There is relatively little tidal flow close inshore on the wreck itself. But after high-water, fairly strong currents will be found further offshore which clear away any disturbed silt.

The wreck is easily located, since the large steel winch used during the salvage operation still stands on the cliffs above the wreck site. The boilers lie almost directly off this winch, with a line of iron rings set into the rock, pointing directly from the winch towards the boilers. At low-water, some exposed wreckage can be seen on the rocks (at 53° 10.710' N 004° 29.300' W / SH 337E 675N). With the wreck being so shallow, this is a good snorkelling site where large parts of a wreck can be seen from the surface.

Directions from Porth Cwyfan to the wreck: Shore-dive the wreck by walking to the left (south) from Porth Cwyfan (53° 11.075' N 004° 29.145' W / SH 339E 682N) for about 750 metres (roughly half a mile) along the cliff-top path. This should preferably be attempted only at high-water, when access is much easier than at low-water. Forget the twin-set or 15-litre cylinder and pony-bottle as it is a long walk, and a single 10-litre cylinder is perfectly adequate for this shallow dive. You will need hard-soled boots on your diving suit. Cross two stiles, but stop just before the third (53° 10.750' N 004° 29.255' W / SH 338E 676N), with a large metal hand-winch to your right. Take care clambering down the slope into the narrow gully. This gives access to the open sea at high-water, but is full of boulders that make access very difficult at low-water. The boilers lie about 20 metres directly off the outer end of the gully, and in reasonable visibility can be seen from the surface. See the following dive-site for directions to Porth Cwyfan.

The Story of the 3 Weight-belts

The first time I went to look for the 'Bothilde Russ', I was unsure of the exact location and decided to identify the site before kitting-up. To split the load, three of us carried our weight-belts until we found the winch, then hid them in a nearby hollow. Returning to the car, we donned our diving-gear and set off back to where we had left the weight-belts, only to bump into an angler walking towards us carrying a creel and two fishing-rods. We wondered why he was staggering along the path until we realised that he was wearing three weight-belts as well! How many fishing-weights can you make with 30kg of diving-weights?

10.2 - Trwyn y Wylan to Porth Cwyfan

Latitude	53° 11.075'N	Longitude	004° 29.175'W
O.S. Reference	SH	338E	682N

Porth Cwyfan is a shallow, sheltered bay suitable for snorkelling or for a shore-dive. Perhaps the greatest attraction of the site is the ample parking very close to the shore-line, but this site is viable only at high-water. Once the tide starts to fall, sharp rocks are exposed, making access to and from the sea very difficult. At low-water, Porth China on the other side of the bay is a much easier dive-site. The bay is exposed to the south-west but can provide a sheltered shore-dive in north, east or south winds. It gradually slopes to about 10 metres, but the seabed unfortunately tends to be covered in kelp. However, nearer the open sea there are a few areas of bare rock, with gullies and crevices holding a variety of life including dog-fish, small edible-crabs and the occasional lobster. The bay is extensively fished for lobsters, so watch out for SMB lines being snagged by pot marker-buoys.

The bay has a small island with a church dedicated to Saint Cwyfan, and gravestones dating back to the 1760s. Known as the 'Church in the Sea', the island is cut off from the shore at high-water but can be visited on foot at all other times. Further offshore, the seabed has many large boulders in around 15 metres of water, but this area is best dived with boat-cover.

Directions to Porth Cwyfan: Take the A55 dual carriageway on to Anglesey. Exit at junction 5 (Rhosneigr, Bryngwran, Aberffraw and Circuit) and turn left for Rhosneigr and Aberffraw. Pass through Engedi and Llanfaelog, following the A4080 road signs for Aberffraw. Pass the turning for 'The Circuit' and, as you enter Aberffraw, turn right by the 'Prince Llewellyn' hotel. Pass the Countryside Centre and follow the road as it winds through Aberffraw village. Pass the church on your left and follow the sign for 'Eglwys Cwyfan' out of the 30mph area. The narrow, twisting lane leads to a dead-end at Porth Cwyfan where there is parking for about a dozen cars. Please don't block any of the farm gates.

10.3 - Porth China and Cribinau Headland

Latitude	53° 11.255'N	Longitude	004° 29.430'W
O.S. Reference	SH	336E	685N

Porth China is a small, sandy bay next to Porth Cwyfan, but is shallower, less rocky and sometimes used for small-boat moorings. The rough access road is very narrow, with sharp bends and only a few passing places. At the end of the track there is parking for about 10 cars close to the beach. A small inflatable could be launched here, but the site is unsuitable for larger boats as the access track is narrow and uneven, and has several sharp bends. At high-water, anyone diving from the shore needs to swim 200 to 300 metres to clear the flat sand, so this site is best visited at low-water. Even then, there is a long swim to achieve any depth, but there is a surprising variety of marine-life including plaice, cuttlefish, lobsters and crabs. Keep close to the rocks rather than venturing out on to the flat sand.

On a nice summer's day, this is a good site for a family outing as there is a sandy beach for the kids or for a barbeque. Porth China is also suitable for a shallow night-dive.

Although several old sailing ships have reportedly been lost here, the only visible wreckage is the remains of a fibreglass boat, scattered around the bay.

Directions: Take the A55 dual carriageway on to Anglesey. Exit at junction 5 and turn left for Rhosneigr and Aberffraw. Pass through Engedi and Llanfaelog, following the A4080 road signs for Aberffraw. Turn right at the sign for the 'Circuit' race-track. Go over the speed bumps and turn left immediately before the 'SLOW / CHILDREN' sign (at 53°11.780'N 004° 29.735'W / SH 333E 696N). This leads to Porth China down a narrow, twisting, bumpy, muddy lane, so don't attempt this route in a heavily-laden saloon or low-slung sports car.

Track to Porth China

10.4 - Porth Trecastell or Cable Bay

Latitude	53° 12.470'N	Longitude	004° 29.810'W
O.S. Reference	SH	332E	709N

The middle of the bay is sandy and shallow, making it suitable for novices, but there is plenty of marine-life to occupy even the more experienced diver who just wants an easy shore dive. You have the choice of either a long walk to the water at low-tide or a long swim at high-tide, but a small inflatable dinghy and lightweight engine could be carried down to the beach. At high-water, this is a useful site for a night-dive and barbeque. The bay is sheltered from any currents but is exposed to a south-westerly wind which quickly reduces underwater visibility, so dive here after a calm period or during easterly winds. One small rocky area along the left-hand side of the bay provides a home for a 1.5 metre-long conger eel, a lobster, several prawns and half a dozen squat-lobsters, all crammed together inside a small cave. Nearby are some broken pieces of aluminium sheet which appear to be from an aircraft or missile, possibly from the old army firing range close by at Ty-Croes and now used as 'The Circuit' car racing track.

Directions: Take the A55 dual carriageway on to Anglesey. Exit at junction 5 and turn left for Rhosneigr and Aberffraw. Set the trip mileometer as you leave the A55. Pass through Engedi and Llanfaelog, following the A4080 road signs for Aberffraw. The car park at Porth Trecastell is on your right, 4.5 miles from the A55.

10.5 - Porth Nobla

Latitude	53° 12.630'N	Longitude	004° 29.970'W
O.S. Reference	SH	331E	711N

Porth Nobla Reef at high water

This beach is situated at the north side of Mynydd Mawr headland and, like Porth Trecastell, has parking facilities which quickly fill up on a sunny day. After a 150 metre walk along a narrow footpath, there is a sandy beach that provides an excellent site for photographers and novice divers, or just for snorkelling. This site needs calm weather, so avoid the area in south-westerly winds.

There are two different areas to dive, separated by shallow, flat sand. Leaving the beach and swimming on the surface 45 degrees to your right, you will see the peaks of an extensive but shallow reef which is partially covered by a layer of wrack seaweed and surrounded by flat sand. At high-water, the maximum depth will only be around 5 metres and there is little current to worry about, thus providing an excellent site for snorkelling. Life on the reef comprises many snakelocks anemones, prawns, shore crabs, hermit crabs, velvet swimming-crabs and small edible-crabs. Fish life is mainly corkwing wrasse, two-spotted gobies, shannies and tompot blennies, with a few dogfish. If you venture off the reef on to the flat sand, look carefully for sand-eels, cuttle-fish, small plaice, sand swimming-crabs and lesser-weevers. The latter are the small fish with black, poisonous dorsal-fins - so leave them well alone.

The other diving route is along the rocky cliffs at the left-hand side of the beach, heading round towards Mynydd Mawr headland and Porth Trecastell. Take care, as there can be quite strong currents as you approach the headland where the underwater visibility tends to be less. Marine-life is similar to the reef, but there are more dogfish, pollack and ballan wrasse, while the seaweed changes to kelp rather than wrack. Many of the rocks have a covering of small mussels, but look carefully along the edge of the kelp-line for swarms of mysid shrimps. The maximum depth after swimming 300 metres out from the shore is unlikely to be more than 10 metres. Close to the cliffs, there are several pieces of timber which have obviously come from an old wreck, but no other wreckage has been seen or reported, so these may have simply been brought inshore by the wind and tide.

Directions: Take the A55 dual carriageway on to Anglesey. Exit at junction 5 (Rhosneigr, Bryngwran, Aberffraw and Circuit) and turn left for Rhosneigr and Aberffraw. Set the trip mileometer as you leave the A55. Pass through Engedi and Llanfaelog following the A4080 road signs for Aberffraw. Parking at Porth Nobla is on your right, 4.3 miles from the A55, immediately after a row of bungalows on the left and a single one on the right. Look out for a red lifebelt box on the right-hand side, with the parking area 50 metres further on.

Boat Dives - Where to Dive

10.6 - Wreck of the 'Segontium'

Name	Segontium	Type	Mussel Dredger
Date Lost	1984	Location	Caernarfon Bay
Cause	unknown	How Lost	Foundered
Hull	Steel	Weight	192 tons
Cargo	Ballast	Access	Boat
Latitude	53° 05.935'N	Longitude	004° 33.245'W
Position Fix	Differential-GPS	Datum	WGS84
Seabed	32 metres	Wreck Height	6 metres
Charted as	Wk 12.6		
Slipway (1)	Ty-Calch	Distance	10 miles
Slipway (2)	Trearddur Bay	Distance	11 miles
Slipway (3)	Trefor	Distance	8 miles
Tidal Data	Slack approx 90 mins before high or low at Liverpool		

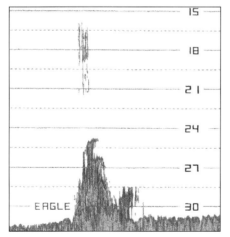

Segontium echo sounder trace.
(metres) note expanded scale

The 'Segontium' really is a superb dive-site, located out in the middle of Caernarfon Bay. This is one of the few intact, upright and almost complete shipwrecks to be found off the Llŷn and Anglesey coast within a reasonable depth. Owned by Severnside Foods Ltd of Bangor, this small vessel had been used as a mussel dredger until it sank in 1984. The name 'Segontium' is taken from that of the Roman military station founded at Caernarfon in about A.D. 50. Originally, the ship was named 'C165' and used by the Royal Navy as an armaments tender. The quality of the ship's fittings such as the porthole (see photo) shows that it was built to a much higher specification than a commercial mussel-dredger.

However, the 'Segontium' was fully refurbished for its new career and a new 'Scania' diesel engine had been fitted.

The wreck lies about 5.5 miles west-south-west of Llanddwyn Island where it is charted as Wk 12.6 in a charted depth of 28 metres, but you will need fuel for a round trip of about 20 miles from the slipway at Ty-Calch in the Menai Strait or from Trefor slipway. After the sinking, the wreck was initially buoyed, but this was removed many years ago.

The 'Segontium' is still largely complete, sitting upright on a sandy seabed and lying north - south with the bows to the south. The single, bronze prop was at a depth of 32 metres at low-water neaps until it was removed in 1992, but the rudder is still in place. The deck lies at about 26 metres, reducing to 20 metres at the wheel-house and funnel. The bows and wheel-house are very prominent and the whole wreck can easily be covered in one dive, making the task of relocating the shot-line very easy. Just about every piece of the vessel is covered in soft corals such as plumose anemones, but perhaps one of the few criticisms of this wreck is that it is difficult to make out any of the finer details of the 'Segontium' because of this thick coating of marine-life. When looking downwards from the deck towards the seabed, it sometimes appears that the whole sand is moving, but this is simply due to a massive shoal of fish viewed from above and not the extreme effects of nitrogen narcosis!

Nets and dead porpoise
nearby at Dinas Dinlle

This wreck is very popular with anglers because of the vast shoals of fish that are attracted to it. Charter and privately-owned boats are often seen over the site, creating friction when both divers and anglers want 'possession' of the wreck at the same time.

The 'Segontium' seems to have a magnetic attraction for fishing nets, and there are currently large trawl-nets wrapped around the remains of the mast, on the port side and on the stern. At one time, the wreck was festooned in monofilament drift-nets, which created a strange effect when diving because of the large number of dead fish suspended in the water. They also meant that the conger were always well fed and very large! Several years ago, one diver found a decomposed body trapped in the monofilament netting - but this was a dolphin, porpoise or seal which had become entangled. Fortunately, most of the netting has now gone, but a net cutter, sharp knife or pair of scissors is still recommended when diving here as there are always lost fishing-lines, lures and hooks entangled in the wreck. Divers must be extremely wary of these nets and fishing-lines, especially if the visibility is poor after a storm or during the plankton bloom. For further details, see 'Diver' magazine, July 2003.

Location: The nearest launching point for dive-boats is at Trefor, with alternative slipways at Ty-Calch, Rhosneigr, Rhoscolyn and Trearddur Bay. This is only a small wreck, lying north-south, so search east-west with the echo-sounder.

140

Llanddwyn Island

Llanddwyn Island is a rocky outcrop which runs about half a mile in a south-westerly direction from the sand dunes at Newborough. Once truly an island, it is now permanently joined to Anglesey by a ridge of sand. There is access to the island from the car park at Newborough, but this entails a long walk along the beach and is impractical with heavy diving equipment. Hence, a boat is the only realistic option when diving here.

The two white-painted buildings, Twr Bach (small tower) and Twr Mawr (large tower), were erected in the early 1800s, with the larger one being converted to a lighthouse in 1846. More recently, in 1972, the situation changed, with Twr Bach becoming the Llanddwyn Lighthouse. In the past, the row of cottages on the island provided homes both for the lighthouse keepers and for the local pilots who would guide ships in and out of the dangerous and constantly changing channel to the Menai Strait. The old signal-gun used by the pilots can be seen on a replica gun carriage outside the cottages.

Signal Gun

Pilot's Cove

10.7 - Pilot's Cove, Llanddwyn Island

Latitude	53° 08.100'N	Longitude	004° 24.760'W	
Position Fix	Differential - GPS	Datum	WGS84	

Pilot's Cove is a small, sandy beach on the eastern side of Llanddwyn Island, suitable for a lunch break or an easy shore-dive. The rock face outside the cove drops to only 3 metres at low-water but has enough life to make an interesting dive for novices. There is a boat-house slightly to the south of the cove, and just off the rocks in only a few metres of water are the remains of some form of trolley. It has been suggested that this is the launching-trolley from the old lifeboat station, but this is difficult to prove as all that remain are the steel girders and wheels.

To the south of the bay, the small underwater cliff consists of smooth rocks with the odd crevice providing a home for edible and green crabs, fish and anemones. Again, at low-tide the water is only a few metres deep. Among the rocks, there are a number of roofing slates jammed into the seabed, suggesting that a ship was probably wrecked here while outbound with such a cargo, but the wreck either lies buried under the sand or was salvaged long ago. On a warm summer's day, the area is very popular with yachts, water-skiers and anglers, so use SMBs and keep a close watch for boats and fishing lines.

10.8 - Ynys yr Adar, Llanddwyn Island

Latitude	53° 08.170'N	Longitude	004° 25.105'W
Position Fix	Differential - GPS	Datum	WGS84

During a south-westerly wind, this small island provides the only sheltered dive-site along this stretch of coast. As with most sites here, the rocks and boulders drop on to flat sand at a depth of only 5 or 6 metres at low-water. Divers will notice large numbers of edible-crabs, green crabs and velvet swimming-crabs, along with the odd small lobster. An interesting gully at the north-west corner of the island has a number of small over-hangs which are covered in anemones, but if you move away from the island, the seabed is mainly flat sand.

10.9 - Wreck of the 'Watkins F. Nisbet'

Name	Watkins F. Nisbet	Type	Steamer
Date Lost	6/12/1940	Location	Llanddwyn Island
Cause	Weather	How Lost	Blown ashore
Hull	Steel	Weight	1,747 tons (gross)
Cargo	Coal	Access	Boat
Latitude	53° 08.795'N	Longitude	004° 24.860'W
Position Fix	Differential-GPS	Datum	WGS84
Seabed	2 metres (low-water)	Wreck Height	2.5 metres
Charted as	Drying wreck		
Slipway (1)	Ty Calch	Distance	5 miles
Slipway (2)	Trearddur Bay	Distance	11 miles
Tidal Data	Little current		

There is a charted wreck lying at low-water on a sandy beach, approximately half a mile north of the tower on Llanddwyn Island. This is all that remains of the 'Watkins F. Nisbet', a Canadian Lakes steamer which ran on to the only piece of rock along a wide sandy beach. Built by Lairds of Birkenhead in 1923, the ship was owned by the Upper Lakes and St. Lawrence Transportation Co. of Toronto, Canada and measured more than 75 metres from stem to stern.

According to the Llanddwyn Pilots' record book kept in Gwynedd Archives, the steamer ran aground at Penrhos Beach, about 1,100 metres north of Llanddwyn Lighthouse. Coastguards and the Holyhead Lifesaving Apparatus Company rescued all 19 men aboard. The forward section was cut off and abandoned, but the after section was refloated and towed away in a joint effort by the tug 'Moore' and the dredger 'Seiont II'. This section was initially towed into the Menai Strait, then on to Birkenhead where the boilers and other machinery were removed, overhauled and fitted into another vessel.

The bow section was left on the sandy beach and now partially dries out at low-water to reveal several horizontal and vertical girders which could cause severe damage to passing boats. The remaining wreckage is only about 10 metres long and 2.5 metres high. At low-water and in calm weather, it is possible to dive or snorkel around the wreck, but the bay suffers from poor visibility in onshore winds.

10.10 - Caseg Malltraeth

Latitude	53° 09.240'N	Longitude	004° 26.315'W
Position Fix	Differential - GPS	Datum	WGS84

Caseg (or Careg) Malltraeth is a steep-sided, isolated rock which is awash at high-water and dries out as the tide falls. Lying about 300 metres off the south-west entrance to Malltraeth Bay, it provides a resting place for cormorants, seagulls and seals. At low-water, the maximum depth around the rock is only about 10 metres, with a varied seabed of rock, silt and coarse sand. There are also many large boulders, providing homes for the odd lobster or edible-crab. Many of the small crevices are full of large prawns and gobies, while dogfish are plentiful. The rocks are covered in dead-men's fingers and plumose anemones, suggesting there are strong currents around this reef. As the seabed around the rock can be rather silty, a reasonable current helps keep the visibility clear.

There are several underwater reefs surrounding Caseg Malltraeth, with at least one submerged pinnacle lying between it and the nearest shore. Since the rock is a danger to navigation, a magnetometer search of the area could prove fruitful - especially as one piece of tubular iron is known to lie slightly north of the rock. Note that the Waterford brig 'Eliza' struck this rock and sank nearby on the 2nd February, 1854, details of which are given in the quotation at the beginning of this chapter.

10.11 - Wreck of M.V. Kimya

Name	Kimya	Type	Tanker
Date Lost	7/1/1991	Location	Porth Twyn Mawr
Cause	Bad weather	How Lost	Blown ashore
Hull	Steel	Weight	1,876 tons
Cargo	Edible oil	Access	Boat
Latitude	53° 09.515'N	Longitude	004°26.965'W
Position Fix	Differential-GPS	Datum	WGS84
Seabed	8 metres (low-water)	Wreck Height	9 metres
Charted as	Drying wreck		
Slipway (1)	Ty Calch	Distance	6 miles
Slipway (2)	Trearddur Bay	Distance	10 miles
Tidal Data	Little current		

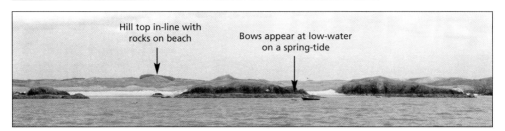

Hill top in-line with rocks on beach

Bows appear at low-water on a spring-tide

Dive boat on mid-section of Kimya

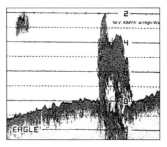

On Monday 7th January, 1991, the motor vessel 'Kimya', a Maltese-registered tanker of 1,876 tons, was carrying 1,500 tons of edible sunflower oil from St.Nazaire to Birkenhead when it capsized in heavy seas about fifteen miles out in Caernarfon Bay. The ship drifted slowly towards the Anglesey shore, keel uppermost, until the masts became embedded in the seabed. Only two crew members could be rescued by helicopter and the remaining ten seamen were lost. Fortunately, the cargo caused less pollution and loss of wildlife than other conventional oil-tanker wrecks.

In order to beach the vessel, the salvage company cut off the superstructure, allowing the hulk to be turned upright and the oil removed. She now lies in shallow water about 500 metres offshore, and makes an excellent dive in a position where there is little current. The steel hull, built in Germany during 1964, is largely complete and even had a large, bronze, 4-bladed propeller until it was removed in July 1992. The wreck sits upright on a sandy seabed at a depth of less than 8 metres at low-water, when the winch on the fore-castle just breaks the surface. At high-water, the top of the wreck is at a depth of about 3 metres. The ship was designed to carry edible oil in several large stainless steel tanks that have access ladders and swivel hatchways made of the same material. These tanks were still giving out traces of yellow sunflower oil in

1993, attracting flocks of seagulls. However, by 1994, there was no longer any sign of the oil and the easy way of finding the wreck was lost.

In a relatively short period of time, the 'Kimya' has attracted a wide variety of sea-life. The bow is partially covered in kelp and mussels, while the surrounding seabed provides a home for many angular crabs, spiny spider-crabs, hermit-crabs, brittle-stars, sea-mice, starfish and dogfish. Small cuttle-fish have been seen sheltering around the wreck, while the engine room is home to a shoal of pouting. The stern appears to be the most badly damaged part of the 'Kimya', with several holes in the hull. Divers who have penetrated the hull report that odd pockets of air have been found underwater, but the air quality is unknown and it should not be breathed.

Divers should be careful near any access hatchways or openings if there is a sea-swell running over the wreck, since quite strong surges can be felt. Underwater visibility quickly reduces to nil in a south-westerly blow.

Location: The wreck is marked on the seawards side by a green buoy marked 'Kimya'. The hull lies about halfway between the buoy and the nearest coast, roughly parallel to the shore. At low-water, the vessel's bow and winch are clearly visible above water, pointing eastwards. At high-water, the transit should be used in conjunction with an echo-sounder or a trailed anchor, heading towards the shore on the northerly transit, but take care that the outboard does not hit the wreck. Alternatively, use a GPS and sounder. The wreck position given opposite is located amidships, while the bows are at 53° 09.520'N 004° 26.932'W.

The superstructure still lies on the seabed some distance south of the hull, where it is shown on the Caernarvon Bay chart as Wk 12.7, but it appears to be slowly sinking into the seabed. As such, it is difficult to locate with the echo-sounder, while a magnetometer registers many contacts over a wide area.

10.12 - Carreg-y-trai Reef

Latitude	53° 10.485'N	Longitude	004° 29.440'W
Position Fix	Differential - GPS	Datum	WGS84

Carreg-y-trai is a low, rocky islet about a hundred metres off the Anglesey shore, and just over a mile south-west of the village of Aberffraw. It is totally covered on the highest spring-tide, but soon reappears once the tide begins to ebb. The GPS position given above is for the seawards point of the visible reef, but this does continue underwater for some distance to the south-west. Around the islet, the rocks drop off rapidly to around 6 metres at low-water before flattening out at around 12 to 15 metres, giving a pleasant, shallow dive where some shelter can always be found from the current. The area immediately to the north-west of Carreg-y-Trai has a succession of interesting gullies which teem with life and provide a hunting ground for the seals which live in the area.

At low-tide, the narrow channel (at 53° 10.565'N 004° 29.340'W) between the reef and the Anglesey shore is only 3 or 4 metres deep and can have quite strong currents. The pieces of wreckage scattered around Carreg-y-Trai are probably from the German steamer 'Bothilde Russ', the main part of which has been described in the 'shore dives' section of this chapter.

10.13 - Wreck of the German steamship 'Bothilde Russ'

Latitude	53° 10.715'N	Longitude	004° 29.380'W	
Position Fix	Differential - GPS	Datum	WGS84	

Details of this wreck have already been given in the 'shore dives' section of this chapter, but the site can easily be visited by boat by anchoring just off the gully. If you snorkel around the gully at low-water, the boilers and other parts of the wreck can be seen from the surface.

10.14 - Ynys Meibion (Boat dive)

Latitude	53° 11.270'N	Longitude	004° 30.535'W	
Position Fix	Differential - GPS	Datum	WGS84	

Ynys Meibion is a small, rocky islet that is linked to Anglesey at low-water, but becomes cut off as the tide rises. Beware of the small out-lying rock off the western point of the island. At low-water, the north side (at 53° 11.300'N 004° 30.440'W) provides a little shelter from southerly winds, where the rock face drops off to around 10 metres with many gullies and small overhangs. Visibility tends to be quite good, but a south-westerly wind soon changes this and creates a heavy swell off the point.

Underwater, there are many yellow boring-sponges, brightly coloured anemones, dead-men's fingers, starfish and squat lobsters, while if you look carefully, you may see an octopus. Keep close to the rocks to enjoy the best of the marine-life. Wooden spars and fragments of copper sheathing have been found on this northern side, along with bricks and ceramic pipes – all presumably from a wreck. The current may have brought in the wood, but the bricks would not have been easily moved by the elements, and they are too far from the nearest path to have been thrown from the shore. Further investigation is required.

10.15 - Wreck of the 'Kyle Prince'

Name	Kyle Prince	Type	Steamer
Date Lost	8/10/1938	Location	Caethle Bay
Cause	Engine failure	How Lost	Ran ashore
Hull	Steel	Weight	409 tons (gross)
Cargo	Cement	Access	Boat
Latitude	53° 11.525'N	Longitude	004° 30.335'W
Position Fix	Differential-GPS	Datum	WGS84
Seabed	9 metres	Wreck Height	4 metres (boiler)
Charted as	Uncharted		
Slipway (1)	Rhosneigr	Distance	2 miles
Slipway (2)	Trearddur Bay	Distance	7 miles
Tidal Data	Little current close inshore		

Kyle Prince   Photo: John Clarkson

In October 1938, the small coaster 'Kyle Prince' was totally wrecked in Caethle Bay, to the north of Ynys Meibion, after being abandoned by its crew in a gale. Built in Dublin in 1908, the vessel was carrying cement from Barry to Liverpool when it developed engine problems in bad weather and dropped both anchors, hoping to ride out the gale. As the weather deteriorated, the Holyhead Lifeboat rescued the crew before both anchor cables snapped and the coaster ran on to the rocky coast.

The wreck has been professionally salvaged over the years, but still makes an interesting – if shallow - dive. A large boiler stands on its end in 8 metres of water, about 20 metres offshore, where it provides a home for conger eels, ballan wrasse and cuckoo wrasse. The boiler resembles a giant baked bean can with three circular holes cut into the top lid. More badly smashed wreckage lies alongside, and continues right up to the cliff face. Steel plates, ship's ribs, bits of brass and the cargo of now solidified cement lie among big boulders, where large areas of rock are covered in multitudes of small mussels. The rudder-post is still evident but the propeller is missing, presumably having been salvaged.

Being close inshore, there is little current, but a westerly wind creates a nasty underwater surge which could sweep a diver into one of several narrow crevices in the cliff-face. There are several sandy patches close inshore that tend to stir up easily to give poor visibility and a ruined dive.

Location: The wreck lies in Caethle bay, to the north of Ynys Meibion and underneath the cliffs by the 'Circuit' car racing track. The boiler lies only about 20 or so metres out from the cliff, at the stated GPS position, but the photograph should put you directly over the boiler, indicated by the red mark, ahead and inshore of the Delta RIB.

Kyle Prince wreck site   Cuckoo wrasse

Vessel on rocks off Anglesey. Crew rescued by lifeboat.

Hundreds of villagers and others from neighbouring districts gathered on the shore at Aberffraw on Sunday, where they witnessed a coasting vessel being battered to pieces by wind and sea. It was a tragic sight to see the masts and funnels carried away, to be smashed like matchwood. The sea was strewn with timber. The vessel was tossed to and fro by the high wind and sea, and dashed against the rocks by the fury of the storm, becoming a total wreck. She was the Kyle Prince of Liverpool, owned by Messrs Monroe brothers. She had left Barry a week previously, with a cargo of cement for Liverpool and had encountered severe weather conditions. Onboard she carried a crew of nine, all of whom were saved by lifeboat.

The plight of the coaster was first seen by Tom Jones, one of the coast watchers at Rhoscolyn and communication was made with Holyhead. The lifeboat was launched on Saturday morning, and after a battling with the elements reached the Kyle Prince two hours later. Her position was then some seven miles off Rhoscolyn. Enquiries on Sunday morning elicited the information that, as there was no sign of the vessel, it was presumed she had sank, but later in the day it was ascertained that she had drifted on the rocks off Aberffraw.

Holyhead Chronicle, 14th October 1938.

10.16 - Trwyn Euphrates and the wreck of the 'Euphrates'

Name	Euphrates	Type	Sailing vessel
Date Lost	January 1868	Location	Trwyn Euphrates
Cause	Bad weather	How Lost	Capsized & ran ashore
Hull	Wood	Weight	618 tons (net)
Cargo	Palm oil	Access	Boat only
Latitude	53° 11.770'N	Longitude	004° 30.380'W
Position Fix	Differential-GPS	Datum	WGS84
Seabed	12 metres	Wreck Height	1.5 metres
Charted as	Uncharted		
Slipway (1)	Rhosneigr	Distance	2 miles
Slipway (2)	Trearddur Bay	Distance	7 miles
Tidal Data	Little current close inshore		

Trwyn Euphrates (Euphrates Headland) is an excellent dive-site where the rocky headland drops off sharply to a depth of about 10 to 12 metres before hitting flat sand. The shore is usually occupied by one or more anglers, with the result that there are many lost fishing-weights and lengths of fishing-line tangled in the kelp. There are several gullies, large boulders, rock overhangs and small caves with prolific marine-life. Despite the many lobster-pots, there are several small lobsters, many spiny spider-crabs and the odd edible-crab in the area. Large wrasse will be found in any of the clefts in the rock. As this is a rocky headland, strong currents will be found away from the cliff face, but some shelter can be found close inshore.

All those aboard the 'Euphrates' lost their lives before the hull was washed ashore at the small headland now marked on large scale Ordnance Survey maps as 'Trwyn Euphrates', close to what is now 'The Circuit' race track. The remains of this wooden barque lie scattered along the edge of the cliff. Two large capstans, an anchor and a large coil of anchor chain mark the bows, with at least one large conger lying well hidden in this pile of chain. Other parts of the ship - such as planks of wood, iron knees, old bricks and copper nails - will be found scattered along the seabed to the south.

Wreck site

Disasters on the Coast of Anglesey.

Yesterday, according to instructions, Captain Jones, Lloyd's agent at Holyhead having engaged a tug boat left Holyhead at 3 am in search of the Euphrates which has been capsized 15 miles off the South Stack. That same boat, with Lloyd's Agents aboard, scoured the channel all day and they experienced severe weather which prevented the boat from returning to Holyhead and they had to land at Bangor without seeing any sign of the capsized vessel. In the course of Thursday afternoon a box containing silver articles was picked up on the south coast of Anglesey near Aberffraw and casks of palm oil, valued at £50 were strewn along the coast. Captain Jones instantly appointed a large number of men by the day to collect the salvage, which is being done with considerable success.

Carnarvon and Denbigh Herald, 25th January, 1868

10.17 - Ynysoedd Duon

Latitude (1)	53° 12.000'N	Longitude (1)	004° 30.300'W
Latitude (2)	53° 12.050'N	Longitude (2)	004° 30.240'W
Position Fix	Differential-GPS	Datum	WGS84

These are two rocky islets, adjoining the cliffs north of Trwyn Euphrates. Away from the rocks, the seabed is flat and fairly shallow, but may be worth further exploration as I have found several interesting items within 20 or 30 metres of the cliffs. The copper pins, brass hinge, brass key and 3 brass castors are possibly all that remains of a cabin trunk which may have come from the 'Euphrates' (see the previous dive-site), or there may be another wreck in this area.

10.18 - Mynydd Mawr Headland

Latitude	53° 12.415'N	Longitude	004° 30.315'W
Position Fix	Differential - GPS	Datum	WGS84

Mynydd Mawr is a rocky headland between the two sandy bays of Porth Trecastell and Porth Nobla, and is the site of an ancient burial chamber. Although it is possible to walk out on to the headland for a shore dive, the entry is not easy and the exit would be extremely difficult even in calm weather. To dive Mynydd Mawr, it is much safer to launch a boat at Rhosneigr, Rhoscolyn or Trearddur Bay. But if you have a small inflatable with a lightweight engine, launch at Porth Trecastell and motor round to the right.

Although only around 8 metres deep and with a sandy seabed, there is a great deal of marine-life here, with the occasional thornback ray. Watch out for anglers' lines. Several divers have reported small pieces of wreckage, but these are mostly buried under the sand and are easily missed. They may be part of the remains of the 'Sarah', a vessel that broke up on the rocks near Trecastell on 7th October, 1835, while outbound from Liverpool for Demerara. The Rev. James Williams, a local vicar, had been instrumental in setting up the 'Anglesey Association for the Preservation of Life from Shipwreck', a forerunner of the R.N.L.I. He took charge of the rescue attempt. His wife, Frances, made a painting of the rescue, showing the vessel on the rocks with a seaman escaping along a rope strung from the mizzenmast to the cliffs.

10.19 - Carreg Goch (Red Rock)

Latitude	53° 12.320'N	Longitude	004° 32.455'W
Position Fix	Differential - GPS	Datum	WGS84

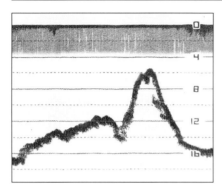

This offshore reef, charted as Rk 1.7, is the seaward end of a long ridge which runs out from Rhosneigr for about 1.3 miles. Overfalls, or an area of disturbed water, usually mark Carreg Goch. The top of the rock is covered in kelp, but the steep sides have been worn smooth and are covered in dead-men's fingers. This is a very exposed site, with the reef lying across the current which, even on a neap-tide, can be extremely fierce. There is at least one cleft in the rock, about 1 metre wide and five metres deep, through which the tide hits you like a giant water-cannon, but some shelter can usually be found on the leeward side of the reef. The seabed around the rock is composed of coarse sand at a depth of 15 to 20 metres and is littered in parts with old lobster-pots.

Slack-water is around 2 hours before high-water at Liverpool, but it is better to be on site early and wait for the current to ease off.

Lesser-spotted dogfish

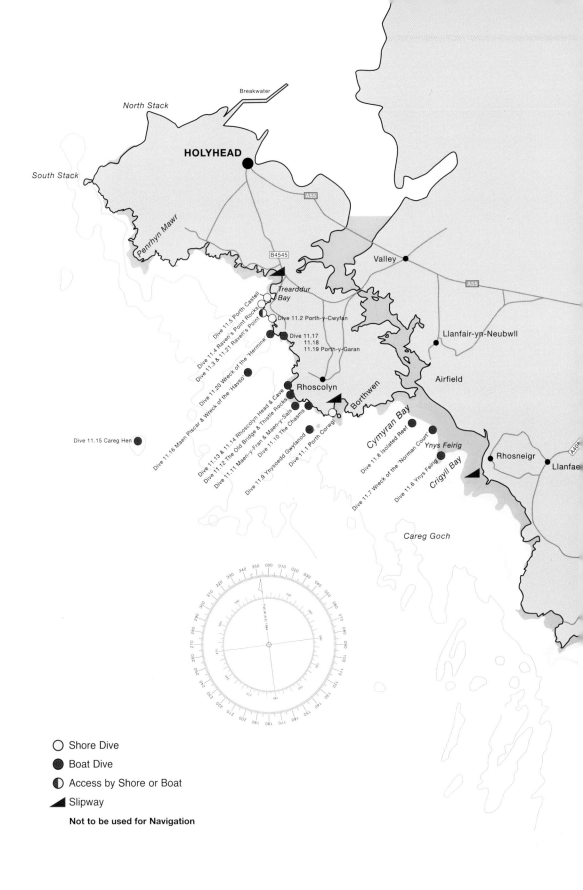

Breakwater

North Stack

HOLYHEAD

South Stack

A55

Penrhyn Mawr

B4545

Valley

A55

Trearddur
Bay

Dive 11.5 Porth Castell
Dive 11.4 Raven's Point Rocks
Dive 11.3 & 11.21 Raven's Point

Dive 11.2 Porth-y-Cwyfan

Dive 11.17
11.18
11.19 Porth-y-Garan

Llanfair-yn-Neubwll

Dive 11.20 Wreck of the 'Hermine'

Airfield

Rhoscolyn

Borthwen

Dive 11.16 Maen Piscar & Wreck of the 'Hayso'

Dive 11.15 Careg Hen

Dive 11.13 & 11.14 Rhoscolyn Head & Cave
Dive 11.12 The Old Bridge & Thistle Rocks
Dive 11.11 Maen-y-Fran & Maen-y-Sais
Dive 11.10 The Chasms
Dive 11.9 Ynysoedd Gwylanod
Dive 11.1 Porth Corwgl

Cymyran Bay

Dive 11.8 Isolated Reef

Ynys Feirig

Dive 11.7 Wreck of the 'Norman Court'
Dive 11.6 Ynys Feirig

Crigyll Bay

Rhosneigr

Llanfae

A40?

Careg Goch

○ Shore Dive

● Boat Dive

◑ Access by Shore or Boat

◣ Slipway

Not to be used for Navigation

CHAPTER ELEVEN

Rhosneigr to Trearddur Bay

The coxswain steered straight for the ship and got alongside. 'Don't leave us this time' was heard from aloft and the answer came 'No, No. We came here to take you away and do so we will. Dead or alive!' And so they did.

Carnarvon and Denbigh Herald, 7th April 1883

General Description

This is one of the most popular sea-diving areas in North Wales. The coastline is mainly rocky, but there are pleasant, sandy beaches at Rhosneigr, Silver Bay, Rhoscolyn and Trearddur Bay. Several rocky islands are found off Rhoscolyn, along with dozens of isolated and jagged reefs that have torn the keels out of many sailing vessels.

During the week, Hawk, Tornado and Jaguar aircraft from the nearby airfield at R.A.F. Valley constantly disturb the peace and tranquillity as they take off and land, but the reassuring clatter of the Sea King rescue-helicopter is always welcomed by divers. They may be noisy, but it is nice to know that they are around, should we ever need them.

Essential Information:-

- Launch sites are available at Rhosneigr, Rhoscolyn and Trearddur Bay.

- There are many shore-diving opportunities, mostly around Raven's Point at Trearddur Bay.

- After high-water, the current at Raven's Point can take a diver out to sea. There have been several life-boat call-outs for this reason.

- Strong currents and heavy overfalls will be found at Rhoscolyn, Maen Piscar and Carreg Hen.

- There are drying rocks at Ynys Feirig, Cymyran Bay, Rhoscolyn and further offshore at Maen Piscar.

- Charts required – 'Caernarvon Bay' (Number 1970) and 'Approaches to Holyhead' (Number 1413).

- Maps – Ordnance Survey Explorer map number 262 (Anglesey West).

Shore Dives or Snorkelling Sites

11.1 - Porth Corwgl at Rhoscolyn

Latitude	53° 14.525'N	Longitude	004° 35.585'W
O.S. Reference	SH	270E	749N

Located about 350 metres from Rhoscolyn car park, Porth Corwgl (Coracle Bay) is useful for a shore dive in a sheltered bay, and suitable for a training dive or snorkelling. It is a narrow, sandy cove with rocky cliffs on either side, and divers should keep within the confines of the bay to avoid the strong offshore currents. The middle of the bay is shallow and sandy.

Directions: Cross Anglesey on the new A55 dual carriageway and exit at junction 3 (Valley, Y Fali). Note – this is the one <u>after</u> the RAF Valley turnoff. Turn right, cross over the A55 and follow the signs for 'Local Services' and 'Valley'. Turn left at Valley traffic lights, cross over the railway line and the A55. Go straight across the roundabout and over the Four-Mile Bridge on to Holy Island, then immediately take the first left on to the B4545 (opposite the Post Office) signposted 'Rhoscolyn'. Follow this lane through the sharp left-hand bend and over the hill. Pass the turning

for Silver Bay, then bear left at the sign for the 'White Eagle' Hotel. Pass the hotel and continue along this narrow, twisty road to the car park. Kit up and walk along the right-hand side of the bay, but note that the beach is totally covered at high-water on a spring-tide. Follow the track with the sign 'Private Land, No Vehicles, Public Footpath Only', and pass the Old Lifeboat House. The track then leads to the cove, only a few metres further on. Note that there is another bay with the same name near Porth Dafarch.

Shore Dives From Raven's Point Road, Trearddur Bay.

One of the most popular diving areas in North Wales, Raven's Point Road has several different shore-diving locations. Most of the road has double-yellow lines along each side and is regularly checked by the local authorities. Note that parking on the pavement by the yellow lines could incur a penalty for obstruction as well as parking. If you leave the car where there are no yellow lines, please park as close to the nearside as possible, and try not to leave your vehicle opposite the driveways of the bungalows. This is a very busy, narrow road.

Directions to Raven's Point Road: Cross Anglesey on the A55 dual carriageway, turning sharp left on to the B4545 for Trearddur Bay at the roundabout (Junction 1) on the outskirts of Holyhead. Pass the Trearddur sign, the garage, the Sea Shanty Café and the Spar shop, then take the next right into Raven's Point Road. All dive-sites on this road are beyond the Seacroft Hotel.

11.2 - Porth-y-Cwyfan (Shore dive from Raven's Point Road)

Latitude	53° 16.040'N	Longitude	004° 37.150'W		
O.S. Reference	SH	253E	778N		

Porth-y-Cwyfan provides an easy shore-dive in a sheltered bay without too long a walk in full diving gear. Diving should not be attempted at low-water or if there are onshore winds. Access to the water is easy at high-water, but as the tide drops, it involves a scramble over sharp rocks covered in bladder-wrack weed. High-water at Trearddur Bay averages around one and a half hours before high-water at Liverpool. At the time of writing, access is uncertain, so note the comments in 'Directions'.

Close-inshore, the seabed is rather boring, being mainly covered in kelp, but this soon gives way to areas of sand and gravel. Colonies of starfish are found on the rocks, with the sandy areas providing a home for shoals of sand-eels which dart out of the seabed when disturbed. The better diving is to be found past the right-hand (westerly) point of the bay. The rocks here drop off to about 15 metres where there is a succession of horizontal clefts, mostly about half a metre deep. In places, these go back into the cliff for up to two metres and, as a result, the area provides many suitable hiding places for the prolific marine-life. Crevices are crowded with prawns, blennies, gobies, crabs and small lobsters. Large wrasse are found patrolling the cliff face and are attracted by any disturbance of the seabed that uncovers even the slightest morsel

of food. Further away from the cliff face, the rocks have been scoured smooth by wave action and have been undercut to give a flat overhang up to three metres high. This provides a home for large areas of bright yellow boring-sponges.

A plaque on the cliff top immediately west of Porth Cwyfan reads 'Figurehead ship 'Jane', Wrecked on this coast December 12th, 1913. All lives saved'.

Directions: Follow Raven's Point Road, passing the Seacroft Hotel, 'Diving Services Anglesey', and the sharp bend at the entrance to the private housing estate. The road climbs up a slight hill before levelling off and dropping into a small dip from where a footpath on the right leads to the dive-site. This path starts about 25 metres before the sign for the 'Bagnol' caravan park. Parking is limited to only one car, so diving gear should be unloaded by the white garage (at 53° 16.065'N 004° 37.075'W SH 254E 778N) and the car parked some distance away. A footpath runs between two walls for about 150 metres down to the shingle beach. This path can be very slippery in wet weather.

Note: In early 2003, a padlocked gate was erected across the path and the access from the path to the shore was blocked. As such, this dive-site cannot currently be easily reached on foot.

11.3 - Raven's Point (Shore dive from Raven's Point Road)

Latitude	53° 16.160'N	Longitude	004° 37.525'W
O.S. Reference	SH	249E	780N

This is an excellent shore-dive but is suitable only for those who can walk a tightrope and rock-climb in full diving gear, so read the directions first. Do not dive here in an onshore wind, as there will be a dangerous surge inside the confines of the gully. Note also that after high-water, there can be strong currents off the point which can carry divers out to sea. Depths are relatively shallow, so a 10-litre cylinder is adequate and much easier to carry back up the cliff than a 15-litre. Raven's Point is a very popular angling venue, so you may find the site already occupied when you arrive. Take a good torch to explore some of the small caves.

From the entry point, swim on the surface to your left (south-east) until you reach a large inlet which has sheer cliffs along one side. This is Raven's Point Gully (See photo: page 172). I usually submerge on the far side of the gully and follow the cliffs back to the entry point. The initial underwater impression is of many large boulders covered with lots of starfish. There is quite a covering of kelp, but this rapidly peters out as you swim into the gully, probably because of the shallow depth (about 6 metres at low-water neaps) and exposed position. Swimming further into the gully, you will find a cave in the right-hand cliff, which is worth exploring with a torch. This is not wide enough for two divers or for making a 'U' turn, so back-pedal out. Note that because of the lack of current in the cave, the silt is quickly stirred up and visibility is lost. Further into the gully, the width decreases rapidly to just a narrow slot in the cliffs, canted over to the right where several boulders have been jammed into the gap. Again, engage reverse gear rather than trying to do a 'U' turn. The seabed is littered with debris which has probably been brought in by storms, with one large piece of ship's timber solidly jammed into the cleft. Parts of a modern fibreglass boat lie scattered around the area, along with several aluminium poles. There are many well-worn bricks and tiles at this point, probably from a shipwreck, but further research is required. Some of the tiles are incised with the words 'Made in Wales', and this author would welcome any information as to the origins of this debris. Continuing the anti-clockwise tour of the gully brings you to small vertical cliffs, and yet another deep cave with massive boulders jammed in the roof. Look upwards to see the light streaming down past these boulders. Swimming further along the edge of the cliffs will bring you back out of the gully to the entry/exit point.

Marine-life inside the gully is quite impressive for such a confined area. Pollack, wrasse, two-spotted gobies, sand gobies, small lobsters, various crabs, sand-eels, prawns, common starfish, sun-stars, feather stars and much more will be seen in one dive.

You then have the option of climbing out on to the rocks or, assuming you have enough air, continuing underwater to finish your dive closer to Trearddur Bay. Outside the gully, the seabed drops off via some nice vertical cliffs to a depth of around 10 to 15 metres, depending on the tide state and the distance offshore. Even further out, the seabed comprises coarse sand and broken rock where the current can be quite strong. Take care if surfacing here, as there is considerable boat traffic off the point. Because of the current, the marine-life is quite different to that in the gully, with dead-men's fingers, yellow boring-sponges and sagartia elegans anemones. The large ballan wrasse found here are very impressive.

As an alternative to diving in the main gully at Raven's Point, head to the right from the entry point and swim back towards Trearddur Bay, exiting onto the rocks or at Porth Castell. This dive is totally different to the gully, with dozens of massive boulders scattered along vertical cliff faces. Many of these boulders have created caves to explore or tunnels to swim through, but take care not to become entangled as there are many lost lobster-pots and ropes along this edge. In addition, there are many metres of lost fishing line waiting to ensnare the passing diver, so a net-cutter is a worthwhile accessory. Again, depths of 10 to 15 metres are possible, depending on the state of the tide.

The exit over the rocks towards Porth Castell is difficult. Ensure that you leave the water beyond the pipe-bridge so you don't have to repeat the balancing act with wet feet. An easier exit is available at Porth Castell, but this entails a longer swim.

Directions: Unload your diving gear by the entrance to the Ravens Point private housing estate (at 53° 16.255' N 004° 37.365' W / SH 251E 782N) and park elsewhere. Kit up and walk 100 metres to the left until you reach a narrow gully blocking the path. Note that although the land is privately owned, public access is still allowed. A cast iron pipe, encased in concrete, crosses this gully (at 53° 16.220' N 004° 37.435' W / SH 250E 781N) but do not attempt to cross it unless you are confident in doing so. It is narrow, does not have a flat surface, and can be slippery in wet weather. Tornado jets have a habit of flying low overhead, just as you reach the middle of the bridge. If you have any doubts about crossing the pipe, either go left and scramble across the gully or enter the water from the rocks at the nearest point. See the following dive-site for details.

Before crossing the pipe bridge, look straight across the gully and note how the pipe continues, being mostly buried in the rock and covered with smaller rocks and concrete. Having crossed the pipe bridge, follow the route of the pipe to the headland and climb down the cliff (at 53° 16.155' N 004° 37.525' W / SH 249E 780N) to the water's edge. As the rocks are covered with barnacles and weed, access is easier at high-water, but take care even then.

11.4 - Rocks between Raven's Point and Porth Castell
(Shore dive from Raven's Point Road)

Latitude	53° 16.230'N	Longitude	004° 37.465'W
O.S. Reference	SH	250E	781N

This dive has slightly easier access and less current than Raven's Point. You don't need to tightrope walk, although it still requires a clamber over the rocks to the entry point. Note that although the site is relatively sheltered, after high-water there may be currents which can carry a diver past Raven's Point and out to sea. The rocks have many overhangs and small caves with rocky reefs running out on to flat sand and boulders at around 13 metres. There is thick kelp close inshore.

Look out for pipefish, squat lobsters, sun-stars and anemones. Following the rocks in a north-easterly direction will bring you to the sandy beach at Porth Castell and an easy exit, but this area has lots of passing boat traffic, so use SMBs and be careful.

Directions: Unload the diving gear by the entrance to the Trearddur Bay housing estate (at 53° 16.255' N 004° 37.365' W / SH 251E 782N) and park elsewhere. Note that the land is privately owned, but public access is permitted. Kit up and walk 100 metres to the left until you reach the narrow gully (at 53° 16.220' N 004° 37.445' W / SH 250E 781N) which blocks the path. Enter the water from the rocks at the nearest point, preferably at high-water.

11.5 - Porth Castell (Shore dive from Raven's Point Road)

Latitude	53° 16.300'N	Longitude	004° 37.280'W	
O.S. Reference	SH	252E	782N	

Best dived at high-water, this site provides a sheltered bay immediately opposite 'Diving Services Anglesey'. It is suitable for novice divers or for a night dive, since entry and exit are from a gently sloping beach. Much of the bay comprises a sand and shingle seabed and, as such, is a useful site for training drills. The more interesting diving, though, is along the base of the rocks or around the reefs just outside the bay. Beware of passing boats or mooring-lines which will snag SMBs. If you bring your own boat into this bay, watch out for submerged rocks as well as divers without marker-buoys.

Despite the sheltered area, the marine-life is interesting, especially for newcomers. Hermit crabs, snakelocks anemones, mussels and wrasse will all be seen. This is one of the few places where I have seen a 15-spined stickleback.

Do not park on the double yellow lines. Parking at 'Diving Services Anglesey' is for customers only, unless you buy a £5 per car parking ticket. This is strongly recommended to avoid having to carry diving gear some distance from a legal parking area and is far cheaper than a parking-fine. This is one of the few places where air and spare parts are available within a few metres of the dive-site, but note that the gate is not normally open before 9.30 am.

Porth Diana, the larger bay between the dive shop and the sailing club, is used for boat moorings and can be very busy during the summer, when it is best avoided by divers.

Directions: Follow Raven's Point Road, passing the Seacroft Hotel and the sailing club car park. Porth Castell is on the right, immediately opposite 'Diving Services, Anglesey'.

Boat Dives - Where to Dive

11.6 - Ynys Feirig and Cerrig-y-Gwyr

Latitude	53° 13.675'N	Longitude	004° 32.755'W
Position Fix	Differential - GPS	Datum	WGS84

Lobster-pot

Ynys Feirig (or Starvation Island) is a long, narrow, rocky island located west of Rhosneigr. The seabed around the island is shallow and sandy, but this may be one of the few sheltered dive-sites available during a westerly wind.

The GPS position given above is for Cerrig-y-Gwyr, a dangerous outlying rock about 200 metres south of Ynys Feirig. Covered at high-water, the tips of several rocks dry out as the tide falls, to create a nasty hazard for boats travelling south of Ynys Feirig. The underwater reef then continues in a south-south-westerly direction for another half mile. Coxswains need to watch out for lobster-pot buoys all over this area, and to be aware of the strong offshore currents.

On the night of the 11th, the brig 'Adelaide' Granby master, from Charente to Liverpool, came ashore at Cymyran, Carnarvon and was soon a total wreck. The cargo, consisting of 500 casks of brandy, out of which 430 have been saved and brought to the Custom House Yard. The vessel being wrecked on a rock about a mile from the shore, causing the cargo to be scattered along the coast to an extent of 6 or 7 miles, the strong disposition to plunder, exhibited by the numerous groups.

Carnarvon & Denbigh Herald, Saturday Feb 20, 1841.

11.7 - Wreck of the 'Norman Court' in Cymyran Bay

Name	Norman Court	Type	Sailing vessel
Date Lost	29/3/1883	Location	Cymyran Bay
Cause	Bad weather	How Lost	Hit rock
Hull	Wood & Iron (comp)	Weight	855 tons (gross)
Cargo	Sugar	Access	Boat only
Latitude	53° 14.310'N	Longitude	004° 32.790W
Position Fix	Differential-GPS	Datum	WGS84
Seabed	5-8 metres	Wreck Height	1.5 to 3 metres
Charted as	Drying wreck		
Slipway (1)	Rhosneigr	Distance	1 mile
Slipway (2)	Trearddur Bay	Distance	5 miles
Tidal Data	Little current		

Cutty Sark

Transit A - Conspicuous chimney

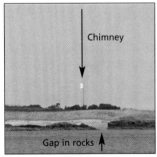

Chimney

Gap in rocks

Transit A

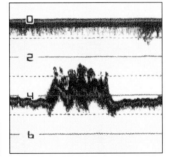

High-water

Low-water

Location: The 'Norman Court' lies in shallow water off the airfield at RAF Valley and immediately east of a drying rock which is visible above water for two or three hours either side of low-water. At this state of the tide and in calm weather, the dark outline of the wreck is usually visible from the surface. At high-water, the rock is completely submerged, so use the transits or a GPS and echo-sounder. This rock has claimed other victims, with the remains of at least one fibreglass cabin cruiser lying scattered around the bay.

Note: There are several other drying rocks and reefs in Cymyran Bay. The direct line from Silver Bay takes you over a cluster of reefs at Cerrig-y-Caw. The direct line from Rhoscolyn Sound (Trearddur Bay or Rhoscolyn) could take you over the isolated reef described in the next dive-site, and the route from Rhosneigr to the south of Ynys Feirig could take you over Cerrig-y-Gwyr.

Located between Rhosneigr and Rhoscolyn, this is one of the most wreck-prone areas on the North Wales coast and includes Crigyll Bay, Cymyran Bay and the barren island of Ynys Feirig, otherwise known as 'Starvation Island'. Any sailing vessel caught in a south-westerly gale stood a chance of becoming embayed (trapped by the wind) and wrecked here, either being smashed to pieces on the rocks or running ashore on the sandy beach. In addition to the natural dangers, any vessel wrecked in this area was liable to attract the attentions of the notorious 'Crigyll Wreckers' who would plunder a wreck within hours. See the following extract from the Carnarvon & Denbigh Herald. Despite that, in March 1883, when poor navigation and bad weather caused yet another shipping disaster, all the local lifeboat crews made incredible efforts to save those stranded on a vessel in the bay.

This was the most famous vessel ever to be lost in Cymyran Bay, the former tea-clipper 'Norman Court'. Having been built by A. & J. Inglis of Glasgow during 1869, they utilised a new but short-

RAF Valley

Transit B
Radar scanner is just to the right of the white gate

lived method known as 'composite construction'. The hull-frames were made of iron and had an outer cladding of teak planks attached by large brass bolts. Any diver visiting Greenwich in London should take the opportunity to visit the 'Cutty Sark', which was built in a similar way.

Named after the home of one of her original owners, the 'Norman Court' had traded on similar routes to the 'Cutty Sark' when they were both involved in transporting tea from China to London. Both were built for speedy ocean voyages carrying a light but valuable cargo. In 1872, the 'Norman Court' took only 96 days to sail from Macao to London while the 'Cutty Sark' needed 122 days.

By 1883, the 'Norman Court' had been re-rigged as a barque and was loaded with a cargo of sugar from Surabaya in Java (Indonesia). Having reached Cork Harbour, her master, Captain McBride, received orders to proceed to Glasgow. Somehow, poor navigation during a gale caused the ship to become embayed off Rhosneigr. Initially grounding well offshore, the ship was relentlessly driven towards the shore and no doubt would have been washed up safely on a sandy beach. Unfortunately, the ship struck one of the few isolated rocks in the bay, causing parts of her hull to be torn apart and the mainmast to collapse.

The nearest lifeboat station was at Rhoscolyn, but the lifeboat was lying damaged at Porth Diana, Trearddur Bay. The Rhosneigr lifeboat made several valiant attempts to rescue the 22 people on board, while lifelines fired out by rocket also failed to reach the wreck. Eventually, a train was used to take the crew of the Holyhead lifeboat to a position as close as possible, allowing them to man the Rhosneigr lifeboat and rescue Captain McBride and 19 of the crew. Two of the crew had already died from exposure, having tied themselves to the rigging to prevent themselves being washed overboard.

The vessel was declared a total loss and was sold as such on 18th April, 1883, after which the wheel, bell and binnacle were recovered. For further details see the 'Chester Chronicle' (28th April 1883), 'Sea Breezes' (May 1969) or a report by the 'Anglesey Antiquarian Society'.

The wreck was first located by local divers and surveyed in 1967 by a team of Royal Air Force divers. The RAF team reported finding a mast, sections of hull, wood, copper sheathing, chains,

copper bolts and dead-eyes. Little has changed since then, although most of the copper bolts have now gone. Individually stamped with the maker's name 'Grenfell Inglis', these bolts prove beyond doubt that this is indeed the 'Norman Court'.

Lying about a quarter of a mile out from the low-tide mark, the site still provides an interesting dive suitable for novices, but it should be avoided in south-westerly winds as the resultant swell soon reduces the underwater visibility to nil and fills the hull with loose seaweed. At high-water, the maximum depth is around 8 metres, with the hull mostly standing about two metres proud of the seabed, but some ribs are up to four metres high and partially dry out at low water on a spring-tide.

Most of the teak hull-cladding has gone, but many of the iron frames and beams can still be found, and it is possible to swim underneath several of them. Look carefully at these frames to see where they are drilled for the bolts which held the outer planks on to the frames. Other noticeable features are some remaining sheets of hull-cladding, a section of tubular iron mast, bitts and an iron cannon. Strangely, every time I have dived this wreck, at least one golf ball has been recovered.

The surrounding seabed is mainly flat sand, with a few rocky patches where there have been unconfirmed reports of other wreckage. Being in a shallow, sandy bay, there is less marine-life than in deeper, rocky areas, but the ever-hopeful wrasse know that divers stirring up the seabed will uncover titbits of food, so you usually have some company on your dive. Otherwise, expect to see pollack, hermit-crabs and small edible-crabs.

The 'Norman Court' is the first site in North Wales to become part of the Nautical Archaeology Society 'Adopt a Wreck' scheme. It is now being surveyed and overseen by Worsley Sub-Aqua Club, so for further details check their website at www.normancourt.homestead.com. Visit the wreck, but please treat it with care and respect.

Wreck and the loss of life near Holyhead - Brave rescue by a Holyhead lifeboat crew. Seldom have services more heroic been rendered by any lifeboat crew than were rendered on Friday night last by the Holyhead lifeboat crew in rescuing the crew of the ship Norman Court of Greenoch. She was wrecked on Thursday night last week during a terrific gale. She was a vessel of 804 tons, of composite build, and 12 years old. A splendid passage of 102 days was made from Sourabaya, and while making for Greenock all being well previously, she was driven onto the rocks in Cymyrau Bay on the most dangerous part of the rugged Anglesey coast, not far from the spot some years ago the ship Palinurus became a total wreck and also the spot where the Earl of Chester was dashed to pieces.

Carnarvon and Denbigh Herald, 7th April 1883

11.8 - Isolated Reef in Cymyran Bay

Latitude	53° 14.300′N	Longitude	004° 33.545′W
Position Fix	Differential - GPS	Datum	WGS84

This is an isolated reef that dries out by 1.2 metres, in a position about half a mile offshore in Cymyran Bay. The reef is covered in thick kelp and is surrounded by a sandy seabed at a depth of around 6 to 9 metres. Although not a particularly inspiring dive-site, I have located copper nails and bars on and around the reef, so further investigation may be worthwhile as many vessels have been lost in this area.

11.9 - Ynysoedd Gwylanod

Latitude	53° 14.300′N	Longitude	004° 35.950′W
Position Fix	Differential - GPS	Datum	WGS84

Rhoscolyn beacon and wreck site, possibly the "Elizabeth Kloosterboer'

Ynysoedd Gwylanod, the Seagull Islands are a string of rocky islands located about a quarter of a mile off the Rhoscolyn cliffs. They are aligned roughly north-east to south-west. The GPS position given above is for the north-east tip of the most northern island, where, even on a neap-tide, there can be very strong currents running through Rhoscolyn Sound. They are easily recognised by the small tower, Rhoscolyn Beacon, erected on their highest point. At high-water, they appear as several separate islands, but these merge together as low-water approaches. Note that the ridge of rock that created these islands does continue underwater further to the south-west, where there are several small, submerged rocks and reefs to create a danger to passing boats. Overfalls are often found off this south-west point.

Lying across the general tidal flow, the islands allow diving at all tidal states as long as care is taken to keep within the shelter of the rocks. Fast drift-dives are possible through the gaps between the islands, but these are full of kelp that can tangle SMBs and buddy-lines. Do not venture here on spring-tides. Weight belts also seem to snag easily on the kelp, and several of these have been found lying deep in the kelp jungle.

The whole area is an excellent site for marine-life enthusiasts, with sun stars, yellow boring-sponges and dead-men's fingers, while the rocky gullies in the more sheltered areas are totally covered in feather-stars. Most diving here is in the 10 to 15 metre range, where there is a wide variety of fish life. Be sure to check out the small caves with their resident conger eel and attendant group of prawns. On one dive here, several pollack were observed working together to corral a small shoal of sand-eels into a narrow gully. These predators then took it in turn to dart into the confused group of sand-eels, picking them off one at a time for an easy meal. The local group of seals have now accepted visiting divers, so you may see one or more of them during your dive.

The area has also attracted many wrecks over the centuries, with their scattered remains lying all around the area. In one gully located immediately to the south-west of the beacon (at 53° 14.176'N 004° 36.253'W), there is a large iron bar with a 90' bend in it. This is either all that remains of a large iron knee, or part of the sternpost. To the south of the tower, more scattered wreckage is possibly all that remains of the Elizabeth Kloosterboer, a small Dutch schooner wrecked here in March 1878, with the loss of 5 crew members. Chains, hinges, bricks, copper bars and hull-sheathing are often seen during a dive.

11.10 - The Chasms

Latitude (1)	53° 14.645'N	Longitude (1)	004° 36.320'W
Latitude (2)	53° 14.625'N	Longitude (2)	004° 36.430'W
Position Fix	Differential-GPS	Datum	WGS84

The 'Chasms'

The Chasms are two deep gashes in the cliffs and hillside. The seabed drops off to around 12 metres in an area that is sheltered from the main current to give pleasant diving in a series of gullies and sandy patches. Look out for the shoals of small squid or cuttlefish that occasionally congregate here, as well as plenty of other marine-life.

Cuttlefish

11.11 - Maen-y-Fran and Maen-y-Sais

Latitude (Fran)	53° 14.590'N	Longitude	004° 36.680'W
Latitude (Sais)	53° 14.550'N	Longitude	004° 36.700'W
Position Fix	Differential-GPS	Datum	WGS84

Maen-y-Fran (Frenchman's Rock) is an isolated rocky islet that lies about 150 metres off the Rhoscolyn cliffs, approximately half a mile north-west of the Seagull Islands and Rhoscolyn Beacon. Maen-y-Sais (Englishman's Rock) is a smaller isolated outcrop, located about 100 metres further offshore than Maen-y-Fran, with a submerged ridge connecting these two rocks. Note that there are discrepancies between how these rocks are known locally and how they are marked on the Ordnance Survey map. Local information has been used in this instance.

Strong currents flow past these rocks on the flood-tide, but it is possible to dive in their shelter at this time or enjoy a long drift-dive. However, once the tide starts to ebb, there is a long period of slack-water.

The seaward side of Maen-y-Sais drops off almost vertically to a depth of about 15 metres and is surrounded by large boulders. To the east, a large cleft exists between Maen-y-Sais and a massive boulder. A large iron hatch-cover at the base of this rock may be part of the wreck of the sailing ship 'Southern Cross'. This Liverpool-registered vessel ran on to Maen-y-Sais on 15th March 1855, and became a total loss. Near the hatch, another piece of wreckage may be the remains of a badly corroded anchor. As mentioned above, a submerged ridge runs from Maen-y-Fran to Maen-y-Sais where a large hollow has been formed between several massive boulders. This hollow is littered with debris, mainly iron bars and plates.

Around the two rocks, the seabed flattens off at about 16 metres, but away from both Maen-y-Fran and Maen-y-Sais there are many boulders and gullies.

A finely-built ship of 509 tons register, 13 years, A1, called the 'Southern Cross', commanded by Captain Moorson, which was launched at Teignmouth about a month ago and had been just a week afloat on her way to Liverpool to be coppered, with a ballast of pipe clay, struck on the rocks off Rhoscolyn between 9 and 10 o'clock on the night of Thursday 15th instant. The weather was very thick and blowing a fresh gale. Soon after she struck, the ship sank and disappeared but the crew consisting of 19 seamen had succeeded to get on the rocks where they remained until about 8 o'clock the following morning in a most pitiful condition, lashed by the waves of a tempestuous sea during an unusually stormy and dark night. They desperately clung onto the rocks and with one exception were able to keep in that perilous position until observed by the inhabitants. She is totally lost and nothing of her remains to be seen.

Carnarvon and Denbigh Herald, 24th March 1855

11.12 - The Old Bridge and Thistle Rocks

Latitude (Old Bridge)	53° 14.660'N	Longitude	004° 36.800'W
Latitude (Thistle Rocks)	53° 14.760'N	Longitude	004° 36.900'W
Position Fix	Differential-GPS	Datum	WGS84

The Old Bridge and Thistle Rocks are two rocky ridges that lie close inshore to the north-west of Rhoscolyn Beacon, Maen-y-Fran and Maen-y-Sais. These are scenic dives in 5 to 15 metres of water, but odd pieces of wreckage have been reported. Strong currents will be encountered on the flood tide, but the rocks do afford some shelter in their lee. However, the ebb-tide tends to run further offshore, so this area is best dived after local high-water.

11.13 - Cave near Rhoscolyn Head

Latitude	53° 14.875'N	Longitude	004° 36.850'W
Position Fix	Differential - GPS	Datum	WGS84

Rhoscolyn Head   Cathedral cave

Known as 'Bangor Cathedral' or 'Cathedral Cave', this makes an interesting but shallow dive-site. Although sheltered from the current, the seabed may be swept clean or, on other occasions, it can be quite silty. The cave goes back about 30 metres into the cliff, narrowing gradually until it becomes impassable. It is possible to surface within the cave and look backwards towards the entrance, but note that canoeists often venture well inside it. Look upwards, in case you surface under a canoe, as I have done. You may also see rock-climbers, abseiling down from the cliffs above.

The seabed outside the cave drops off to about 10 metres and is littered with many large boulders which have fallen from the cliffs. Ballan wrasse, cuckoo wrasse and pollack inhabit the secluded areas under and between these rocks.

11.14 - Rhoscolyn Head

Latitude	53° 14.915'N	Longitude	004° 36.890'W
Position Fix	Differential - GPS	Datum	WGS84

Lying adjacent to 'Cathedral Cave', this headland has quite strong currents, yet at times it may be quite silty close to the rocks. Depths are around 15 metres, where there are large boulders, many of which are covered in bright-yellow boring-sponges.

11.15 - Careg Hen

Latitude	53° 13.980'N	Longitude	004° 41.100'W
Position Fix	Differential - GPS	Datum	WGS84

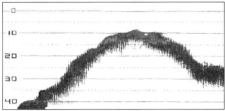

Careg Hen echo-sounder trace. (metres)

Careg Hen (Old Rock) is an isolated, underwater reef nearly 3 miles west of Rhoscolyn Beacon and 3.5 miles south-west of Trearddur Bay slipway. Charted as R 5.6, the reef is very exposed to weather and tide and is usually marked by lobster-pots, whirlpools and overfalls. An Admiralty survey has described it as covering an area about 300 metres by 100 metres, and having four patches under 10 metres at chart datum. The position given is for the shallowest part of the reef, although there is quite a large area which can be covered without going particularly deep. Diving at low-water neap-tide, the shallowest depth recorded was 8 metres, although Careg Hen is surrounded by deep water with a charted depth of 39 metres immediately north-west of the rock.

The rock has many vertical or steeply sloping faces, with the top few metres covered in red seaweeds. Below about ten metres, the rock is covered in white and yellow sagartia elegans anemones. A large shoal of pollack shelters from the current, while large wrasse swim along the vertical cliffs. Large dogfish can be seen, with one having claimed a small hollow in the top of the reef as its home, sharing it with several tom-pot blennies.

Timing: A very good diving site, this is for experienced divers and competent boat handlers – mainly because of the strong currents. It should be dived only at slack-water on a neap-tide. Slack-water is about 1.5 to 2 hours before low-water Liverpool, but dives should start well before this if two waves of divers are to be catered for. On one occasion when diving here at low-water on a neap-tide, by one hour before low-water at Liverpool the current had already turned and started to run towards the north. By low-water Liverpool, the current was extremely strong, although we did find shelter from the current in the lee of the rock at a depth of about 15 metres. Emerging from the protection of the rock, we had to cling on tightly in order to avoid being carried away by the tide. In similar circumstances, delayed SMBs should be deployed as divers may be swept away before surfacing some distance away from the actual dive-site.

Dogfish

11.16 - Maen Piscar and the wreck of the 'Havso'

Name	Havso	Type	Steamer
Date Lost	21/7/1937	Location	Maen Piscar
Cause	Hit rock	How Lost	Foundered
Hull	Steel	Weight	1,843 tons (gross)
Cargo	Scrap Iron	Access	Boat only
Latitude	53° 15.195'N	Longitude	004° 37.985'W
Position Fix	Differential-GPS	Datum	WGS84
Seabed	0 to 25 metres	Wreck Height	1 metre
Charted as	Uncharted wreck	Maen Piscar is a drying rock	
Slipway (1)	Trearddur Bay	Distance	1.5 miles
Slipway (2)	Rhosneigr	Distance	4 miles
Tidal Data	As Carreg Hen		

Steamer on the rocks - Vessel sinks at Trearddur Bay. Crew of Norwegians saved. There was some excitement in Trearddur Bay in the early hours of Wednesday morning when the S.S. Havso struck on the rocks near Ravens Point. She was carrying a cargo of scrap iron from Virginia to Birkenhead. Within 15 minutes of striking the rocks she capsized and sank. She carried a crew of 16 foreigners, all of whom were saved. The crew came ashore in the steamer's lifeboats and were fed at the home of Colonel Walker. Captain Brunn said there was a gale blowing, it was raining heavily, and very hazy, rendering visibility very poor. A cat, belonging to a member of the crew, went down with the ship.

When the radio call was received by Seaforth wireless station, a steamer and tug dashed at full speed to the rescue, but long before they arrived, the ill-fated vessel had disappeared. As the result of an inspection at dawn yesterday by officials of the Association, the Liverpool Salvage Association have definitely abandoned all hope of salving the Havso.

Holyhead Chronicle, Friday 23rd July 1937

Maen Piscar is another isolated reef lying about three-quarters of a mile offshore and one and a half miles south-south-west of Trearddur Bay slipway. Popular with boat anglers, this rock dries out at low-water on spring-tides to a maximum height of 1.7 metres and can be easily seen from the shore at this time. At low-water on a neap-tide, the rock is awash but can still be located visually by the disturbance of the sea. Alternatively, Maen Piscar can be located by GPS and an echo-sounder at the position given above, but take care to avoid propeller damage unless searching at high-water. The surrounding seabed drops off gradually to sand and stone at around 25 metres.

As with all offshore sites in this area, tidal streams can be extremely strong, so avoid diving here on spring-tides. Slack-water is around one and a half hours before low-water at Liverpool, with overfalls appearing as the current picks up afterwards. Many divers visit the site just for the wreck of the 'Havso', but wreckage from older ships has been reported here and the prolific marine-life on the reef justifies Maen Piscar as a dive-site in its own right.

The 1,843 ton steel steamship 'Havso' was carrying a cargo of scrap iron when it ran on to Maen Piscar during a heavy rainstorm. Despite sinking in only 15 minutes, all aboard were saved with the exception of the ship's cat. Subsequent salvage operations blew the ship apart. The remains of the ship and its cargo now lie mostly to the north and north-west of Maen Piscar, at a depth of about 16 to 18 metres. Very little now stands proud of the seabed, with many of the hull-plates lying totally flattened, but parts of the ship's machinery such as pipe-work and two boilers are still recognisable. Other wreckage such as anchors, lie further south.

The wreck attracts a considerable amount of marine-life, with crabs, lobsters, conger eels, pollack, and wrasse being seen. Because of this, angling boats can usually be seen over the site, making 'A' flags and SMBs essential.

11.17 - Porth-y-Garan Reef

Latitude	53° 15.665'N	Longitude	004° 36.995'W
Position Fix	Differential - GPS	Datum	WGS84

Porth-y-Garan Reef

This dive-site lies tucked away behind a ridge of rocks which, even at high-tide, provides some shelter from onshore winds when all other local sites are exposed to the weather. There are some vertical walls up to 4 metres high, and a small cave at a depth of about 8 metres which has formed underneath a massive boulder. Despite being a rather narrow channel, depths of up to 15 metres will be found, and there can be quite a strong current. Large wrasse, shoals of two-spotted blennies and crevices full of leopard-spotted gobies can be seen.

Take care when approaching the site by boat, as there are several drying rocks and many lobster-pots.

11.18 - Porth-y-Garan

Latitude	53° 15.710'N	Longitude	004° 37.130'W
Position Fix	Differential - GPS	Datum	WGS84

Porth-y-Garan is a rocky inlet which has a narrow entrance but opens up to produce a sheltered mooring area. The seabed inside the mooring area is littered with large lumps of scrap-iron, probably formerly used as mooring weights, but a brief search with an underwater metal detector has also uncovered a brass belt buckle among all the other junk. Several fibreglass sheets are also visible - all that remains of one or more cabin cruisers.

To the south-east of the entrance are several isolated rocks, all surrounded by thick kelp and the odd area of clear sand. Large shoals of sand-eels can be seen, with predatory pollack lurking among the kelp. A rocky islet protects large parts of the bay from onshore winds, so the bay may be used for shallow training dives when south-westerly winds are blowing. But watch out for boat traffic, as Porth-y-Garan is used as a small harbour.

11.19 - Porth-y-Garan West Point

Latitude	53° 15.710'N	Longitude	004° 37.150'W
Position Fix	Differential - GPS	Datum	WGS84

The cliffs west of Porth-y-Garan provide an easy dive-site, sheltered from northerly or easterly winds. The few areas which are out of the current are very silty, but most of the seabed is swept clean, with dead-men's fingers and yellow boring-sponges attached to many of the rocks. The remains of a modern fibre-glass boat lie scattered about the area, in 10 to 15 metres of water, but older wreckage has also been seen nearby. There are several narrow gullies here, one being about 1 metre wide and 3 metres deep. A large lobster sits at the bottom of this gully in the full knowledge that it is totally inaccessible to any diver without an extremely long crab-hook!

If you are using a Surface Marker Buoy, look out for the overhanging cliffs that tend to snag the line.

11.20 - Wreck of 'Hermine'

Name	Hermine	Type	Sailing vessel
Date Lost	16/6/1890	Location	West of Porth-y-Garan
Cause	Thick fog	How Lost	Ran ashore
Hull	Iron	Weight	538 tons (gross)
Cargo	Sugar	Access	Boat only
Latitude	53° 15.760'N	Longitude	004°37.270'W
Position Fix	Differential-GPS	Datum	WGS84
Seabed	5 to 16 metres	Wreck Height	2 metres maximum
Charted as	Uncharted		
Slipway (1)	Trearddur Bay	Distance	1 mile
Tidal Data	Away from the cliffs, currents can be strong		

The Liverpool-owned iron barque, 'Hermine', ran ashore between Porth-y-Garan and Raven's Point in June 1890, when all the crew were rescued by a breeches-buoy system. Lying against the cliffs a mile south of Trearddur Bay slipway, this wreck is a very popular dive-site, being

Tunnel | Life-belt above wreck site

Site of tunnel leading to wreck (at low-water)

Hermine wreck site

suitable for novice and experienced divers alike. The cargo of Peruvian sugar has long gone, but the wreck lies spread over a large area. This consists of iron plates, pipes, ribs, bitts, tubular iron masts, lengths of chain and halliard winches. Now well smashed up, the remains lie close to the shore in 10 to 16 metres of water. At the deepest part of the wreck lie some wooden planks. There has been speculation that they could be from an earlier wreck lying underneath the 'Hermine', although they could simply be decking planks from the 'Hermine'. Immediately to the west of the wreck is a 20-metre long underwater tunnel that has been formed by a boulder resting between the cliffs and an off-lying reef. (See photo above) Dangerous only if there is a severe underwater swell, this passageway emerges in an underwater gully that leads directly on to the wreck. Although there is always sufficient light in the tunnel, it is worth taking a torch to shine on the rocky walls and illuminate the anemones. As you emerge on to the site of the wreck, there are several overhangs, vertical cliffs and other gullies.

Wrecks always attract marine-life, so on a single dive expect to see octopus, conger, wrasse, leopard-spotted gobies, starfish, squat-lobsters, hermit crabs and much more. Many parts of the wreck are completely covered in small mussels. There are many lobster-pots around the wreck, and although lobsters and edible-crabs are often seen on it, few are large enough to be taken legally. Several lobster-pots have lost their buoys, so you may encounter loose lengths of rope.

Strong currents will be found on the flood-tide, so delayed SMBs are strongly recommended. Note that the site is very popular with shore-anglers, so it is often strewn with lost fishing line, hooks and weights.

Directions: Leaving Trearddur Bay by boat, bear left, passing Raven's Point (the first headland) and the next bay with the caravan site and slipway. The 'Hermine' is located close inshore against the rocks on the next headland, almost directly underneath the lifebelt mounted on top of the cliff.

The barque 'Hermione' (537 tons) of Liverpool, Captain Sparks, owned by J S Fletcher and company, Liverpool, went ashore near Holyhead on Monday. When she grounded the wind was blowing from the southward, a very thick fog prevailing. She was an iron vessel and was laden with a cargo of sugar from Peru to Liverpool. She carried a crew of 13 hands all told. Everything went well until Sunday when the Tuskar was sighted, after which it became a dense fog and shore objects could not be discerned. It was between 9 and 10 on Monday morning that the master found himself within a short distance of a most dangerous coast of Anglesey, viz, near Towyn Capel. He immediately endeavoured to tack, but the vessel would not do so. He therefore hove to, and in doing so the vessel got stern onto a rock where she stuck. In about half an hour's time there appeared a danger of her heeling over and it was evident that her hold was filling with water. The captain and crew has scarcely considered the position when the vessel heeled over on her beam end and the men with great difficulty clung to the side of the vessel. There are on this coast always ready and willing hands, prepared to assist those in distress and on this occasion a group of the noted Rhoscolyn men who have so often distinguished themselves were on the cliff to render assistance.

Immediately on the crew landing, the vessel foundered. Little or nothing was saved by the crew and the cargo, it is said, will be worthless. It is doubtful whether the barque will ever be raised from her sunken position, because if a heavy sea prevails she must be dashed to pieces.

Carnarvon and Denbigh Herald, 20th June, 1890

11.21 - Raven's Point & Gully

Latitude	53° 16.120'N	Longitude	004° 37.515'W
Position Fix	Differential - GPS	Datum	WGS84

For details of this dive, see the previous section regarding shore dives from Raven's Point Road. The site gives a nice, easy dive in depths of 5 to 18 metres, and is not far from Trearddur Bay slipway. Note that the cliffs are popular with anglers. Access is much easier by boat than by clambering over the rocks, and boat cover gives a greater safety margin if there is a strong current.

Directions: As you leave Trearddur Bay by boat, keep to the left of the bay, passing the old lifeboat station and 'Diving Services Anglesey'. Raven's Point is the first headland, underneath the housing estate.

A 'Bloody Henry' starfish

Hermit crab

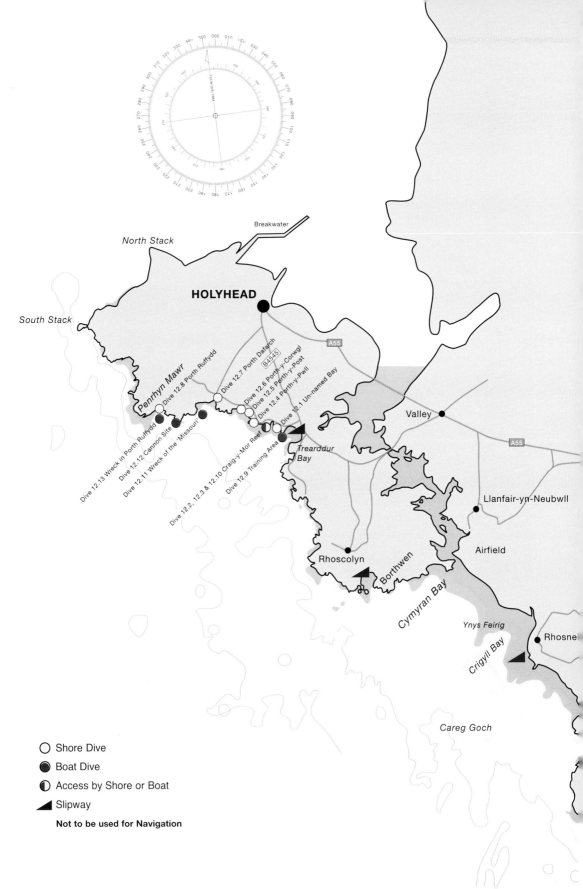

Breakwater

North Stack

HOLYHEAD

South Stack

A55

B4545

Penrhyn Mawr

Dive 12.8 Porth Ruffydd
Dive 12.7 Porth Dafarch
Dive 12.6 Porth-y-Corwgl
Dive 12.5 Porth-y-Post
Dive 12.4 Porth-y-Pwll
Dive 12.1 Un-named Bay

Dive 12.13 Wreck in Porth Ruffydd
Dive 12.12 Cannon Site
Dive 12.11 Wreck of the 'Missouri'
Dive 12.2, 12.3 & 12.10 Craig-y-Mor Reef
Dive 12.9 Training Area

Trearddur
Bay

Valley

A55

Rhoscolyn

Borthwen

Llanfair-yn-Neubwll

Airfield

Cymyran Bay

Ynys Feirig

Rhosne

Crigyll Bay

Careg Goch

○ Shore Dive

● Boat Dive

◑ Access by Shore or Boat

◀ Slipway

Not to be used for Navigation

CHAPTER TWELVE

Trearddur Bay to Porth Ruffydd

Holyhead – Shipwreck. On the morning of Friday 2nd instant, about 3 o'clock, the John Bannerman of St. Johns N.B. struck on shore near Porth-y-Post, Penrhos Feilw, about 2 miles from this town. She was a fine vessel of 1,139 tons register, bound from New Orleans for Liverpool with a valuable cargo of cotton. The commander, Captain Robertson, with most of the crew (of whom there were 26 in all) got ashore at Holyhead about 11.30 am the same morning and saved their clothes. The mate, with 5 hands, took to the jolly-boat and have not since been heard of. During the night, the vessel became much damaged and about 8 on Saturday morning broke up and has since become a total wreck. Her cargo and pieces of the vessel being strewn about the shore in every direction. Most of the cotton will be saved in a damaged state, the cargo consisting of 3,500 bales.

Carnarvon and Denbigh Herald, 10th March, 1855

General Description

The coastline in this area is also mainly rocky, but there are popular beaches at Trearddur Bay and Porth Dafarch. This is probably the busiest sea diving area in North Wales because of the relatively easy access, good facilities and excellent diving services.

Essential Information:-

- The main launching site for this area is at Trearddur Bay, but this slipway becomes very congested on a nice summer's day.
- There are many shore-diving opportunities between Trearddur Bay and Porth Dafarch.
- There are strong currents along this coast.
- Charts required – 'Caernarvon Bay' (Number 1970) and 'Approaches to Holyhead' (Number 1413).
- Maps – Ordnance Survey Explorer map number 262 (Anglesey West).

Shore Dives or Snorkelling Sites

Trearddur Bay

The main beach at Trearddur Bay is shallow and sandy and has considerable boat traffic, so do not dive in this area. There are shops, a petrol station, a chandler, cafes, newsagents and grocers. Toilets and a large pay-and-display car park (at 53° 16.700' N 004° 36.930' W / SH 256E 790N) can be found near the Sea Shanty Café and the Spar shop.

Shore dives from Lon Isallt, between Trearddur Bay and Porth Dafarch.

Lon Isallt is the narrow, twisty coast road between Trearddur Bay and Porth Dafarch which gives easy access to several small, shallow bays, rocky reefs and small islands.

Directions to Lon Isallt: Cross Anglesey on the new A55 dual carriageway, turning sharp left at the roundabout in Holyhead. After about a mile, pass the Trearddur sign. Half a mile further on, turn right at the bottom of the hill, opposite the garage. This road is Lon Isallt (Cliff Lane).

12.1 - Un-named Rocky Bay

Latitude	53° 16.820'N	Longitude	004° 37.485'W
O.S. Reference	SH	250E	792N

This site is suitable for shallow training dives or snorkelling but, as the rocks are close to the slipway, it is important to keep well within the bay and clear of any boat traffic. Trearddur Bay is very popular with jet-skis, dive boats and angling boats. Being only 30 metres from the car park, this is probably the easiest access around here, but should only be dived at high-water. As the tide falls, there are sharp, slippery rocks to contend with.

Directions. See directions above to Lon Isallt. Pass the lifeboat station, the slipway and the Trearddur Bay Hotel, then turn into the public car park on the right. Leave the vehicle at the far end of the carpark, kit up and cross the road.

12.2 - Craig-y-Mor Reef - Off the 'Haunted House'

Latitude	53° 16.850'N	Longitude	004° 37.875'W
O.S. Reference	SH	246E	793N

Access to this reef is from a small road close to 'Craig-y-Mor' house, an easily recognised and rather sombre-looking building of dark stone with red drainpipes, long known to divers as the 'Haunted House'. The GPS position given is for the parking area by an old winch on the shore, but be aware of the rocks which block vehicle access.

Craig-y-Mor reef is a string of islets about 200 metres offshore, which run almost parallel to the coast to form a sheltered lagoon used for boat moorings. Note that strong currents may be found on the outer edge of the reef and in the channels between the islets, especially after local high-water. In the summer months, there may be more than two dozen boats moored here, so divers need to take care to avoid boat traffic. The lagoon is only a few metres deep with a flat, sandy seabed. It is most useful as a training area, but also provides an interesting dive-site as old anchors, lost lobster-pots and even a brass belaying-pin have been found here.

The eastern island is easily explored and circumnavigated in a single dive, but can be rather silty. Immediately around the island, the seabed is covered in thick kelp, but it is worth exploring the many small caves and hollows formed either by erosion or by the numerous piles of large rocks. Further offshore, depths are around 10 to 15 metres with a seabed of sand, gravel and rock. The only wreckage to be found here appears to be the scattered remains of a modern, fibreglass boat.

Other rocky islands extend for about 300 metres to the west, with several reefs appearing above water only as the tide falls. This area appears to have suffered several shipwrecks over the years, but fierce waves have dispersed the remains over a large area. Underwater metal detectors give many positive contacts. Several iron plates and what appear to be iron ballast-weights have been found here. The western-most point of the reef may be the site of an old wooden sailing vessel, but the timbers are well buried in the sand. They were located by an underwater metal detector responding to copper nails and rivets firmly embedded in the wood. Other divers have reported further wreckage. One found an upturned iron hull, while another discovered what he described as the remains of a steam yacht.

Broken pottery, with the word 'Marine' and a picture of an anchor, has been found off the reef. Similar, but complete, pottery has been recovered from a wreck in Liverpool Bay. This was made by Minton around 1910, but further research would be needed to date the wreck or wrecks at Trearddur Bay. Octopus, cuttlefish, sand-eels, conger, wrasse and pollack are usually encountered, while a rarely seen triggerfish was reported here in the summer of 2002.

Directions: From the A55, follow the directions for Lon Isallt. As you pass the Lifeboat Station, zero your mileage trip-meter. At 0.4 miles from the Lifeboat Station, turn left on to a narrow track that will take you past the distinctive 'Craig-y-Mor' house. If you pass the 'Cliff Hotel' on the main road, you have missed the turning for the track. Limited parking is on the left of the track, just after the house.

12.3 - Craig-y-Mor Reef - Alternative access

Latitude	53° 16.860'N	Longitude	004° 38.030'W
O.S. Reference	SH	244E	793N

Parking by Craig-y-Mor house is very limited, so this parking spot is given for alternative access to 'Craig-y-Mor reef' (described in dive number 12-2). Once again, parking is limited, but this time your car can be left alongside the main road. Access to the sea involves a slight scramble down the bank to a shingle and rock bay. Preferably dive here at local high-water, about one and a half hours before Liverpool, as access is difficult at all other states of the tide.

Directions: From the A55, follow the directions for Lon Isallt. As you pass the Lifeboat Station, zero your mileage trip-meter, then pull in to the left on a small piece of rough ground, 0.6 miles from the Lifeboat Station.

12.4 - Porth-y-Pwll

Latitude	53° 16.925'N	Longitude	004° 38.105'W
O.S. Reference	SH	243E	794N

This is another site with easy access, suitable for training or for a night dive, but again this is best dived only at high-water. Avoid this site in a south-westerly wind. Close inshore, there is sand and shingle, with a rocky reef along the left side of the bay and a large drying rock at the mouth of the bay.

Directions: From the A55, follow the directions for Lon Isallt. As you pass the Lifeboat Station, zero your mileage trip-meter, then pull in to the left on a small piece of rough ground, 0.7 miles from the Lifeboat Station. Park by the wall, almost opposite the private road to 'Bay View'. Steps lead from the road down to the beach.

12.5 - Porth-y-Post

Latitude	53° 17.065'N	Longitude	004° 38.210'W
O.S. Reference	SH	242E	797N

Porth-y-Post has parking for 3 or 4 cars, with easy access to a rock, sand and shingle beach. An old wooden wreck will be found partially buried in the sand, in only two or three metres of water at low-tide (at 53° 17.015'N 004° 38.335'W / SH 241E 796N). This wreck comprises several large baulks of timber and lies broadside on to the beach, towards the left-hand side of the bay where it occasionally dries out at low-water on spring-tides. It may be what remains of the American ship 'John Bannerman', which Lloyd's List reported as being ashore and bilged on March 2nd 1855, while carrying a cargo of cotton. Other reports say this vessel was lost further north, or that it was repaired and refloated. However, a later Lloyds report said the 'John Bannerman' had broken up and that people were being employed to collect the cotton. See the quotation from the local newspaper at the beginning of this chapter.

Away from the wreck, the bay is shallow and sandy with two small reefs, making the site suitable for snorkelling, training or a night dive. In the summer, you will see shoals of sand-eels as well as weever fish, lying partially buried in the sand with only their eyes and poisonous fins showing.

Porth-y-Post is south-west facing, so the under-water visibility quickly suffers from the onset of onshore winds.

Directions: From the A55, follow the directions for Lon Isallt. As you pass the Lifeboat Station, zero your mileage trip-meter, then pull in to the right, 0.9 miles from the Lifeboat Station. The beach is immediately adjacent to the road.

12.6 - Porth-y-Corwgl, near Porth Dafarch

Latitude	53° 17.100'N	Longitude	004° 38.400'W
O.S. Reference	SH	240E	798N

Porth-y-Corwgl (Coracle Bay) is another shallow, sandy dive-site suitable for training or snorkelling. Access is easier at high-water, when there is about 8 metres of water against the rocks on either side of the bay. There is a shallow, kelp-covered reef further out.

Directions: Park at Porth-y-Post (see the previous site – 12.5) and carry your diving equipment for a further 150 metres along the road towards Porth Dafarch. Just after the 'Henoed / Elderly

People' sign, there is a narrow footpath (at 53° 17.135'N 004° 38.300'W / SH 241E 798N) leading to the beach, 100 metres away. Note that there is another bay with the same name at Rhoscolyn.

12.7 - Porth Dafarch

Latitude	53° 17.255'N	Longitude	004° 39.020'W
O.S. Reference	SH	233E	801N

Porth Dafarch is a pleasant, south-westerly facing, sandy bay, bordered by high, jagged cliffs. Although long known to divers as 'Bog Bay', the water quality is good, with regular monitoring carried out. There are ice cream vans, toilet facilities, limited car parking and a narrow slipway. Access for boats is normally blocked by padlocked bollards, so only lightweight inflatables can be launched here. During the summer months, surfers, windsurfers, speedboats and water-skiers use the bay, so take great care when diving here, and always use SMBs. However, the site provides a shallow shore dive with very easy entry and exit in a relatively confined area with lots of marine-life. All these features combine to give a site ideal for training, or for anyone with a young family who needs a dive-site next to a safe, sandy beach.

At high-water, a long swim is necessary to clear the flat sand, but at low-water there is a long walk to the tide-line where, out in the bay, maximum depths will be only around 6 to 8 metres. Access from the sandy bay to the open sea is via a relatively narrow channel where the rocks are usually occupied by anglers, so watch out for their lines or lost fishing tackle. This channel is shallow and out of the main current, so night dives can be enjoyed here - especially if combined with a barbecue.

From 1819 to 1820, Porth Dafarch was used as an alternative harbour for the mail packet crossing to Dublin, should the wind be blowing directly into Holyhead Harbour. The old stone-built structure to the right was erected for this purpose. Old telegraph cables run down the middle of the bay but these are sometimes buried under the sand. More modern optic-fibre telecommunications cables may also be seen. You may also find the remains of what appears to be a riveted, iron-hulled vessel with large 'U'-shaped girders, though these are often hidden under the sandy seabed. During one mid-winter dive, a small marine boiler, about the size of a small car, was seen mostly buried in the sand after swimming out of the bay to the left. Is this an auxiliary boiler from the wreck of the 'Missouri' further offshore, or is there is a second wreck closer inshore?

Pollack, wrasse, blennies and gobies will be seen, while large numbers of sand-eels lie buried in the sandy seabed, darting out of their hiding places when disturbed. This is especially noticeable during a night-dive, when the rocky areas become alive with free-swimming lobsters and conger-eels.

Underwater visibility can be extremely good, but quickly deteriorates in a south-westerly wind when there can be heavy surf in the bay.

Directions: Take the A55 across Anglesey to the roundabout at Holyhead. Turn sharp left, then immediately right by the 'Foresters Arms' into Porth Dafarch Road. Turn left at the 'T' junction and Porth Dafarch is immediately on your right. Alternatively, follow Lon Isallt from Trearddur Bay, and Porth Dafarch is 1.5 miles from the Lifeboat Station.

12.8 - Porth Ruffydd

Latitude	53° 17.145′N	Longitude	004° 40.540′W
O.S. Reference	SH	216E	799N

It is possible to dive from the shore at Porth Ruffydd, but the entry point is 500 metres from the car park and the return journey is uphill and tiring, and especially difficult in wet weather. Depths within the bay are fairly shallow, so a single 10-litre cylinder is perfectly adequate. This site should be shore-dived only at local high-water, about one and a half hours before high-water at Liverpool, as access is difficult at other times. Divers should not venture too far out to sea as there can be fierce currents outside the bay. For further information, see the Porth Ruffydd boat-dive, further on in this chapter.

A lifeboat station was established at Porth Ruffydd in 1891, but was closed in 1904. The old lifeboat building was demolished in March 1997, and only the foundations now remain.

Directions: Take the A55 across Anglesey to the roundabout at Holyhead. Turn left, then immediately right by the 'Foresters Arms' into Porth Dafarch Road. Turn right at the 'T' junction and follow this road. Pass the old Penrhos Feilw chapel and a large white house called Glan Gors Coch Isaf. Turn left into a narrow dead-end road (at 53° 17.560N 004°40.490′W / SH 217E 807N) to the car park (at 53° 17.370′N 004°40.660′W / SH 215E 804N). Follow the left-hand path for 500 metres down to the concrete steps at Porth Ruffydd. These steps lead down to a narrow, shingle beach, with access to the open sea via a narrow gully.

Alternatively, from Trearddur Bay, take Lon Isallt (the coast road) and zero your mileage trip-meter as you pass the Lifeboat Station. Pass Porth-y-Post, Porth Dafarch, the old Penrhos Feilw chapel and a large white house called Glan Gors Coch Isaf. After 2.8 miles from the Lifeboat Station, turn left into a narrow dead-end road (at 53° 17.560N 004°40.490′W / SH 217E 807N) to the car park (at 53° 17.370′N 004°40.660′W / SH 215E 804N). Follow the left-hand path for 500 metres down to the concrete steps at Porth Ruffydd. These steps lead down to a narrow, shingle beach with access to the open sea via a narrow gully.

Boat Dives - Where to Dive

12.9 - Training area, south of Cod Rocks

Latitude	53° 16.670'N	Longitude	004° 37.490'W
Position Fix	Differential - GPS	Datum	WGS84

This sheltered area is often used for boat-based training-drills such as navigation or rescue skills. Lying out of the current and the boat traffic into Trearddur Bay slipway, the seabed is mostly flat sand.

12.10 - West Point of Craig-y-Mor Reef

Latitude	53° 16.660'N	Longitude	004° 38.140'W
Position Fix	Differential - GPS	Datum	WGS84

For details of this dive, see shore-dive 12.2 from Lon Isallt road, but using a boat is much easier as it saves the long swim home. The site offers an easy dive in depths of up to around 15 metres, and is not far from Trearddur Bay slipway.

The remains of several ships lie scattered around this reef, details having been given in the shore-diving section.

Directions: Heading out of Trearddur Bay, turn right (westwards) and follow the coastline for about half a mile. Craig-y-Mor Reef is the series of rocky islets located off the prominent 'Haunted House', but be aware that several smaller rocks lie underwater at high-tide.

Diving on the 'Missouri' (see opposite)

12.11 - Wreck of the 'Missouri'

Name	Missouri	Type	Barque-rigged steamer
Date Lost	1/3/1886	Location	Porth Dafarch
Cause	Snowstorm	How Lost	Ran ashore
Hull	Iron	Weight	5,146 tons (gross)
Cargo	Cattle, general cargo	Access	Boat
Lat. (Bow)	53° 17.035'N	Long. (Bow)	004° 39.420'W
Lat. (Mid)	53° 17.020'N	Long. (Mid)	004° 39.455'W
Lat (Stern)	53° 17.040'N	Long. (Stern)	004° 39.540'W
Position Fix	Differential-GPS	Datum	WGS84
Seabed	14 metres	Wreck Height	1 to 3 metres
Charted as	# (Bow section)		
Slipway (1)	Trearddur Bay	Distance	1.5 miles
Tidal Data	Little current except on spring-tides		

Wreck of the Missouri.
Photo: Gwynedd Archive Services

The largest vessel ever wrecked close inshore on the west coast of Anglesey was the 5,146 gross-ton 'Missouri', which ran ashore at Porth Dafarch on March 1st 1886, while carrying a mixed cargo of cattle, hides, palm-oil, 3,000 bales of cotton and 4,000 sacks of flour. A heavy snowstorm had reduced the surface visibility, causing navigation problems. The 'Missouri' was a large, iron screw-steamer but had four masts to provide sail assistance or for use in an emergency. It was a fairly new vessel, having been built only five years earlier by G. Connell of Glasgow. The salvage vessel 'Hyena' was sent to help recover the cargo, but a heavy ground-swell prevented diving operations. By March 12th, the 'Missouri' had fallen over on to her starboard side, and the masts were almost parallel to the surface of the sea. Hatches were cut into the sides of the vessel to allow access to the cargo holds.

This is now probably the most visited wreck along the whole west coast of Anglesey. The vessel was about 130 metres long and is best treated as two different dive-sites. The forward section will be found in the middle of Porth Dafarch bay, with the stern against the rocky cliffs to the west. Until fairly recently, much of the 'Missouri' was covered in sand, but in recent years much more wreckage has been exposed. Located in a shallow, south-westerly facing sandy bay, the underwater visibility varies considerably depending on the prevailing wind direction and strength.

Transit A

Dip in skyline

Toilet Block
just visible

Water pipe

Missouri forward section

The most prominent feature of the wreck is the forward section, lying in 10 to 12 metres of water, just over a quarter of a mile off the middle of Porth Dafarch beach. This part is often buoyed, courtesy of 'Anglesey Divers', making location much easier, but if the buoy is missing, the wreck does give a small indication on the echo-sounder. See diagram.

Many pieces of iron plate, ribs, and girders lie on a flat, sandy seabed, but there are many rocks and boulders all around the wreck. Five massive boilers and a smaller one will be seen, along with several upright pairs of mooring-bitts. Large areas of wooden planking will be seen if a thin layer of sand is washed away. The actual bow is easily recognisable, still standing almost upright and nearly 3 metres proud of the seabed. The other main features of the 'Missouri' are the many sections of tubular iron masts and spars which

remain here. Take a good torch to examine the various nooks and crannies for small lobsters, crabs, wrasse, pollack, sea-scorpions, octopus and two-spotted gobies. Shoals of sand-eels congregate around the security of the boilers, while large plaice have been spotted (pardon the pun) on the sandy areas amongst the debris.

Currents are generally weak, although there will be some movement on a spring-tide.

Transit B

Right hand edge of middle house
lines up with small drop

Location: Launch at Trearddur Bay and motor westwards for just over a mile until you can see the sandy beach and toilet block at Porth Dafarch. If the wreck-buoy is missing, start well out to sea and run in on Transit A, with the water-pipe in-line with the left-hand side of the dip on the skyline. In clear weather, use Transit B to the east to judge when to drop the shot-line. Line-up the small vertical drop with the right-hand edge of the middle of the three large, white houses, shown in the photo.

Alternatively, use the GPS co-ordinates for the bow section in conjunction with the echo-sounder. The wreck does give a noticeable trace on the echo-sounder, but use the zoom feature, as the wreck is only 2 or 3 metres high.

Expanded trace

Missouri stern section

This section lies close to the rocks at the western side of the bay and comprises large iron plates and ribs on a rocky seabed. The main identifiable feature is the steering-quadrant, a semi-circular girder with a centre rod which operated the rudder. This stands nearly 3 metres high in a maximum depth of about 12 metres. The curved girder on the steering-quadrant is grooved, with parts of the old steering chains still in their

original place. As the whole assembly stands inclined at about 45 degrees, a diver could easily swim underneath it, so take care in poor visibility if using a surface marker-buoy. The rocks drop off to a sandy seabed at a maximum depth of 14 metres. This area can be a little silty but has a good deal of fish life, mainly wrasse. In the early 1980s, a small brass bell was recovered from this area, possibly from one of the live cattle carried as cargo.

Location: The stern lies close to the cliffs, about half a mile south-west of Porth Dafarch beach. Look for the cave as shown in the photograph. Most of this section lies on a rocky seabed that masks the outline of the wreck, but the steering quadrant does give a small blip on the echo-sounder at the GPS position given for the stern.

12.12 - Cannon Site

Name	Unknown	Type	Sailing vessel
Date Lost	Unknown	Location	West of Porth Dafarch
Cause	Hit rock	How Lost	Ran ashore
Hull	Wood	Weight	Unknown
Cargo	Various	Access	Boat only
Latitude	53° 16.890'N	Longitude	004° 40.095'W
Position Fix	Differential-GPS	Datum	WGS84
Seabed	5 to 17 metres	Wreck Height	0.5 metres
Charted as	Uncharted		
Slipway (1)	Trearddur Bay	Distance	1.5 miles
Tidal Data	Slack at high-water Liverpool		

Narrow gully and drying rock

Wreck site

The badly smashed wreck of a wooden sailing ship lies close inshore on the next headland past Graig Lwyd. The wreck is easily found, since the ship ran straight into a deep cleft in the cliff face with the small cave on the right-hand side. As you approach this cleft, beware of the large rock that dries out as the tide falls. Underwater, there are several narrow gullies, one of which contains a pile of cannon balls and a single, iron cannon. I understand that several other cannon were removed many years ago. Where the gully walls have been worn smooth, many dead-men's fingers cling to the bare rock.

The wreck has been continuously salvaged over many years, but many artefacts remain - especially right against the cliff face, where there are several massive boulders with large baulks of timber solidly jammed underneath. Careful searches have uncovered a great deal of grape shot or musket shot. The cliffs are very popular with shore anglers, who have lost many fishing weights. Some of these are almost identical to musket balls, but are easily identified as they have a small hole drilled

Musket shot

through them. Although the vast majority of the recovered musket balls are spherical, some have been flattened, giving the impression that they have already been fired from a gun. Small lead bars have also been seen, possibly for melting down to make more musket shot.

The site is very exposed to the winter gales, so the amount of visible wreckage varies from year to year. In recent years, a large quantity of shingle has covered the wreck, but this may be swept away in the future to reveal even further wreckage.

12.13 - Wreck in Porth Ruffydd

Name	Unknown	Type	Sailing vessel
Date Lost	Unknown	Location	Porth Ruffydd
Cause	Unknown	How Lost	Ran ashore
Hull	Wood	Weight	Unknown
Cargo	Unknown	Access	Boat only
Latitude	53° 17.020'N	Longitude	004° 40.505'W
Position Fix	Differential-GPS	Datum	WGS84
Seabed	14 metres	Wreck Height	1.5 metres
Charted as	Uncharted		
Slipway (1)	Trearddur Bay	Distance	2 miles
Tidal Data	Little current but note back-eddy		

There is some wreckage at the GPS position given above, located about 100 metres east of the Porth Ruffydd gully and about 100 metres offshore. A large pile of wire-rope, possibly the rigging from a sailing ship, lies on the seabed, along with several bricks and baulks of timber. Muntz-metal sheathing has been found here, dating the wreck from the 1830s onwards, but the presence of wire-rope makes it more likely to be from the late 19th century. The area is very rocky, with a seabed covered in large boulders and small patches of coarse sand. Octopuses are often seen, along with plaice, goldsinnys, cuckoo-wrasse and small lobsters. Close inshore, the rocks are covered in very thick kelp.

As the wreck is close inshore, the currents here are not as fierce as further out, but note that a counter-current forms in the bay on the flood tide. At times, Porth Ruffydd can be very silty, making exploration difficult, so ensure you have a good torch and a buddy-line handy.

Sun star

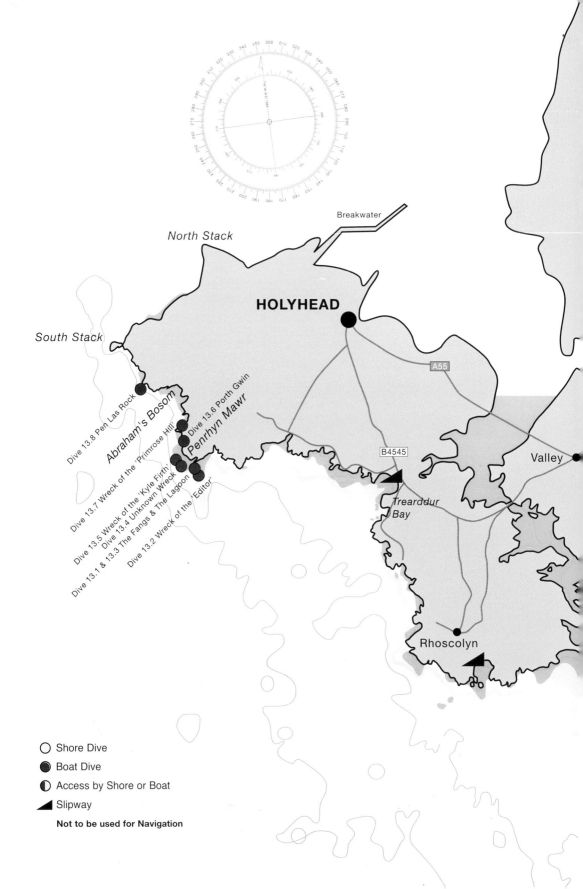

Breakwater

North Stack

South Stack

HOLYHEAD

A55

B4545

Valley

Dive 13.8 Pen Las Rock

Abraham's Bosom

Dive 13.6 Porth Gwin

Penrhyn Mawr

Dive 13.7 Wreck of the 'Primrose Hill'

Dive 13.5 Wreck of the 'Kyle Firth'

Dive 13.4 Unknown Wreck

Dive 13.1 & 13.3 The Fangs & The Lagoon

Dive 13.2 Wreck of the 'Editor'

Trearddur Bay

Rhoscolyn

○ Shore Dive

● Boat Dive

◑ Access by Shore or Boat

◢ Slipway

Not to be used for Navigation

CHAPTER THIRTEEN

The Fangs to South Stack

Wreck and the loss of 10 lives off Holyhead. On Tuesday evening a dense fog prevailed on this coast, and guns were fired incessantly from the South Stack. About seven o' clock in the evening, guns were fired and the lifeboat crew assembled, and in a very short space of time, the boat was in the surging waves, gallantly making in the direction of the ship in distress beyond the South Stack, in the very identical place where the Niagara became a total wreck. The vessel proved to be the Tenby Castle of Liverpool (Captain Davies). After striking on the rocks, the vessel rapidly began to go to pieces, the sea dashing with terrible fury against her. Her boats were soon swamped, and all hope of raising them was despaired of by the ill-fated crew, who, with the officers, clung to the breaking vessel, in the rigging and elsewhere, endeavouring to save themselves. One after another however, was washed away by the relentless sea that broke over them. Their position was becoming more and more desperate, when a boat was seen to approach. It was in charge of Mr William Owen, Holyhead pilot, and managed deftly to get alongside the parting ship, that at imminent peril to himself and the other brave fellows who were with him. On getting on board and shouting for some time, the rescuers were about to conclude that their mission had been in vain, when one man descended from the rigging, speedily followed by two others. Instantly their brave deliverers got them into the boat and after a tough battle with the elements, managed to get out of the rock and surf, and they landed the exhausted mariners on shore. The coastguards described the wreck as one of the most harrowing ever witnessed by them and these brave fellows were almost wild with frenzy when they found they could render no aid to the distressed mariners. Out of fourteen hands, ten perished in the angry billows, whilst another died immediately on landing. Nothing like this has happened for years on this coast.

Holyhead Mail, Thursday 19th December 1889

General Description

This whole area consists of bare rocky islets and jagged, volcanic rocks under steep, rocky cliffs. It is an area of outstanding natural beauty, enhanced by the spectacular sight of South Stack Lighthouse. There are no easy landing places, but the cliffs are a popular venue for rock climbers and bird watchers.

The main diving area is around Tide-rip Rock and the Fangs, which together form a series of small islets and submerged reefs where you'll encounter extremely strong currents, overfalls, whirlpools and undertows. Take extreme care here. The 'Fangs' are a pair of drying rocks, about 100 to 150 metres south of 'Tide-rip Rock', but an underwater reef continues further southwards for some distance. Abraham's Bosom is a wide, rock-fringed bay between the 'Fangs' and the rocky island on which South Stack Lighthouse stands.

Essential Information:-

- There are strong currents and overfalls at the 'Fangs', Penrhyn Mawr, South Stack and North Stack.

- To reach any of these sites from Trearddur Bay, you will need to pass the 'Fangs'.

- The 'Fangs' are appropriately named, so don't get bitten by them! They may appear placid and calm, but be well aware that conditions here can deteriorate rapidly. Always check your tide-tables and the weather forecast.

- To dive here, you need a seaworthy boat, a competent coxswain and observant passengers. The standing waves and overfalls found here have swamped even large RIBS.

- There are drying rocks all around the 'Fangs', along with many other dangerous obstructions close to the cliffs.

- Ferries heading to or from Holyhead create a large wake, which takes some time before it arrives at any of the dive-sites mentioned. A dive-boat anchored close inshore could easily be washed on to the rocks by these waves.

- Helicopters frequently practise their rescue drills here by hovering above the cliffs.

- Charts required – 'Caernarfon Bay' (Number 1970) or 'Approaches to Holyhead' (Number 1413).

- Maps – Ordnance Survey Explorer map number 262 (Anglesey West).

Shore Dives or Snorkelling Sites

There are no easily accessible sites for shore-diving in this area, and nowhere to go ashore easily from a boat.

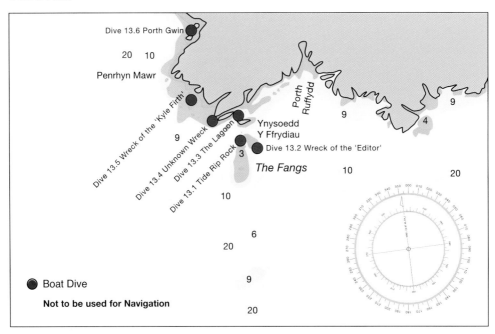

Boat Dives - Where to Dive

13.1 - The Fangs (Ynysoedd Ffridiau) and Tide-Rip Rock

Latitude	53° 16.750'N	Longitude	004° 40.830'W
Position Fix	Differential - GPS	Datum	WGS84

The Fangs at low-water on a spring tide

The 'Fangs' (See photo above) are a pair of drying rocks which lie about 100 metres south of the Tide-Rip Rock. They are totally covered at high-water, but as the tide falls they are often marked by white water and breaking waves. Two other reefs lie even further south, but these do not dry out at low-water. Standing waves and overfalls are created by the north-westerly current on the flood tide, so it is not the place to take an un-seaworthy boat!

Timing: Because of the horrendous currents, this area can be dived only at slack-water on a neap-tide. There is very little slack at low-tide. Arrive on site about half an hour before high-water at Liverpool and wait for the current to ease. The current tends to swirl around before stopping altogether, giving plenty of time for two consecutive waves of divers.

View from the shore on a calm day

View from the shore on a stormy day

191

Wreck of a liner off Holyhead - On Monday morning, shortly after one o'clock, in a dense fog, the Harrison Line, 'Editor', homeward bound to Liverpool with a cargo of sugar and cotton from the Brazilian coast, went ashore at Penrhyn Point. The captain (Captain Waterson) had been on the bridge in consequence of the fog for two days and soundings had been constantly taken. Immediately on striking, the fog lifted and the South Stack Light was observed some short distance away and it was then ascertained for the first time their actual position. She proved to be in precisely the same place as the ill-fated Tenby Castle, the crew of which, without exception, perished. The engines were at once set to work, but the stern going downwards, the engine-rooms soon filled with water and the danger becoming so great the captain decided that the best course would be to endeavour to save their lives, and they took to the four boats. A few articles of clothing were saved, but saturated with water. A monkey and some parrots died on the passage to Holyhead, so intense was the cold. The boats were filling with water, and not withstanding that, the poor sailors were up to their waists in water in a semi-starved condition for want of food and from cold. One of the boats well-nigh foundered and but for the timely appearance of the Number 1 (Cene) lifeboat (coxswain Edward Jones) being towed by Tanrefail's tug, it is feared that the men, six in number, would have perished. The men presented a most pitiful appearance, having left the steamer hurriedly and got wet through on the passage to Holyhead, which occupied four hours. The crew praised the conduct of Captain Waterson and Mr Sargeant, the second officer, and ascribe not to blame them, one of the crew declaring that at the time she went on the rocks, that the fog was as thick as a hedge. The Porth Ruffydd and the Thomas Fielding lifeboats were out. The coastguards proceeded with their rocket apparatus on receiving the news from the mounted messenger who rode into town. Signals of distress were heard about the same time at the South Stack, and the Holyhead coastguard who, in charge of Mr Dawes, soon proceeded to the place, but found the crew had already left by their own boats. It was a welcome sight to see the Holyhead lifeboat in tow of the ' Briton' coming to rescue them. Captain Parry, the hon. agent of the Shipwrecked Mariners Society, took the poor fellows to Mr Turner's establishment and has supplied them with articles of clothing and shoes, and sent them to their homes, mostly in Liverpool. The ship is breaking up rapidly and the 2080 tons of cargo is being scattered with the tide and bales of cotton are floating about in all directions. It is a foregone conclusion that she will never come away, having partly disappeared under water. A message from South Stack on Tuesday stated that the wrecked steamer 'Editor' had slipped off the rocks into deep water, a spar showing indicated the position of the wreck. The Liverpool Salvage Association reports that on Tuesday morning the vessel was entirely submerged. The wind was south-west fresh and still rough. The ship, it is added, may be considered a total loss. A large quantity of cotton has been washed ashore and arrangements are being made for getting it up the cliffs and for collecting the loose.

Carnarvon and Denbigh Herald, 26th March 1897

Inquiry - The jury found that the stranding was caused by steering an improper course and the non-use of the lead after midnight on 21st March. The vessel was not navigated with either a proper or seaman-like care. The loss of the 'Editor' was caused by the wrongful act and default of her master, Mr Henry W. Waterson. The court feels they have no alternative but to suspend the master's certificate for six calendar months.

Carnarvon and Denbigh Herald, 16th April 1897

13.2 - Wreck of the steam-ship 'Editor'

Name	Editor	Type	Screw-steamer
Date Lost	22/3/1897	Location	Tide-rip rocks
Cause	Hit rock	How Lost	Ran ashore
Hull	Steel	Weight	1,701 tons (gross)
Cargo	Cotton & sugar	Access	Boat only
Latitude	53° 16.810'N	Longitude	004° 40.780'W
Position Fix	Differential-GPS	Datum	WGS84
Seabed	16 metres	Wreck Height	3 metres (boiler)
Charted as	Uncharted		
Slipway (1)	Trearddur Bay	Distance	2 miles
Tidal Data	See text		

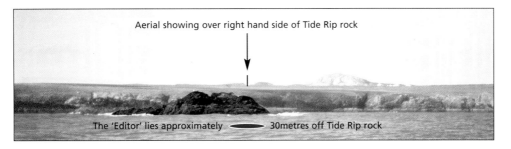

Aerial showing over right hand side of Tide Rip rock

The 'Editor' lies approximately ⬤ 30metres off Tide Rip rock

Carrying a cargo of cotton and sugar from Maceio (Brazil) to Liverpool, the 76 metre-long 'Editor' ran on to the 'Fangs' during bad weather in 1897. The crew escaped from the wreck in their own boats before the ship slipped off the rocks and broke up. Built by M. Pearse & Co. at Stockton-on-Tees in 1885, the vessel was propelled by a 170 nautical horsepower triple-expansion steam engine.

A 3-metre high boiler, believed to be from the 'Editor', still lies on its end in about 16 metres of water, roughly 30 metres south of Tide-rip Rock. The outer plating of the boiler has worn away in places to reveal the internal pipe-work, and, with good underwater visibility, it is possible to see completely through it. Large amounts of hull-plating and iron ribs lie scattered to the south of the boiler, covering the bare, rocky seabed. Tubular iron mast-sections, a winch and lengths of anchor chain litter the site, with at least one large anchor still jammed among the debris. All this wreckage is well broken up and scattered, making identification of the various parts of the ship very difficult. There is virtually no silt around this dive-site, undoubtedly because of the fierce currents that rip over the whole area. Several large boulders lie on top of the wreck, presumably having been flung there by violent underwater surges.

Bright-red sea-scorpions are often found on this wreck, but despite their name, sharp spines and aggressive appearance, they are not poisonous. Goldsinnys, pollack, cuckoo wrasse and conger are also seen here, while lobsters and crabs hide away under the hull sections, out of the current. The seabed and some of the vertical rock walls are partially covered with sargatia elegens anemones and bright-yellow boring-sponges

Timing: Because of the horrendous currents, this site can be dived only at slack-water on a neap-tide. There is very little slack at low-tide. Arrive on site about half an hour before high-water at Liverpool and wait for the current to ease. The current tends to swirl around before stopping altogether, giving plenty of time for two consecutive waves of divers.

13.3 - The Lagoon

Latitude	53° 16.915'N	Longitude	004° 40.870'W
Position Fix	Differential - GPS	Datum	WGS84

As the tide falls, a sheltered lagoon becomes apparent between the coastline and the more northerly edge of Tide-rip Rock. At low-water, depths of around 10 metres are found at the west edge of this lagoon but there are several drying rocks to watch out for. The seabed has many large boulders, cliffs and overhangs, as well as a series of 2 to 3 metre deep gullies, many of which are partially filled with shingle. There is no silt here.

Strong currents run through the lagoon on the flood-tide, so arrive here about half an hour before high-water at Liverpool and wait for the current to stop.

13.4 - Unknown Wreck

Name	Unknown	Type	Sailing vessel
Date Lost	Unknown	Location	Penrhyn Mawr
Cause	Unknown	How Lost	Unknown
Hull	Wood	Weight	Unknown
Cargo	Unknown	Access	Boat
Latitude	53° 16.890'N	Longitude	004° 40.970'W
Position Fix	Differential-GPS	Datum	WGS84
Seabed	8 to 15 metres	Wreck Height	1 metre
Charted as	Uncharted		
Slipway (1)	Trearddur Bay	Distance	2.5 miles
Tidal Data	Sheltered close in. Fast flowing currents further out.		

The coastline immediately west of Tide-Rip Rock and the Fangs provides interesting diving, with little current close inshore but with strong currents further offshore. While the rocks above water are sharp and jagged, those underwater have been worn smooth by winter gales, in effect 'shot-blasting' them. The depth initially drops off rapidly to about 8 metres, with many vertical walls and deep gullies, before gradually deepening to around 15 metres. In places, large boulders lie piled upon one another, creating small tunnels and caverns.

The remains of at least one vessel lie hard against the shore-line. It appears to have been a wooden-hulled, wire-rigged sailing ship, probably lost after the middle of the 19th century. All that are left are several concreted masses of muntz-metal sheathing, lead sheets, copper bars and sheathing-tacks, with a pile of old anchor-chain lying a further 50 metres offshore. A copper-jacketed .303 bullet has been found on this site, but this is probably not associated with the wreck. Identical bullets have been found on another wreck-site several hundred metres away, presumably originating from the old rifle range on the clifftops above Porth Ruffydd. Other items, including golf balls, are regularly found in this area.

The whole area gives very pleasant diving with very little silt, undoubtedly due to the tremendous currents found here. Look out for the large wrasse and pollack that swim over the bare bedrock and boulders.

Location: Having negotiated the Fangs, follow the coastline keeping a close watch for submerged reefs. Look for a prominent, long, narrow gully in the cliffs that runs north-eastwards for about 150 metres. The wreck lies immediately to the east of the gully.

13.5 - Wreck of the 'Kyle Firth'

Name	Kyle Firth	Type	Screw-steamer
Date Lost	13/5/1940	Location	Tide-rip rocks
Cause	Navigation error	How Lost	Ran ashore
Hull	Steel	Weight	450 tons (gross)
Cargo	Stone chippings	Access	Boat only
Latitude	53° 16.950'	Longitude	004° 41.085'
Position Fix	Differential-GPS	Datum	WGS84
Seabed	10 to 12 metres	Wreck Height	2 metres
Charted as	Uncharted		
Slipway (1)	Trearddur Bay	Distance	2 miles
Tidal Data	Within a sheltered bay, out of main current		

'Kyle Firth'   Photo: John Clarkson

For security reasons, the lighthouse at South Stack was extinguished for the duration of the Second World War. Although this removed a navigation point for enemy bombers, it also removed a reference point for British coastal shipping. At 4.38 am on the 13th of May, 1940, a coastal watchman reported that a steamer had run on to the rocks at Penrhos Point. The Holyhead Life-Saving Apparatus Company rushed to the scene and sent a line over to the steamer. The crew initially refused to leave, but by 5.50am the situation had deteriorated and they were taken off by lifeboat. Owing to the age of the vessel, the extent of the damage and the exposed position of the vessel, it was soon declared that there was no hope of salvage. The steamer proved to be the 'Kyle Firth', which had been transporting stone chippings from Porth Nant (near Trefor) to Liverpool.

Scattered wreckage still litters the seabed in a small cove just west of the Fangs. The propeller, thrust-bearing, stern-post and the remains of the rudder will be found on a flat, rock and shingle seabed, at a depth of around 10 metres. Nearby, a large section of iron girders stands about 2 metres high with a small portion of netting wrapped around it. This piece of wreckage has several curved beams and may possibly be the upside-down bed-plate for the single boiler which can still be found slightly further west. Wooden beams and planks will be found in a rocky cleft at around 12 metres, but these did not originate from the Kyle Firth as the embedded copper pins and nails are from a much earlier era. At around 13 metres, one massive rock lies close against an underwater cliff to provide an interesting swim-through. Only attempt this in good visibility.

Location: Having negotiated the Fangs, follow the coastline keeping a close watch for submerged reefs. Look for a prominent, long, narrow gully in the cliffs that runs north-eastwards for about 150 metres. The Kyle Firth lies in the next small bay to the west at the GPS position given. A partially hidden ridge of rocks runs southwards from the west side of this bay to create a nasty hazard for the unwary cox'n.

13.6 - Porth Gwin

Latitude	53° 17.180'N	Longitude	004° 41.160'W
Position Fix	Differential - GPS	Datum	WGS84

This large bay lies immediately north of the headland at Penrhyn Mawr, where it provides a dive-site sheltered from the fierce currents which run off Penrhyn Mawr and the Fangs. The underwater cliffs drop off rapidly to a depth of around 15 metres, but the seabed then slopes away only gradually to around 20 metres. Many of the underwater rock faces have been 'sand-blasted' clean by the waves to give smooth, bare bedrock broken up by patches of coarse gravel.

Strong currents run across the mouth of the bay, but there is less current closer inshore where the seabed can be rather silty.

13.7 - Wreck of the 'Primrose Hill'

Name	Primrose Hill	Type	Sailing vessel
Date Lost	28/12/1900	Location	Abraham's Bosom
Cause	Bad weather	How Lost	Ran ashore
Hull	Iron	Weight	2,520 tons (gross)
Cargo	General cargo	Access	Boat
Latitude	53° 17.520'N	Longitude	004° 41.040'W
Position Fix	Differential-GPS	Datum	WGS84
Seabed	12 metres	Wreck Height	2 metres max.
Charted as	Uncharted		
Slipway (1)	Trearddur Bay	Distance	3.5 miles
Tidal Data	See text		

Primrose Hill Memorial

Location: Launch at Trearddur Bay and motor westwards past Porth Dafarch, Porth Ruffydd and the 'Fangs'. Clear Penrhyn Mawr headland before heading north, keeping towards the eastern cliffs of Abraham's Bosom. Keep about 200 metres offshore so you can see the two lifebelts on the cliffs, then move inshore looking carefully for several iron rings which were set into the rock during salvage operations. These iron rings are difficult to see from a boat, but once you locate them, look to the right for the three prominent cracks in the rock face. The wreck lies directly out from these fissures.

Timing: Slack-water occurs at approximately 2 hours before high-water at Liverpool and 4 hours after high-water at Liverpool.

Lying close inshore at a depth of around 10 to 12 metres, the 'Primrose Hill' has been battered by the elements for more than a century and is now almost totally flattened. Iron ribs and sections of riveted iron plate lie scattered around the seabed, along with a piece of one of the tubular iron masts. A number of bricks can be seen, all incised with the maker's name 'Cartcraig', a Glasgow company that manufactured firebricks from 1900 to 1959. The off-white objects lying around are the remains of chalk-filled casks where the staves have rotted away to leave a solid, barrel-shaped lump of chalk. Intact beer bottles have been recovered, while one complete stoneware jar from the wreck is marked 'Thorpes Old-fashioned Ginger Beer. Red Hand Brand' and is presumed to have originated in Northern Ireland.

Several lobster-pots have become entangled in the wreck and been abandoned. Their lines remain wrapped round the wreckage, so take care to avoid them, especially as the underwater visibility can be poor. Another problem with the site is that although it is some distance from the Holyhead to Dublin ferry route, it is quite badly affected by the swell caused by the Sea-Cat ferry. Underwater visibility is decreased for a short period, while any boat anchored close inshore could be washed on to the rocks.

The 2,520 ton, four-masted, iron barque 'Primrose Hill' was owned by the 'Sailing Ship Primrose Hill Co.' when she was towed out of the River Mersey on Christmas Day 1900. En route for Vancouver, Canada, the barque carried a general cargo and was manned by a mixed crew of British, Norwegian, Swedish, Finnish, American, German, Philippine and Russian sailors. Bad weather was soon encountered, so the 'Primrose Hill' and the attendant steam-tug 'William Jolliffe' sheltered off the east coast of Anglesey until the weather moderated and the tow could continue. By early evening on the 27th, the tow-line was still connected and they had almost reached Bardsey Island, but later that evening the weather deteriorated and the tow-line snapped. Later evidence suggests that the 'Primrose Hill' was inadequately manned, so it is not surprising that the crew found it impossible to reconnect the tow-line and that they had difficulty in raising sail either to steer back to the shelter of Holyhead or to head westwards, away from the Anglesey coast. As the wind increased to a gale, several sails were carried away by the wind and the vessel was gradually forced back towards South Stack Lighthouse. The following day, the 'Primrose Hill' was showing distress flags when she was sighted by the lookout at South Stack, so the following telegram was sent to Holyhead. 'Primrose Hill, 4-masted barque, no canvas, lying-to, one mile N.W. Send tug William Jolliffe to her at once'.

Unfortunately, in the north-westerly gale, not even the steam-powered lifeboat 'Duke of Northumberland' could leave the shelter of Holyhead Harbour. Help did appear in the form of the passenger steamer 'Hibernia' as it approached Holyhead from Dublin, but the force-11 violent storm made it impossible to launch the lifeboats, and when the steamer suffered problems with her steering equipment, this rescue attempt was abandoned. Fortunately, the

'Hibernia' had twin-screws and managed to reach safety by engine-power alone. Otherwise, there would have been a tremendous loss of life.

Eventually, having passed close to South Stack Lighthouse, the 'Primrose Hill' had no option other than to drop anchor, but the cables soon parted and the barque ran on to the jagged rocks in Abraham's Bosom, just south-west of Porth-y-Gwyddel. The weather was so fierce that the vessel broke up within five minutes. Only one man was saved, and even he was badly injured and lucky to survive, having been grabbed from the rocks by a local farmer, John Owen. Thirty-three seamen were lost that day, with ten being buried at Maeshyfryn Cemetery, Holyhead.

13.8 - Pen Las Rock

Latitude	53° 17.995'N	Longitude	004° 41.530'W
Position Fix	Differential - GPS	Datum	WGS84

Pen Las rock

Pen-Las Rock is a submerged reef that lies only 30 metres off the cliffs, roughly half a mile south-south-east of South Stack Lighthouse and where it is shown on the chart as Rk. 1.4. At low-water on a neap-tide, the echo-sounder showed two distinct peaks, with a least depth of 4 metres. The shoreline has spectacular cliffs that rise vertically to around 50 metres above sea level and are regularly used by rock climbers.

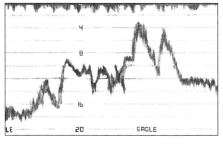

Sometimes marked by overfalls, Pen-Las Rock has many large boulders and small canyons. It is split by a long, deep gully, where divers have reported metal pipe-work, possibly from a wreck. The surrounding seabed drops off rapidly to 16 to 20 metres. The sides of the rock are either steep or sheer, giving a little protection from the strong current which flows over the whole area. Away from Pen Las Rock, the seabed is around 20 metres deep with a sprinkling of various sized rocks and boulders.

South Stack lighthouse

Slipways

General advice

- For accurate predictions of high-water times, log onto www.easytide.com and let the Hydrographic Office do the calculations for you. They will provide free tidal height and time predictions for up to 6 days ahead.

- Unless otherwise stated, all tidal predictions given in this book are with reference to Liverpool tide-tables.

- Many slipways are only viable for a few hours either side of high-water.

- Always carry a copy of your boat insurance certificate with you. Without it, you may be denied permission to launch.

- Several of the slipways lead onto soft sand and mud. Even if you have a four-wheel drive vehicle, always investigate before taking a vehicle onto the beach and make sure you have a long rope, sand-mats and a shovel.

- Even four-wheel drive vehicles have been bogged down on our beaches and submerged as the tide comes in. Are you insured for this eventuality?

- Always check the weather forecast before setting out. Many of the slipways face towards the south-west and cannot be used if the wind is from that direction.

- Where-ever possible, photographs of slipways have been taken at low-water to illustrate any problems at this state of the tide. Launch or recovery at high-water makes life much easier.

Use the following addresses to apply for slipway permits:-

Maritime Services, Gwynedd County Council, Pwllheli, Gwynedd. LL53 5AA

Tel: 01758 704066

Nefyn Town Council

Clerk to the Council, Muriau, Ffordd Dewi Sant, Nefyn, Pwllheli, Gwynedd. LL53 6EA

Tel: 01758 720507

Barmouth Harbour

Barmouth slipway at low water

Latitude	52° 43.150'N	Longitude	004° 03.100'W
O.S. Ref	SH	614E	156N

Access type: A concrete slipway leads into the sheltered estuary of the River Mawddach.

Four-Wheel Drive needed?: No.

Directions: The slipway runs into the estuary of the River Mawddach, between Barmouth town centre and the railway-bridge.

Toilets: Yes, within 50 metres.

Car Parking: Yes, there is a pay & display car park along the sea-front at £1.50 per day. (2002) Parking alongside the slipway is limited to 30 minutes only.

Fuel: Barmouth (nearest garage 200 metres away)

Approximate local high-water time: Three hours earlier than high-water at Liverpool.

Fee payable: Launching charges apply, but it is covered by the season ticket from Gwynedd County Council.

- The slipway is only viable for about 2 and a quarter hours either side of high-water but these times will vary slightly depending on the tide height and weather conditions.
- The concrete slipway runs parallel to the harbour wall. As the tide drops, hard sand is exposed, but within a few metres there is a large area of very soft mud. Do not take a vehicle anywhere near this mud as it is difficult even walking in this area.
- There are moorings, overfalls, strong currents and drying sandbanks in the estuary.
- Do not launch without the Harbourmaster's permission. His office is by the Lifeboat Museum, 100 metres from the slipway or ring him on 01341 280671 (office) or 07879 433146 (mobile).
- There is a 5-knot speed limit within the harbour limits.
- Power-driven vessels need to register and provide proof of third-party insurance.
- If necessary, contact the Beach Patrol on either 01341 280671 or 07879 443146.

Shell Island

Entrance to the Artro River, Shell Island

Latitude	52° 49.520'N	Longitude	004° 07.980'W
O.S. Ref	SH	563E	275N

Access type: This concrete slipway leads onto sand in a sheltered but tidal lagoon.

Four-Wheel Drive needed?: No

Directions: Shell Island is situated off the A496, about 7 miles north of Barmouth and 3 miles south of Harlech. Turn westwards off the A496 at Llanbedr for Mochras / Shell Island. Follow the road over the railway and past the airfield onto the causeway which runs across the beach to Shell Island. Note that the island may be cut off from the mainland at high-water on spring-tides.

Toilets: Yes   Car Parking: Yes   Fuel: Llanbedr, Dyffryn, Harlech.

Approximate local high-water time: About three hours earlier than high-water at Liverpool.

Fee payable: Yes, £5 entry to Shell Island plus £2.50 launching fee. (2002)

- The slipway is only viable for about 2 and a quarter hours either side of high-water but these times will vary slightly depending on the tide height and weather conditions.

- Although Shell Island was an island many years ago, it is now so in name only. Drifting sand and a changing river channel have converted the area into a peninsular which can only be reached by a tarmac road across a sandy bay. At high-water on spring- tides, the road is flooded, so check the web site for access times before setting out. The tides cover the causeway twice a day but only on spring-tides. These occur every other week.

- The island comprises 300 acres of camping sites, large areas of sand dunes, a long sandy beach and a sheltered but tidal lagoon. The camp-site has a holiday centre with a supermarket, camping shop, tavern, snack bar, licensed restaurant and a games room. The site caters for tents and motor-homes, but not caravans.

- On the ebb-tide, strong currents and overfalls occur in the channel leading from the open sea into the lagoon.

- The road through Harlech town centre is narrow and difficult. Use the lower road if towing a boat.

- You will need to provide proof of insurance for your boat.

- For further details, phone 01341 241453 or check the website on www.shellisland.co.uk.

Porthmadog / Portmadoc Harbour (Greaves Wharf)

Latitude	52° 55.440'N	Longitude	004° 07.810'W
O.S. Ref	SH	568E	385N

Access type: A stone slipway leads into the harbour and narrow tidal-estuary of the River Glaslyn.

Four-Wheel Drive needed?: No.

Directions: Travelling westwards on the A487, cross the causeway into Porthmadog. Turn left immediately after the Craft Cymru and Edinburgh Woollen Mill retail outlets and then left again opposite the children's playground. The slipway is then on the left.

Toilets: Yes, by the main road.

Car Parking: Yes, but the area is very busy during the summer months. Fuel: Porthmadog

Approximate local high-water time: Two and three-quarter hours earlier than high-water at Liverpool.

Fee payable: Launching charges apply, but it is covered by the season ticket from Gwynedd County Council.

- The slipway is only viable for about 3 hours either side of high-water but these times will vary slightly depending on the tide height and weather conditions.
- The A487 running westward from Minffordd into Porthmadog crosses over a toll-road which can cause long delays in the height of summer.
- The channel to the open sea is narrow, with moorings and extensive sandbanks.
- Within the harbour, there is soft mud and a 6-knot speed-limit.
- Permits are available at the nearby Harbourmaster's office.

Black Rock Sands, (West end), Porthmadog

Latitude	52° 54.760'N	Longitude	004° 11.350'W
O.S. Ref	SH	528E	373N

Launching at low-water

Access type: Black Rock Sands is a mile-long, flat, open beach comprised mainly of hard sand.

Four-Wheel Drive needed?: Not essential, but it makes life easier. Cars have been stuck in the soft sand.

Directions: From the centre of Porthmadog, take the turning by Woolworth's for Black-Rock Sands and Borth-y-Gest. Follow the road through Morfa Bychan until you reach the beach.

Toilets: Yes, near the beach access gate. Cold showers are also provided.

Car Parking: Yes, on the beach. Cost £2.00 per car or £8.00 for car & boat. (2002)

Fuel: Porthmadog.

Approximate local high-water time: Three hours earlier than high-water at Liverpool.

Fee payable: Launching charges apply, but it is covered by the season ticket from Gwynedd County Council.

- The beach is controlled by the local council who allow access only from 9.30 am until 8.00 pm.
- By-laws are enforced by a regular beach patrol, so pay attention to the speed limit inshore of the yellow buoys.
- Only launch between the red buoys.
- Black Rock Sands can be very crowded on hot summer days.
- There may be high surf in south-westerly winds.
- You will need lots of manpower to launch a heavy RIB on a falling tide, as the water is very shallow for some distance offshore. Take a long rope to assist recovery.
- Watch out for pot-holes where children have built sand-castles.
- Ensure that you park above the high-water mark!

Criccieth

Latitude	52° 55.040'N	Longitude	004° 13.825'W
O.S. Ref	SH	502E	379N

RIB recovery

Access type: This is a concrete slip which is viable for most of tide and is sheltered from the south and west by a small breakwater.

Four-Wheel Drive needed? No, except at low-water.

Directions: Take the A497 from Porthmadog, heading west and as you enter the 30 mph speed limit in Criccieth, turn left (signposted 'Traeth/Beach') opposite the Texaco garage. Cross the railway line and bear right along the seafront where the slipway is opposite the lifeboat station. See photo below.

Toilets: Yes, close to the sea-front car-park, about 300 metres to the east.

Car Parking: Yes, there is Pay & Display parking along the sea-front. Fuel: Criccieth

Approximate local high-water time: Three hours earlier than high-water at Liverpool.

Fee payable: Launching charges apply, but it is covered by the season ticket from Gwynedd County Council.

- Do not block the slipway or the approaches to it. Avoid the life-boat slipway.

- Keep within the marine speed-limit designated by the yellow buoys.

- Beware of rocks.

- On a spring-tide, the concrete does not reach all the way down to the low-water mark.

Pwllheli (by the Harbourmaster's office)

Latitude	52° 52.980'N	Longitude	004° 24.185'W
O.S. Ref	SH	383E	345N

Access type: A narrow concrete slipway runs down to low-water, inside the shelter of the estuary.

Four-Wheel Drive needed?: No

Directions: Take the A497 from Porthmadog and Criccieth into Pwllheli, turning left at the mini-roundabout just after the Black Lion. Follow the signs for 'Through Traffic/Nefyn/Abersoch', pass the Co-op Supermarket and turn left by the station, following the sign for the Lifeboat Station. Pass the War Memorial on the left and the Council Offices (Swyddfa Dwyfor) on the right. Turn left for the Lifeboat Station and Gimblet Rock Caravan Park, taking care over the speed bumps. Turn left, at the sign for the Harbwr Feistr/ Harbourmaster, immediately before 'Firmhelm' marine.

Toilets: No

Car Parking: Yes

Fuel: Pwllheli

Approximate local high-water time: Three hours earlier than high-water at Liverpool.

Fee payable: Launching charges apply, but it is covered by the season ticket from Gwynedd County Council.

- The slipway is available at all states of the tide.

- A 4-knot speed limit applies inside the harbour.

- Beware of the sudden drop-off at low-water on spring-tides.

- The Harbourmaster's office is alongside the slipway.

Abersoch Beach

Flioedd a Thaliadau		Fees and Charges
Cychod Pwer		**Power Boats**
Lansio Dyddiol	£8.50	Daily Launching
Lansio Wythnosol		Weekly Launching
Lansio Misol	£70	Monthly Launching
Lansio Bleyddyn (1 Ebrill - 31 Mawrth)	£86	Yearly Launching (1 April - 31 March)
Beiciau Dŵr		**Jet Skis**
Cofrestru	£18	Registration
Lansio Dyddiol	10.00	Daily Launching
Lansio Wythnosol		Weekly Launching
Lansio Misol	£80	Monthly Launching
Lansio Bleyddyn (1 Ebrill - 31 Mawrth)	£112	Yearly Launching (1 April - 31 March)
☎ 01758 704081		☎ 01758 704081
Cychod Heylio Dydd Gyda/Heb Peiraint (Dyddiol)	4.00	Selling Dayboats with / Without Outboards (Daily)
Cychod Heylio Dydd Gyda/Heb Peiraint (Tymhorol)	£36	Selling Dayboats with / Without Outboards (Seasonal)
Hwylfyrddio (Dyddiol)	3.50	Windsurfing (Daily)
Hwylfyrddio (Tymhorol)	25.00	Windsurfing (Seasonal)

Latitude	52° 49.255'N	Longitude	004° 30.065'W
O.S. Ref	SH	315E	278N

Access type: A narrow concrete slipway leads onto a wide sandy beach.

Four-Wheel Drive needed?: Advisable, unless launching a small boat. Beware of soft sand at high water.

Directions: Drive into the centre of Abersoch from Pwllheli. Go straight through the one-way system, following the road for Sarn Bach and Cilan. Pass the shops, the St. Tudwal's Inn and the Police station before turning left immediately after the Wylfa Hotel. The car park and slipway are at the end of this road.

Toilets: Yes, in the car park.   Car Parking: Yes. (Charges apply)   Fuel: Abersoch, Llanbedrog.

Approximate local high-water time: Three and a quarter hours earlier than high-water at Liverpool.

Fee payable: Launching charges apply, but it is covered by the season ticket from Gwynedd County Council.

- This is a very shallow area, with the deeper water being to the east. In the summer months, this beach is very popular with swimmers and children, so drive slowly both on the beach and whilst at sea.
- Marine speed limits apply inside the line of yellow buoys, but slow down also when passing moored boats.
- Trailers may be left on the beach to the right, but vehicles must be returned to the car-park.
- The beach is regularly patrolled by Dwyfor Council. It becomes very congested at high-water on spring-tides.
- Beware of hollows in the sand left by anglers digging for lugworm.
- The access road is narrow, so this slipway can be chaotic at high-water on sunny days.
- The gate is locked at 8pm.
- Beware of the speed bumps.
- Refreshments are available close to the slip in the summer months. Abersoch possesses several pubs, hotels, chandlers, restaurants, supermarkets etc.

Abersoch South Beach (Machroes)

Launching from Abersoch beach

Latitude	52° 48.615'N	Longitude	004° 29.925'W
O.S. Ref	SH	316E	266N

Access type: A narrow slipway leads onto a wide sandy beach.

Four-Wheel Drive needed?: Advised, unless launching a small boat.

Directions: Drive through the centre of Abersoch, heading for Sarn Bach and Cilan. Pass through Sarn Bach and take the first left after leaving the 30 mph speed-limit zone, signposted for 'Porth Tochyn Hotel'. Follow this narrow lane up the hill, past the summit and through the double-bend. Turn left, again following the 'Porth Tochyn Hotel' signs. Pass the 'Beach View' camping site but instead of following the road sharp right for the 'Porth Tochyn Hotel', go straight on, signposted 'Traeth/Beach. This narrow, twisting hill leads to the slipway and car-park.

Toilets: Yes, in the car park.

Car Parking: Yes.

Fuel: Abersoch, Llanbedrog.

Approximate local high-water time: Three and a quarter hours earlier than high-water at Liverpool.

Fee payable: Launching charges apply, but it is covered by the season ticket from Gwynedd County Council.

- This slipway is difficult to find and is located down a narrow, steep hill.
- It can be very busy on a sunny day.
- Beware of hollows in the sand left by anglers digging for lugworm.
- On the approach road, overhanging branches may be low enough to damage a boat's aerial or mast.

Aberdaron

View down the slipway

Latitude	52° 48.245'N	Longitude	004° 42.725'W
O.S. Ref	SH	172E	265N

Access type: A short concrete slip leads onto a wide beach with very soft sand. Wooden slats have been laid down, but they may be buried under the sand.

Four-Wheel Drive needed?: Essential, unless you have a small inflatable dinghy which can be launched by hand. Note that even tractors get stuck on this beach!

Directions: Take the A499 from Pwllheli, heading for Abersoch. At Llanbedrog, turn right onto the B4413 for Aberdaron, passing through Mynytho, Bottwnog, Sarn Meyllteyrn and Rhoshirwaun. Stop and read the notes below before going down the hill into Aberdaron.

Toilets: Yes - Westwards along the beach and in the village, by the bridge.

Car Parking: Yes, in the village (fee charged), but the car park is usually locked at 7 PM. Note that a vehicle attempting to turn right out of the car-park will need to do a three-point turn. This is totally impossible if towing a trailer, so do not take them into the car park.

Fuel: Rhoshirwaun / Nefyn / Abersoch

Approximate local high-water time: Three hours earlier than high-water at Liverpool.

Fee payable: Launching charges apply, but it is covered by the season ticket from Gwynedd County Council.

- Severe congestion will occur in the village should a single vehicle or boat block the slipway. Do not take a boat down into Aberdaron unless you have the means to launch it. Bank holidays can be total grid-lock! If in doubt, park at the top of the hill, walk down into the village and investigate.

- Long or wide boats will have difficulty crossing the hump-back bridge in the centre of the village.

- Tractors are the only vehicles allowed to park on the beach, so do not leave four-wheel vehicles there. Tractors should turn left at the bottom of the slipway and park beyond the end of the wall while four-wheel drive vehicles should return to the village car-park. Trailers can be left at the top of the beach, beyond the end of the wall to the east.

- Anything left on the beach will become immersed at high-water on a spring-tide.

- There is often a sharp drop at the bottom of the slipway. This can cause trailers to scrape along the concrete.

- To avoid damage at the bottom of the slipway, outboard motors should be locked in the tilted-up position.
- Although there is lots of room at low-water, there is little or no space on the beach at high-water on a spring-tide.
- On sunny days, Aberdaron is very popular with families, so all drivers should watch out for children running along the beach. Likewise, be aware of swimmers, especially in surf conditions.
- A local bye-law prohibits the use of a rope for towing boats off the beach.
- A maritime speed-limit applies inside the line of yellow buoys.
- Strong south-west winds will cause heavy surf. Kedge anchors may be required to safely bring a boat ashore.
- Note that there are many rocks on this beach which dry out, or are awash at low water. Care must be taken when approaching shore at any state of the tide other than at high-water. The safest approach is to head straight toward the beach at the point where the east wall of the grave-yard meets the sea-wall. (See photo) This gives a 50 metre-wide clear, sandy patch.

- Strong currents and whirlpools occur in Bardsey Sound, while overfalls are present off Pen-y-Cil and Braich-y-Pwll headlands, the south tip of Bardsey Island and on the Tripods reef. Further offshore, Bastram Shoal and the Devil's Ridge are to be avoided.
- Ring the Bardsey Island Trust office in Aberdaron on 01758 760667 to see if it is possible to arrange a tractor for launching. Always ring well in advance.
- This slipway is quite steep, but all the hills out of Aberdaron are even steeper. Don't rely on the winch ratchet alone: - boats have fallen off!

The hump-back bridge

Aberdaron slipway   note: sharp drop

Porth Colmon

Latitude	52° 52.510'N	Longitude	004° 41.020'W
O.S. Ref	SH	194E	343N

Access type: A narrow, bumpy, curving slipway leads onto a small rock and gravel beach.

Four-Wheel Drive needed?: Not essential for small boats, but is recommended, since 2-wheel drive vehicles may have insufficient ground clearance and traction. Larger boats need a four-wheel drive vehicle, preferably with a front-mounted tow-ball.

Directions: Take the B4417 southwest from Morfa Nefyn, passing through Edern and Tudweiliog, then climb up the hill with the nasty 'S' bend. Pass the signs for Llangwnnadl and the Carrog Guest House before turning right, signposted for Porth Colmon and Llangwnnadl. Pass the church on the right before stopping at the crossroads. Carry straight on, down a narrow, twisty lane to the slipway.

Toilets: No (Nearest ones in Tudweiliog)

Car Parking: Yes, but very restricted.

Fuel: Rhoshirwaun, Morfa Nefyn and Nefyn.

Approximate local high-water time: Two and a quarter hours earlier than high-water at Liverpool.

Fee payable: No

- Beware of lobster-pot buoys and divers without surface marker-buoys.
- Avoid low-water, when there is a carpet of dead kelp about 1 metre thick which makes launch and recovery impossible.
- There is little room to turn round on the beach, even at low-water.
- Some of the rocks on the beach are sharp and have caused punctures.
- There are air stations and campsites nearby.
- Do not block access to the public footpath along the cliff, or to the private house.
- There are uncharted rocks directly out from the slipway which dry out at low-water on a spring-tide.

Porth Ysgaden

Latitude	52° 54.255′N	Longitude	004° 38.925′W
O.S. Ref	SH	219E	375N

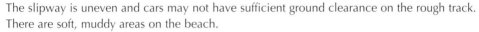

Access type: This is a narrow, curved, rough slipway that leads onto a sandy beach.

Four-Wheel Drive needed?: Advisable.

The slipway is uneven and cars may not have sufficient ground clearance on the rough track. There are soft, muddy areas on the beach.

Directions: Take the B4417 south-west from Morfa Nefyn and pass through the village of Tudweiliog. After leaving the 30mph area, pass a parking area on the left before turning right at the sign for 'Penrallt Coastal Campsite'. After a short distance, where the main road goes sharp left, you need to go straight on into a narrow lane marked 'Beach/Camping'. Pass a house called 'Minafon', currently painted cream and blue with a motif of an anchor on the chimney. The main road then bears to the right, but take the narrower lane straight on. As the tarmac lane then goes sharp left, carry straight on into a narrow dirt-track which leads to Porth Ysgaden. See photo above.

Toilets: No (Nearest ones are in Tudweiliog)

Car Parking: There is parking for about 20 cars at the top of the slipway.

Fuel: Morfa Nefyn, Nefyn, or Rhoshirwaun.

Approximate local high-water time: Two and a quarter hours earlier than high-water at Liverpool.

Fee payable: No (2003)

- This is a hard sandy beach, but beware of soft areas where bait-diggers have been active.
- Look out for submerged rocks just off the point, mooring lines, lobster pots, and divers without surface marker-buoys.
- During gales, large amounts of sea-weed are washed onto the beach and it remains here for some time afterwards.
- At high water, the beach becomes isolated from the slipway, so that any vehicle on the beach will be cut off from the exit point.
- At high-water, there is no room on the beach to turn round. Reversing down the slipway is difficult but four-wheel drive vehicles with front-mounted tow-balls make life much easier.
- There are air stations and campsites nearby.
- Trailers should not be left on the beach. (Council advice)

Morfa Nefyn / Porth Dinllaen

Latitude	52° 56.230'N	Longitude	004° 33.445'W
O.S. Ref	SH	281E	409N

Access type: This is a long, shallow, hard beach with odd areas of soft sand. The concrete part of the slipway is only of use at high-water.

Four-Wheel Drive needed?: Strongly recommended for launching RIBs, as I have seen several cars stuck here. Although the beach is mainly hard sand, there are many areas of soft sand, especially near the high-water mark.

Directions: Take the A487 from Caernarfon, passing through Bontnewydd and Dinas. From Llanwnda, follow the A499 through Aberdesach, Clynnog, Gyrn Goch and Llanaelhaearn, heading for Pwllheli. Avoid the B4417 through Llithfaen, as it is unsuitable for towing boats. Turn right onto the B4354 at Y Ffor, heading for Nefyn but take care crossing the narrow bridge at Pont Penprys. Turn right onto the A497 (Beware of this hidden road-junction). Go straight on at the roundabout, passing the Y Bryncynan public house and following the B4412 into Morfa Nefyn. Go straight on at the diagonal crossroad into Lon Pen Rhos and pass the garage. Turn right into Lon Bridlin, opposite the 'Linksway' hotel. The slipway is at the bottom of the steep hill.

Toilets: Yes - 25 metres up the hill from the slipway and also on the beach, near the Ty-Coch Inn.

Car Parking: Yes. After launching, turn right at the top of the hill, where the National Trust charges a separate fee. (Free to members) Note that there is a short cut from the car park to the beach down a steep footpath.

Fuel: Morfa Nefyn and Nefyn

Approximate local high-water time: Two hours earlier than high-water at Liverpool.

Fee payable: Yes (summertime only). The slipway is administered by Nefyn District Council, so is not covered by the Gwynedd County Council launching permit.

- Don't block the turning area at the bottom of the hill or park on the beach. (Local Bye-laws apply)
- Speed limits are enforced close inshore.
- There are many lobster pots in the area, so keep a close watch for pot-buoys.
- A strong rope is useful for recovering boats, as the beach has a very shallow slope.
- At high-water on a spring-tide the sand is completely covered, so it is unwise to leave vehicles on the beach. They will either be cut off from the slipway or even submerged.

- The Ty-Coch Inn (at 52° 56.615'N 004° 34.065W / SH 275E 416N) at the west end of the beach is popular with sailors, divers and holiday-makers, but note that persons wearing wet-suits are not allowed in the bar.

- The beach in front of the pub is very popular with families, so beware of children when using vehicles or boats.

Porth Nefyn

Latitude	52° 56.230'N	Longitude	004° 31.735'W
O.S. Ref	SH	301E	408N

Access type: A narrow concrete slipway leads onto a hard, sandy beach.

Four-Wheel Drive needed?: Recommended. The hill is very steep.

Directions: Take the A487 from Caernarfon, passing through Bontnewydd and Dinas. From Llanwnda, follow the A499 through Aberdesach, Clynnog, Gyrn Goch and Llanaelhaearn, heading for Pwllheli. Avoid the B4417 through Llithfaen as it is unsuitable for towing boats. Turn right onto the B4354 at Y Ffor, heading for Nefyn but take care crossing the narrow bridge at Pont Penprys. Turn right onto the A497 (Beware of this hidden road-junction) and then turn right at the roundabout, following the A497 into Nefyn. Turn left at the mini-roundabout in the centre of Nefyn, pass the garage and the school before turning right at the 'Traeth/Beach' sign into Lon-y-Traeth. Go down this narrow, steep, twisting hill to the slipway.

Toilets: Yes, further up the hill.

Car Parking: Yes, but there is only a limited amount of parking on the hill.

Fuel: Nefyn & Morfa Nefyn

Approximate local high-water time: Two hours earlier than high-water at Liverpool.

Fee payable: Yes (summertime only). The slipway is administered by Nefyn Council, so is not covered by the Gwynedd County Council launching permit.

- Access and parking is difficult as the road is steep and narrow.

- At high-water, the beach is totally covered.

- Speed limits are enforced close inshore.

- Vehicles and trailers can slowly sink into the sand if left stationary for any length of time. Avoid any patches of wet sand.

Trefor

Latitude	52° 59.930'N	Longitude	004° 25.410'W
O.S. Ref	SH	374E	474N

Access type: A short concrete slip leads onto wooden boards followed by hard sand and mud within the harbour area.

Four-Wheel Drive needed?: Recommended, unless using the slipway only around high-water. Although the beach is mainly hard sand, there are soft areas and dead kelp at high-water. Cars have been stuck in soft mud at low-water.

Directions: Take A487 from Caernarfon and pass through Bontnewydd and Dinas before turning onto the A499 at the second roundabout at Llanwnda. Pass through Pontllyfni, Aberdesach, Clynnog and Gyrn Goch before turning right for Trefor / Plas yr Eifl Hotel. Immediately after the 30 mph sign, take the first right, signposted 'To the Beach' and drive between the bungalows down a very narrow, steep, twisting road. Beware: the local kids have a habit of turning the post to point in the wrong direction. The road runs alongside the beach and the slipway is next to the break-water. Beware of the speed-humps.

Toilets: Yes, in the car park near the beach. Car Parking: On the sea-front and alongside the pier.

Fuel: Dinas, Y Ffor, Penygroes.

Approximate local high-water time: 2 hours earlier than high-water at Liverpool.

Fee payable: Launching charges apply, but it is covered by the season ticket from Gwynedd County Council.

- The village of Trefor has a sandy beach protected from the west by a stone breakwater. On a sunny day, the beach makes a pleasant sun-trap and safe beach for families.

- The short slip is wide enough for two trailers and leads onto a hard sandy beach with the distance to low-water being about 200 metres.

- Beware of rocks, soft mud and mooring chains as the tide recedes. You have been warned!

- At low-water, there is an area of rock and shingle near the end of the breakwater which can cause hull or propeller damage. Keep close to the breakwater when launching at low tide.

- Beware of the soft sand where bait-diggers have been active.

- Beware of mooring-ropes laid down for local fishing-boats.

- Keep clear of the anglers' lines around the pier.

- There are many lobster-pots close to Trefor, so watch out for the marker buoys.

- Trefor Pier is a popular diving site, so be alert for divers' marker buoys or any surfaced divers.
- Launching charges apply, but it is covered by the season ticket from Gwynedd County Council.

Ty-Calch (White Cottage)

Latitude	53° 07.675'N	Longitude	004° 18.640'W
O.S. Ref	SH	454E	615N

Access type: A rocky beach leads onto sand and mud.

Four-Wheel Drive needed?: No

Directions: Take the A487 from Caernarfon, heading south for Porthmadog and Pwllheli, passing MacDonald's and Tesco's. Go straight across the small roundabout with the vertical slate pillars and take the next right turn, signposted Llanfaglan, Saron, Caravan Park, Golf and Nature Reserve, then immediately turn right again into Coed Helen Road. The road winds round and becomes very narrow before passing Coed Helen Holiday Park, Castle Marine and Caernarfon Harbour. It then runs alongside the Menai Strait and past the golf club. The slipway is immediately after a white cottage (Ty-Calch), located 2.4 miles from the A487 turning.

Toilets: Yes (For slipway users only)   Car Parking: Yes, on sea-front.   Fuel: Caernarfon

Approximate local high-water time: One and a half hours earlier than high-water at Liverpool.

Fee payable: Yes

- For those who do not possess a four-wheel drive vehicle, the slipway at Ty-Calch on the Menai Strait is ideal. This privately-owned slipway is situated between Caernarfon and Fort Belan and offers the luxury of a tractor-assisted launch at reasonable cost. Parking is available close by and all one has to do on arrival is remove the lighting board, fit the electronics and load the diving equipment. The tractor then launches the boat and parks the trailer. On returning to the slipway, the tractor is usually waiting in the water with your trailer ready for recovery.
- Take care at low-water as the water is shallow and rocky.
- Note the Direction of Buoyage changes off Caernarfon. See page 113, Chapter 8 for details.
- The Menai Strait is usually well sheltered, so there is rarely any surf to complicate matters, but strong south-westerly winds will cause heavy seas off Fort Belan, especially on the ebb tide.

Y Felinheli (Port Dinorwic)

Latitude	53° 10.990'N	Longitude	004° 12.725'W
O.S. Ref	SH	522E	675N

Access type: This is a concrete slipway which leads onto a hard beach which is comprised of rock and broken slates.

Four-Wheel Drive needed?: Not at high-water, but is recommended at low-water.

Directions: Take the A55 heading west and exit at junction 10 for Caernarfon (A4087/487). Turn left at the exit roundabout and then at the next roundabout, follow the signs for Llanberis (B4547) and Y Felinheli. Ignore the left turn for Llanberis and continue along the old road through the town of Y Felinheli (Port Dinorwic). Pass the Half-way House hotel, the War Memorial and the Central Garage. As you climb up the hill and before the speed limit de-restriction sign, turn right, sign-posted 'Traeth/Beach', into Rowen. Go down the steep hill and follow the road round to the right. Pass the 'Dinas Boat-yard' and the sailing club. The slipway is by the children's playground, opposite the Menai Bakery and the Sail-loft Restaurant.

Toilets: Yes.   Car Parking: Yes, there is limited parking along the sea-front.

Fuel: Caernarfon, Bangor

Approximate local high-water time: One hour earlier than high-water at Liverpool.

Fee payable: No

- A 5-knot speed limit applies to this part of the Menai Strait.
- Note the direction of buoyage changes off Caernarfon.
- Seaweed on the concrete makes this slipway very slippery.
- The concrete ends with a considerable step, so check before launching.

Menai Bridge (Porth Aethwy)

Latitude	53° 13.430'N	Longitude	004° 09.675'W
O.S. Ref	SH	557E	719N

View from the water

Access type: This is a narrow concrete slipway, usable at all states of the tide, except low-water on a spring-tide.

Four-Wheel Drive needed?: No, but the slipway can be very slippery at low-water, so take a strong rope to aid recovery.

Directions: Take the A55 from Conwy and cross over the Britannia Bridge. Take the first exit (junction 8A) after the bridge signposted 'Menai Bridge, Porth Aethwy, Plas Newydd, Sea Zoo', then immediately turn right at the 'T' junction. After about a mile, go straight on at the roundabout and down the hill into Menai Bridge town-centre. At the crossroads, go straight across between the Bulkeley Arms and the Post Office into Water Street. Pass the Liverpool Arms public house and the William Roberts wood-yard. The slipway is about 200 metres further on.

Toilets: Yes, at the adjacent bowling green and in Menai Bridge town centre.

Car Parking: Parking near the slipway is very limited. Some spaces are available behind the house opposite, owned by Welsh Water but please don't block access to the private houses or garages. Otherwise use Menai Bridge town-centre car-park after launching.

Fuel: Menai Bridge (Porth Aethwy).

Approximate local high-water time: Half an hour earlier than high-water at Liverpool.

Fee payable: No

- This location provides a sheltered concrete slip all the way down to low water, but beware of the sharp drop at low-water on a spring-tide.
- Parking is limited, the whole area becoming congested during strong winds when this is often the only viable launch site in the area.
- Very strong currents are present in the Menai Strait.
- Beware of the wind-over-tide effect when passing under the suspension bridge.
- There are many unmarked, shallow reefs between the two bridges, but the drying rock close to the slipway is marked by a post and cone.
- The town of Menai Bridge has shops, cafes, restaurants and public houses.

Rhosneigr

Latitude	53° 13.580'N	Longitude	004° 31.400'W
O.S. Ref	SH	316E	730N

Access type: This is an open beach, mainly comprised of hard sand, but with some very soft areas above the high-water mark.

Four-Wheel Drive needed? Strongly recommended.

Directions: Take the A55 dual carriageway onto Anglesey, exiting at junction 5 and turning left for Rhosneigr. Pass through Engedi into Llanfaelog, then turn right for Rhosneigr (A4080) and pass the 'Maelog Lake Hotel'. Turn 90 degrees left (signposted 'Toilets, Library & Car-park') in the centre of Rhosneigr, immediately after 'Anglesey Motor & Marine' and just before the 'Spar' shop. This is where the main road turns 90 degrees to the right. Having turned left, pass the 'Sandymount' club, the shops and cafes and then the 'Paran' chapel on the left. Turn right, about 100 metres further on, immediately before the house on the right with a 'MIDSHIPS' sign in the window. Access to the beach is immediately ahead, by the old lifeboat station.

Toilets: Yes, in the main car-park.

Car Parking: Yes, in the village. Bylaws state that vehicles should not be left on the beach.

Fuel: Rhosneigr.

Approximate local high-water time: One and three-quarter hours before high-water, Liverpool.

Fee payable: No

Notes:

- The beach has only a slight slope, so the water is shallow for some distance offshore. A good length of strong rope makes boat recovery easier.
- Beware of off-shore reefs and isolated rocks.
- There is an 8-knot speed limit close inshore.
- The beach is mainly hard sand, but there are soft areas above the high-water line.

- Tractors cause the sand to become deeply rutted, making it possible for cars to belly-out and become stranded.
- Tractor launching is available at Anglesey Motor & Marine (01407 810338).
- Keep to the buoyed channel.

Silver Bay Caravan Site

Beware - drying rocks

Latitude	53° 14.750'N	Longitude	004° 33.980'W
O.S. Ref	SH	288E	752N

Access type: This is a flat, open beach, mainly consisting of hard sand, but there are some soft areas, mostly above the high water mark.

Four-Wheel Drive needed? Recommended.

Directions: Cross Anglesey on the new A55 dual carriageway and exit at junction 3 (Valley, Y Fali). Note – this is the one after the RAF Valley turnoff. Turn right, cross over the A55 and follow the signs for 'Local Services' and 'Valley'. Turn left at Valley traffic lights, cross over the railway-line and the A55. Go straight across the roundabout and over the Four-Mile Bridge onto Holy Island, then immediately take the first left onto the B4545 (opposite the Post Office) sign-posted 'Rhoscolyn'. Follow this lane through the sharp left-hand bend and over the hill. Turn left into a very narrow lane sign-posted 'Silver Bay'. This lane is only wide enough for one vehicle and has few passing places. Beware of speed-ramps.

Toilets: Yes, on the caravan site.

Car Parking: Yes, close to the beach, but do not leave vehicles on the sand.

Fuel: Valley / Trearddur Bay / Holyhead

Approximate local high-water time: One and three-quarter hours earlier than high-water at Liverpool.

Fee payable: Yes (Camp-site residents only)

- This is a privately owned caravan site where launching is for residents and campers only. Day permits are no longer available. Ring the site on 01407 860860 for further details.

- Please obey the speed limits.

- Static caravans are available for hire, otherwise bring your own caravan or tent. The site has a shop, a children's play area, horse riding, showers etc.

- The beach is rather shallow for launching boats, so a four-wheel drive vehicle and a long rope make boat-recovery easier.

- Beware of areas of very soft sand at high-water and at low-water.

- Beware of drying rocks on the west end of the beach. See photo above.

- Keep a close look out for swimmers and children.

- There is a partially-submerged reef, located about 500 metres directly off the beach.

Rhoscolyn (Borth Wen)

Latitude	53° 14.705'N	Longitude	004° 35.475'W
O.S. Ref	SH	271E	752N

Access type: A rough, stony slip leads onto a hard sandy beach.

Four-Wheel Drive needed?: Yes, except for small boats. It is a long way to low-water.

Directions: Cross Anglesey on the new A55 dual carriageway and exit at junction 3 (Valley, Y Fali). Note – this is the one after the RAF Valley turnoff. Turn right, cross over the A55 and follow the signs for 'Local Services' and 'Valley'. Turn left at Valley traffic lights, cross over the railway-line and the A55. Go straight across the roundabout and over the Four-Mile Bridge onto Holy Island, then immediately take the first left onto the B4545 (opposite the Post Office) sign-posted 'Rhoscolyn'. Follow this lane through the sharp left-hand bend and over the hill. Pass the turning for Silver Bay then bear left at the sign for the 'White Eagle' Hotel. Pass the hotel and continue along this narrow, twisty road to the car-park and launch-site.

Toilets: Yes.

Car Parking: Yes, but the spaces are often fully taken on a sunny day.

Fuel: Trearddur Bay / Valley

Approximate local high-water time: One and three-quarter hours earlier than high-water at Liverpool.

Fee payable: No

- Access to this beach is via a very narrow road with several sharp bends and few passing places. These are very difficult to negotiate if towing a boat.
- Watch out for children and horses on the beach.
- Beware of submerged rocks inside the bay.
- There are strong currents outside the bay.

Trearddur Bay

Access type: A steep, curved, concrete-ramp leads onto a wide, sandy beach.

Four-Wheel Drive needed?: Preferred, but not essential unless you have a large boat.

Latitude	53° 16.820'N	Longitude	004° 37.275'W
O.S. Ref	SH	253E	792N

Directions: Cross Anglesey on the new A55 dual carriageway, turning sharp left at the roundabout (Junction 1) in Holyhead. After just over a mile, pass the Trearddur Bay sign and turn right opposite the garage at the bottom of the hill. The slipway is on the left, just after the Lifeboat Station.

Toilets: Yes (in the car park, along the sea-front)

Car Parking: Yes. After leaving the beach, turn left and there is a large car-park on the right, about 200 metres towards Porth Dafarch at: 53° 16.800'N 004° 37.445'W / SH 251E 792N

Fuel: Trearddur Bay / Valley / Holyhead

Approximate local high-water time: 1.75 hours before high-water at Liverpool.

Fee payable: No (2002), but this varies from year to year.

- The tide is only on the concrete for about 2 hours either side of high-water.
- At high-water, in good weather, this slipway becomes very congested. On a hot summer's day, you may have to queue for up to two hours.
- As high-water approaches, trailers and vehicles can become marooned on the beach.
- Use the car-park or beach to prepare and load your boat, not the main road.
- Long, low trailers may ground at the top of the slip.
- Beware of passing road traffic when coming off the slipway.
- On occasions, the sand may be stripped away from the beach, revealing the remains of old tree trunks and roots. These have decayed over the centuries, creating soft, muddy areas. Care is also needed to avoid soft sand.
- Beware of divers without SMBs, children on the beach, rocks, windsurfers, water skiers etc.
- There are shallow areas, reefs and rocks as you move out from the beach.
- Watch out for swimmers. There is a designated area, where all boat-traffic is prohibited.
- There is an 8-knot speed limit close to the beach.
- Don't block the adjacent R.N.L.I. slipway.
- This slipway is quite steep; so don't rely on the winch alone when leaving the beach.
- At low-tide, the water is very shallow, so take a rope to assist recovery.

Diving Services

Equipment outlets

Anglesey Divers, Trearddur Bay. (Martin & Caroline Sampson)

Latitude	53° 18.425'N	Longitude	004° 37.945'W
O.S. Ref	SH	246E	822N

1, Church Terrace, Kingsland Road, Holyhead, Anglesey LL65 2HP

Telephone no: 01407 764545 Mobile: 07775 643889

Web site: www.diveanglesey.co.uk E-mail address: info@diveanglesey.co.uk

- Air to 240 bar. Nitrox and trimix on request. Equipment sales & hire.
- PADI / TDI school, re-breather & RYA training.
- Boat charter arranged. Cylinder testing. Regulator servicing.
- Closed Sunday. • Air is available out of normal hours but please ring first.
- Full workshop facilities for diving kit repair. Emergency overnight repair service.

Directions: Take the A55 across Anglesey to the roundabout (Junction 1) at Holyhead. Take the second exit off the roundabout, passing the Fire Station and the 'Builder Center'. Anglesey Divers is on the left, the corner shop at the end of the row. It is located on the corner of Holborn Road and opposite the sign for the 'Blossoms' public house.

Diving Services Anglesey, Trearddur Bay. (Mike & Joyce McGee)

Latitude	53° 16.295'N	Longitude	004° 37.290'W
O.S. Ref	SH	252E	782N

Heathercliff, Raven's Point Rd., Trearddur Bay, Anglesey, LL65 2AQ

Telephone no: 01407 860318

- Air to 300 bar. Nitrox. Equipment sales & hire. • PADI school,
- Cylinder testing. Regulator servicing. Air test. • Watch & dive computer batteries replaced.
- Chandlers. Large stocks of boating equipment and all-weather clothing.
- Full workshop facilities for diving kit repair.

Directions: Cross Anglesey on the A55 dual carriageway, turning sharp left for Trearddur Bay at the roundabout (Junction 1) on the outskirts of Holyhead. Pass the Trearddur Bay sign, the garage, the Sea Shanty Café, and the Spar shop, and then take the next right into Raven's Point Road. Pass the Seacroft Hotel and the Trearddur Bay Sailing Club. The dive-shop is on the left, before the sharp left-hand bend.

A.K.S. Diving, Conwy (Adam Stubbings)

Latitude	53° 17.200'N	Longitude	003° 51.500'W
O.S. Ref	SH	761E	783N

Hadley Buildings, Bangor Rd., Conwy LL32 8DN

Telephone no: 01492 580300 Mobile: 07968 061177

Web site: www.aksdiving.co.uk E-mail address: adam@aksdiving.co.uk

- Air to 300 bar. Nitrox. Trimix. Equipment sales & hire.
- PADI & IANTD school.
- Boat charter.
- Cylinder testing. Regulator servicing.
- Accommodation arranged. UK & overseas excursions.
- Closed Monday
- AKS Diving will happily open at other times by previous arrangement.

Directions: Travelling westwards towards Anglesey on the A55, take the first exit immediately after the Conwy Tunnel (Junction 17 – signposted 'Conwy/Marina/A547). Turn left and take the second turning on the right, about 100 metres from the A55. AKS Diving is then about 300 metres on the right.

Frogsborn Diving, Hawarden. (Richard Frost)

Latitude	53° 10.740'N	Longitude	002° 59.415'W
O.S. Ref	SJ	338E	652N

Unit 2, Eastwood Court, Hawarden Industrial Park, Manor Lane, Hawarden, Clwyd, CH5 3QB

Telephone no: 01244 520333 Mobile: 07710 465449

Web site: www.frogsborn.co.uk E-mail address: richard@frogsborn.co.uk

- Air to 300 bar. Nitrox. Trimix.
- Equipment sales.
- BSAC & SSI school.
- Boat charter arranged. Dry-suit repairs
- Cylinder testing. Regulator servicing.
- Closed Sunday & Monday.

Please call in, the kettle is always on!

Directions: Travelling west on the A55 Chester Southerly By-pass, take Junction 35A for Hawarden (Penarlag) and the Retail Park (A5104). Go straight on at the first roundabout, through Broughton and straight across the second roundabout, following the B5129 for Hawarden. Half a mile from Broughton and just after the bottom of a dip, turn right into Manor Lane (signposted 'Sandycroft, Industrial Estates'). Go straight on at the next roundabout, then immediately turn right into Airfield View. Go along this road and turn left into Clwyd Close, following it round to the right and into Eastwood Court.

Dee Sports, Chester. (Stewart & Joyce Tattersall)

Latitude	53° 11.715'N	Longitude	002° 53.160'W
O.S. Ref	SJ	408E	669N

67, Brook St., Chester. CH1 3DZ

Telephone no: 01244 314204

Web site: www.deesports.co.uk E-mail address: Joyce@deesports.co.uk

- Air to 250 bar. Nitrox. Trimix.
- Equipment sales.
- PADI & TDI school.
- Boat charter arranged.
- Cylinder testing. Regulator servicing.
- Closed Sunday.

Directions: Brook Street is a one-way street located about half a mile towards the city centre from Chester Station. Dee Sports is on the right, about halfway along the street.

Neptune Diving & Water-sports, Wirral. (Wilf Williams)

Latitude	53° 17.340'N	Longitude	002° 53.530'W
O.S. Ref	SJ	405E	773N

South Pier Rd., Telfords Quay, Ellesmere Port. CH65

Telephone no: 0151-356-5550 Mobile: 07986 630051

E-mail address: wilfwil@hotmail.com

- Air to 240 bar. • Equipment sales. • Cylinder testing. Regulator servicing.
- Dry-suit repairs. • Closed Sunday.

Directions: Leave the M53 at Junction 9 (A5032), following the signs for the Boat Museum. Turn into South Pier Road, pass the Museum entrance and continue down the hill towards the Manchester ship-canal. Neptune Diving & Water-sports is on the left, opposite the 'Rotate' restaurant and 100 metres before the BSAC Headquarters building.

Other Air Supplies

Llyn Diving / Shearwater Boat Charter, Llanbedrog (Alan & Susie Gray)

Latitude	52° 51.635'N	Longitude	004° 29.710'W
O.S. Ref	SH	320E	322N

'Eriador', Lon Pin, Llanbedrog, Pwllheli, Gwynedd LL53 7PG

Telephone no: 01758 740899 Mobile: 07815 717241

Opening hours: By appointment. Please ring first.

Web site: www.shearwater.info E-mail address: info@shearwater.info

- Air to 232 bar. • Bed & Breakfast. Boat charter

Directions: From Pwllheli, head west on the Abersoch road (A499), and after approximately 3 miles you will pass the Llanbedrog village sign. Follow the road up the hill and turn right opposite the Glyn-y-Weddw Arms. This is sign-posted 'Aberdaron B4413'. Follow the road for less than a half a mile, passing the Post Office on your right. Look for a road on the right called 'Lon Pin', just before a shop called 'Grandma's Attic'. Turn right into 'Lon Pin' and follow this road for a few hundred metres. As you start to rise out of a dip in the road, "Eriador" is on your right.

Marine Electronics, Abersoch (Richard Bufton)

Latitude	52° 49.304'N	Longitude	004° 30.435'W
O.S. Ref	SH	311E	278N

Fron Haul, Abersoch, Pwllheli LL53 7EE

Telephone no: 01758 712845 Mobile: 07775 777222

Opening hours: By appointment only. Please ring first.

Web site: www.users.globalnet.co.uk/rbuft E-mail address: rbuft@globalnet.co.uk

- Air to 300 bar. Nitrox by previous arrangement. Large air bank. Oxygen clean air
- Marine electronics sales & repair.

Directions: Take the A499 from Pwllheli into Abersoch, passing Land and Sea Marine. Go straight through the one-way system in the centre of Abersoch, following the signs for Sarn Bach and Cilan. Pass the shops, the St. Tudwal's Inn and the Police station. Marine Electronics is on the right, almost immediately opposite the Wylfa Hotel.

The Dive Inn (Penrallt Coastal Campsite), near Porth Ysgaden

Latitude	52° 53.655'N	Longitude	004° 39.300'W
O.S. Ref	SH	214E	364N

Penrallt, Tudweiliog, Pwllheli, Gwynedd LL53 8PB

Telephone no. 01758 770654 Opening hours: By appointment. Please ring first.

Web site www.penrallt.co.uk E-mail address penrallt@aol.com

• Air to 300 bar. Caravan & Camping site. Static Caravan for hire. Boat storage. Close to Porth Ysgaden

Directions: Take the B4417 south-west from Morfa Nefyn and pass through the village of Tudweiliog. After leaving the 30mph area, pass a parking area on the left before turning right at the sign for 'Penrallt Coastal Campsite'. After a short distance, follow the main road round the sharp left-hand bend and pass the Tyddyn Sander Caravan site. The turning for Penrallt is on the right, immediately after the B&B and before the phone-box. Follow this single-track lane to the camp-site.

Tynrhos Diving, Near Abersoch (Chris & Val Green)

Latitude	52° 51.685'N	Longitude	004° 31.590'W
O.S. Ref	SH	299E	324N

Tynrhos, Mynytho, Abersoch, Pwllheli, Gwynedd LL53 7PS

Telephone no: 01758 740712

Opening hours: Open 7.30 am - 7.00 pm, 7 days

E-mail address: Tynrhosdiving@btinternet.com

• Air to 232 bar. • Bunkhouse. Camping

Directions: Take the B4413 heading west from Llanbedrog and into Mynytho. Pass the Post Office, the 'School' sign and bear right just after the old garage. Turn right by the children's playground, following this lane up to the 'T' junction where you should turn left for Nanhoron. 'Tynrhos Diving' is on the left, about half a mile further on. Look out for the 'A' flag.

Penrallt Divers, Tudweiliog, near Porth Ysgaden

Latitude	52° 54.355'N	Longitude	004° 37.210'W
O.S. Ref	SH	238E	376N

'Isfryn', Rhoslan, Tudweiliog, Pwllheli.

Telephone no: 01758 770246

Opening hours: By appointment. Please ring first.

• Air to 232 bar.

Directions: Take the B4417 south-west from Morfa Nefyn and pass through Edern. Just after the 'Tudweiliog' sign, take the first turning on the right signposted 'Traeth/Beach'. Penrallt Divers are located about a quarter of a mile on the right, at the bungalow with the anchor on the front lawn.

Newsham Diving (George Newsham)

Latitude	52° 55.510'N	Longitude	004° 23.660'W
O.S. Ref	SH	391E	391N

Llwyn Ffynnon, Y Ffor, Pwllheli, Gwynedd.

Telephone no: 01766 810356 Mobile: 07971 349724

Opening hours: By appointment. Please ring first.

- Air to 270 bar. Nitrox. Trimix.
- Accommodation. Caravan hire. Camping & Caravan site. Boat storage

Directions: From Caernarfon, follow the A499 signs for Pwllheli, passing through Clynnog and Llanaelhaearn. Turn right in at the main crossroads in Y Ffor, just after the Post Office. Leave the 30mph zone and go round the first right-hand bend. The air-station is located at the first detached property on the left, about half a mile from the junction in Y Ffor. This is a cream-coloured house, with two stone dogs sitting on the gateway.

Dive North Wales, near Caernarfon (Jason Owen)

Bryn Awel, Nebo, Caernarfon LL54 6DY

Telephone no: 01286 882611 Mobile: 07990 683901

Opening hours: By appointment only. Please ring first.

Web site www.divenorthwales.ukdiver.com E-mail address info.divenorthwales@ukdiver.com

- Air to 250 bar.
- Boat charter. Guided dives. Equipment hire.

Directions: Telephone first.

Diver's Air, (Graham McLeod)

Latitude	53° 00.805'N	Longitude	002° 56.270'W
O.S. Ref	SJ	371E	467N

The Bungalow, Cross Lanes, Marchwiel, Wrexham, North Wales LL13 0TG

Telephone no: 01978 780630 Mobile: 07831 551170

Opening hours: By appointment. Please ring first.

- Air to 232 bar.
- Cylinder testing. IDEST Test Centre No: 1U

Directions: Take the A525 south-east from Wrexham, passing through Marchwiel and heading towards Bangor-on-Dee. Turn right at the traffic lights after the Cross Lanes Hotel. Pass the 'Kiln' public house and 'Diver's Air' is located at the first bungalow on the left.

Dive-boat Charter

Shearwater Diving Alan & Susie Gray

'Eriador', Lon Pin, Llanbedrog, Pwllheli, Gwynedd LL53 7PG

Based in Pwllheli, 'Shearwater' is a 12.3 metre, twin-engine, fast catamaran that caters for up to 12 divers. The boat runs diving trips to the North Llyn, Bardsey, South Llyn, St. Tudwal's Islands and Sarn Badrig. In addition to diving trips, they cater for coastal nature-cruises, evening-cruises, and barbeques. Enjoy the taste of freshly-caught mackerel as you view the setting-sun over Bardsey Island.

Tel: 01758 740899 Mobile: 07815 717241

Web: www.shearwater.info E-mail: info@shearwater.info

North Wales Diving (Jason Owen)

Bryn Awel, Nebo, Caernarfon LL54 6DY

Catering for up to 10 divers, the 11.5 metre hard-boat 'Hafaled' normally operates out of Pwllheli but can be moved to a base on the North Llyn if required. Dive sites include North Llyn, Bardsey, South Llyn, St. Tudwal's Islands and Sarn Badrig.

Tel: 01286 882611 Mobile: 07990 683901

Web: www.divenorthwales.ukdiver.com

E-mail: info.divenorthwales@ukdiver.com

Water-line (Paul Turkentine)

Ty Newydd, Carmel, Caernarfon, Gwynedd LL54 7AG

Why tow your boat all the way to the coast when you can have a boat waiting in the water where-ever you want? Waterline can provide a 5.2 metre RIB with a 90 hp four-stroke outboard to cater for a small group of divers, thus avoiding the inherent problems of organising a large group. A 'shuttle service' for a larger group can be organised if conditions and choice of site allow. Waterline specialises in scenic, photographic, and marine-life, especially around the Llŷn Peninsula, but they also cover Anglesey, the Menai Strait and Puffin Island.

Tel: 01286 882619 Mobile: 07768 490320

Web: www.water-line.co.uk E-mail: info@water-line.co.uk

SBS Boat Charter (Aubrey Diggle)

By the time you have towed a boat all the way to Anglesey and launched it, you will be ready for a rest rather than a dive. SBS Boat Charter will have one or two RIBs already in the water, ready and waiting for you. Catering for up to 8 divers per boat, all you have to do is don your dry-suit and load your diving-gear. 'Cobra' and 'Arctic Wolf' are both twin-engine, 6.8-metre RIBs which operate from Trearddur Bay or Holyhead to cover the whole area from Llanddwyn Island to the Skerries.

Tel: 01407 740083 Mobile: 07866 014393 E-mail: sbsdiverib@lineone.net

Quest Diving Services (Scott Waterman)

Based at Menai Bridge, Quest Diving operates a 40 foot hard-boat to cover dive-sites at Menai, Puffin Island, Anglesey, Caernarfon Bay, Liverpool Bay, the Isle of Man and Ireland.

Catering for up to 12 divers, it has a 700 hp engine and features a tail-lift for ease of boarding.

Tel: 01248 716923 Mobile: 07974 249005 E-mail: questcharters@aol.com

ESP Boat Charter (Keith Forster)

ESP Boat Charter operates a 33 foot Aquastar from Menai Bridge pier, taking parties of up to 10 divers to sites in Liverpool Bay, off East, North and West Anglesey, and as far away as the Isle of Man.

Tel. 0151-608-7901or 07885 884388 for further details.

A.K.S Diving (Adam Stubbings)

Hadley Buildings, Bangor Rd., Conwy LL32 8DN

Normally based in Conwy Marina, AKS Diving operates a 7-metre, inboard-powered RIB that takes up to 8 divers. It visits dive-sites at Anglesey, Puffin Island, the Menai Strait and in Liverpool Bay.

Tel: 01492 580300 Mobile: 07968 061177
Web: www.aksdiving.co.uk
E-mail: adam@aksdiving.co.uk

Underwater Photography

For your specialized underwater photography needs, contact Paul Kay of the Marine Wildlife Photo Agency, based in Llanfairfechan, North Wales. Paul holds an honours degree in Scientific Photography from the University of Westminster, is a Fellow of the Royal Photographic Society and holds an HSE Part 4 commercial scuba-diving certificate.

He imports and sells Seacam Silver housings into the UK, including new digital housings for Nikon D100, Nikon D1X, Fuji S2 Pro, & Canon EOS1D Cameras

Also analogue housings for: Nikon F5, F100, F90, F70 & F50, Canon EOS1V/HS/V/D & EOS5 Minolta Dynax 700si, 9xi & 7xi Cameras.

Contact him for details and prices. He also specialises in second-hand Seacam & Subal housings and believes that he has the best selection of used housings in the UK!

Tel: 01248 681361   Web site: www.marinewildlife.co.uk   E-mail: paul@marinewildlife.co.uk

Maritime Photography

Martin Turtle has photographed in the Abersoch area since 1985. His photos have appeared in Yachts and Yachting, Classic Boat, & Carve as well as many others. His postcards are available throughout the area as well as in his gallery in Abersoch.

He specialises in local landscapes around the area, as well as marine photography, especially sailing and surfing events.

Visit The Craft Centre, Lon Garmon, Abersoch, Gwynedd LL53 7UG
You can contact him on 01758 713641 or by e-mail at martin@turtlephotography.co.uk
Check his on-line gallery at www.turtlephotography.co.uk

See his photo's on pages 34 & 40.

Diving with a purpose

Whether you are a diver or not, there are volunteer schemes that you can take part in to help improve our knowledge of the wildlife and maritime history of our seas.

Seasearch

Seasearch is a national project for volunteer sports divers who have an interest in what they're seeing underwater, want to learn more and want to help protect the marine environment.

The main aim of Seasearch is to map the various types of sea bed up to about 5 miles off the coast or up to 30 metres depth around the whole of the British Isles. Seasearch helps record information about what lives in each area, establishing the richest sites for marine life, the sites where marine life is being effected and the sites which need protection.

Any dive can be a Seasearch dive! The support of divers all around the UK is needed to make the project a success. Divers can take part in dives with their buddy, diving club or on Seasearch organised dives and expeditions.

 www.seasearch.org.uk

For more information contact: Marine Conservation Society,

Tel: 01989 566017; e-mail: info@seasearch.org.uk;

or check the web-site at www.seasearch.org.uk

Other marine wildlife recording schemes

If you prefer to stay above water, you can still take part in recording marine life. For more information about the following schemes, contact the organisations listed below:

- Basking shark watch: Marine Conservation Society; Tel 01989 566017; www.mcsuk.org

- Marine turtles: Marine Conservation Society; Tel 01989 566017; www.mcsuk.org

- Sealife survey and shore survey: MarLin (Marine Life Information Network for Britain & Ireland); Tel: 01752 633336; www.marlin.ac.uk

- Skates and rays in Wales and The Great Egg Case Hunt: National Museums and Galleries of Wales; Tel: 029 02573233 / The Shark Trust; Tel: 0870 128 3045; www.sharktrust.org

- Whale and dolphin sightings: Seawatch Foundation; Tel: 01865 717276; www.seawatchfoundation.org.uk

- Welsh strandings project and turtle sightings: Marine Environmental Monitoring; Tel: 01239 682405; www.strandings.com

- UK Marine fish recording scheme: National Marine Aquarium;

  Tel: 01752 275216; e-mail: fishreports@national-aquarium.co.uk

Nautical Archaeology Society & the 'Adopt a Wreck' scheme

The Nautical Archaeology Society is a non-government organisation formed to further interest in our underwater cultural heritage. A number of full and part-time employees run the NAS, with assistance from NAS members who work on a voluntary basis. Their time and help is gratefully acknowledged.

The aims of the NAS:

- To preserve our archaeological heritage in the marine environment.
- To act as a focus for coastal and marine archaeology.
- To involve divers and non-divers.
- To provide education, training and information.
- To improve techniques of surveying, recording, excavation and conservation.
- To promote publication and research.

What can you do in the NAS?

- Assist in the search for evidence of past marine activities in seas, rivers, lakes or on land.
- Survey historic wrecks and other archaeological sites.
- Receive training in underwater archaeological techniques.
- Record and publish new discoveries.
- Help reconstruct and test early water-borne craft.
- Attend conferences and lectures.
- Choose your own involvement based on time available and level of expertise.
- Or just sit back and read about current activities.

NAS Training Courses:

- Provide first-class training in all aspects of archaeology in the marine environment.
- Promote high standards of archaeological work.
- Develop skills and techniques.
- Are certified, supported by Government, and are recognised internationally.

What else does the NAS do?

Publishes the International Journal of Nautical Archaeology (the foremost publication in the field) and provides regular, lively newsletters.

Builds contact through its meetings.

If you would like to join the NAS, you can do so by contacting the Office at the address below.

Nautical Archaeology Society

Fort Cumberland, Fort Cumberland Road, Eastney, Portsmouth PO4 9LD

Tel/fax: 023 9281 8419. Or by e-mail: nas@nasportsmouth.org.uk

Getting Involved

Under the overall project title, Diving with a Purpose anyone can get involved in Nautical Archaeology. There are a number of projects, so you can decide on the level of your commitment. Each project aims to provide information about maritime sites around the UK for a number of reasons:

- To add information to the records of various organisations.

- These include local organisations such as the Dorset Coast Forum and the Dorset Wildlife Trust as well as national bodies including the Royal Commision on the Historic Monuments of England and the Joint Nature Conservancy Council.

- To provide additional information on a variety of maritime sites for members of the general public.

- To enhance the understanding and appreciation of our maritime heritage by all.

- To help divers get more enjoyment out of their sport.

- To help understand the impact we are having on our maritime heritage.

Archaeological Needs

Archaeologists know very little about many of the wrecks that are regularly dived by sport divers. Even the precise location of wrecks is often unknown. It is also important to begin to understand how sites and wrecks are changing.

Many wrecks are beginning to break up, so we are losing the opportunity of recording them before they finally collapse. After the point of collapse, it might be much more difficult to record these sites. In many cases, the only evidence for industrial technological change or changes in ship design, lie on the seabed. It is often a misconception that we possess written records and plans of modern wreck.

Adopt a Wreck

This is a NAS initiative, aimed at those groups, clubs or individuals who regularly dive a site, have developed more than a passing interest and are keen to get involved in research or site survey. This scheme will appeal to those wanting to take on a club project which will have a genuine scientific outcome. Information resulting from these projects will then be passed, with the name of the contributor, to the appropriate agency.

The Norman Court

Worsley Sub-aqua Club have adopted the wreck of the Norman Court off Rhosneigr, Anglesey. The group dive and monitor the site several times each year, so please visit the wreck but do not disturb anything. More information about their activities can be found on their website at www.normancourt.homestead.com

Countryside Council for Wales

The Countryside Council for Wales is the statutory advisor to government on sustaining natural beauty, wildlife and the opportunity for outdoor enjoyment throughout Wales and its inshore waters. With English Nature and Scottish Natural Heritage, CCW delivers its statutory responsibilities for Great Britain as a whole, and internationally, through the Joint Nature Conservation Committee.

One of CCW's roles is to contribute towards the conservation and environmentally sustainable management of the Welsh coast and seas. To do this, CCW is involved in a number of different areas of work:

- participating in the management of marine Special Areas of Conservation and other marine conservation sites;

- undertaking and commissioning surveys and research about the distribution of habitats and species and their sensitivity to different impacts;

- using this information to provide advise to the National Assembly for Wales, Government departments and other statutory organisations with marine responsibilities, as well as users of the sea about the effects of developments and activities on our coast and sea;

- providing information about the marine environment of Wales thorough leaflets, posters, talks and attending local events;

- funding other organisations and groups to undertake conservation work in marine and coastal areas.

For more information about CCW and its work, contact CCW at Maes y Ffynnon, Penrhosgarnedd, Bangor, Gwynedd, LL57 2DN

Tel: CCW Enquiries Line 0845 1306229

or log on to www.ccw.gov.uk

Cyngor Cefn Gwlad Cymru
Countryside Council for Wales

North Western and North Wales Sea Fisheries Committee

The North Western and North Wales Sea Fisheries Committee administer the sea-area around the North Wales coast.

Contact - NW&NWSFC, Lancaster University, Lancaster, Lancs. LA1 4YY.

Telephone 01524 68745 or e-mail nwnwsfc@lancaster.ac.uk

Full details of the bylaws are available at www.nwnwsfc.org

Fish and Shellfish sizes

Shellfish	Minimum Size or Weight
Clam	40mm
Cockle	Shall not pass through 20mm grid
Crawfish	95mm (carapace length)
Edible crab	130mm (across the shell)
Lobsters	87mm (carapace length)
Mussels	45mm
Octopus	750 grams
Queen scallop	40mm (maximum width)
Scallops	110mm (maximum width)
Spider Crab	120mm
Whelk	45mm

Fish	Minimum Size (m.m.)
Bass	360mm
Cod	350mm
Ling	630mm
Mackerel	200mm
Plaice	270mm
Pollack	300mm
Whiting	270mm

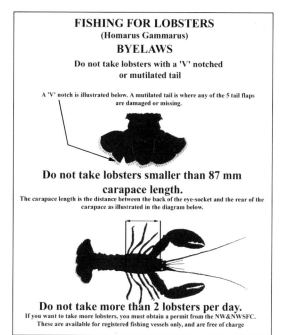

FISHING FOR LOBSTERS
(Homarus Gammarus)
BYELAWS
Do not take lobsters with a 'V' notched or mutilated tail

A 'V' notch is illustrated below. A mutilated tail is where any of the 5 tail flaps are damaged or missing.

Do not take lobsters smaller than 87 mm carapace length.
The carapace length is the distance between the back of the eye-socket and the rear of the carapace as illustrated in the diagram below.

Do not take more than 2 lobsters per day.
If you want to take more lobsters, you must obtain a permit from the NW&NWSFC. These are available for registered fishing vessels only, and are free of charge

235

Important Fisheries Bylaws Effecting Divers

- Unregistered fishermen such as divers may take no more than two lobsters or 5 kg of whelks per day.

- Do not take any lobster that has a notch cut in its tail or one that has a mutilated tail. As a conservation method, 'V'-shaped notches are being cut in the tails of trapped female lobsters before they are returned to the sea to breed. It takes one or two annual moults for the notch to completely grow out of the tail, thereby allowing the lobster one or two chances to breed. Female lobsters can only mate just after they have moulted. It is an offence not only to take a lobster with a notched tail, but also to be in possession of one with a mutilated tail. Simply removing the tail-flap with the 'V' notch will not help.

- Do not take scallops south of Braich-y-Pwll between July 1st and December 31st. (i.e. the area covered by the dive sites in chapters 1 to 5)

- Penalty for infringement of bylaws – a fine of up to £5,000.

The fisheries patrol vessel 'Aegis'.

Codes of Conduct

You can minimise your impact on the marine environment by following the appropriate codes of conduct.

Sea Wise code

At sea, follow the Sea Wise code. This code has been produced by CCW and the four Welsh police authorities to help you understand how the wildlife that use the seas and coasts of Wales is protected. It also advises what actions you can take to help look after it and make sure you stay within the law. Copies are available from CCW or can be downloaded at www.ccw.gov.uk

There are other codes of conduct that give guidance about specific activities. For more information, contact the following:

Diving

British Sub Aqua Club; www.bsac.com   NAUI; www.naui.org   PADI; www.padi.com
Scottish Sub Aqua Club; www.scotsac.com   Sub Aqua Association; www.saa.org.uk

Marine Mammals

Seawatch Foundation; www.seawatchfoundation.org.uk

Whale and Dolphin Conservation Society; www.wdcs.org

Friends of Cardigan Bay; www.fraw.org.uk

Marine Conservation Society; Tel 01989 566017; www.mcsuk.org

Underwater photography

Code of conduct at: www.marinewildlife.co.uk

Historic Wreck Sites

Within the area covered by this book there are, at the time of writing, three legally protected wrecks that have been designated under the Protection of Wrecks Act 1973. It is illegal to dive within these areas without a licence. In addition, Her Majesty's Submarine 'H5' has been designated under the 1986 Human Remains Act, so diving is not permitted at this site either. There are penalties for attempting to carry out any form of salvage operations, tampering with, damaging or removing any part of these wrecks or even undertaking any form of fishing activity in these areas.

In Wales, if you wish to apply for a licence to visit, survey or excavate any wreck site designated under the Protection of Wrecks act 1973, you should contact CADW, the government department for Welsh Historic Monuments.

Contact CADW, Welsh Historic Monuments, National Assembly for Wales, Cathays Park, Cardiff CF10 3NQ

Telephone 029 2050 0200 or e-mail them at cadw@wales.gsi.gov.uk

Bibliography

Hydrographic Charts

Cardigan Bay (Central) – Number 1972; Cardigan Bay (North) – Number 1971; Plans on the Llŷn Peninsula– Number 1512; Caernarfon Bay– Number 1970; Menai Strait– Number 1464; Approaches to Holyhead– Number 1413; Holyhead to Great Orme's Head– Number 1977.

Pilot Information

Glazebrook, Henry and Norman Sheldrick (1961) Anglesey & North Wales Pilot
Morris, Ralph Cruising Anglesey
Morris, Lewis (1748, Reprinted 1987) St. Georges Channel
Hydrographer of the Navy (1870 onwards) West Coast of England and Wales Pilot

Marine-life

Kay, Paul (1996) The Hidden World of the Menai Strait.
Kay, Paul (2000) The Shallow Seas of Wales.
Dipper, Dr. Frances (Second edition, 2001) British Sea Fishes
Naylor, Paul (2003) Great British Marine Animals.
Hayward, Peter & others (1996) Collins Pocket Guide to the Sea Shore.
Miller, Peter & Michael Loates (1997) Collins Pocket Guide to Fish

North Wales Shipwrecks

Jones, Ivor Wynne. (2000) Shipwrecks of North Wales (new revised edition)
Shears, Andy and Scott Waterman. (2002) Anglesey Wrecks & Reefs (Volume 1)
Larn, Richard & Bridget. (2000) Shipwreck Index of Britain, Volume 5, West Coast & Wales
Stubbs, John M. An Index to Shipwrecks on the North Wales Coast 1807 - 1914
Various contributors. BSAC Wreck Register (Edited by Bill Butland)
Bennett, Tom. (1995) Shipwrecks Around Anglesey
Bennett, Tom. (1987 & 1992) Shipwrecks Around Wales, Volumes 1 & 2
Gater, Dilys (1992) Historic Shipwrecks of Wales.
Hocking, Charles (1989) Dictionary of Disasters at Sea in the Age of Steam 1824 - 1962
Eames, Aled. (1981 reprint) Ships & Seamen of Anglesey.
Skidmore, Ian (1979) Anglesey & Lleyn Shipwrecks.
Zanelli, Leo. (1970 & 1974) Shipwrecks around Britain & Unknown Shipwrecks Around Britain
Masefield, John (1953, revised edition) The Conway
Carradice, Phil (1993) Welsh Shipwrecks in Camera
Parry, Henry. (1969) Wreck & Rescue on the Coast of Wales, Volumes 1 & 2

Historical Maritime Information for North Wales

Various Authors. (1976 – present day) Maritime Wales -- Volume 1 onwards.
Lloyd, Lewis. (1993) Whatever Freights Might Offer -- The History of Barmouth 1565 - 1920.
Lloyd, Lewis. (1989) The Port of Caernarfon -- 1793 - 1900.
Senogles, David (1969) Ynys Gorad Goch.
Elis-Williams, Myrvin (1984) Packet to Ireland
Williams, Wil The Manganese Mines of Gwynedd

Index of Dive sites